AA003768

7th Workshop on Narrative Understanding

Albuquerque, New Mexico, USA
4 May 2025

ISBN: 979-8-3313-1931-1

Printed from e-media with permission by:

Curran Associates, Inc.
57 Morehouse Lane
Red Hook, NY 12571

Some format issues inherent in the e-media version may also appear in this print version.

Printed with permission by Curran Associates, Inc. (2026)

Association for Computational Linguistics
209 N. Eighth Street
Stroudsburg, Pennsylvania 18360

Phone: 1-570-476-8006
Fax: 1-570-476-0860

acl@aclweb.org

Additional copies of this publication are available from:

Curran Associates, Inc.
57 Morehouse Lane
Red Hook, NY 12571 USA
Phone: 845-758-0400
Fax: 845-758-2633
Email: curran@proceedings.com
Web: www.proceedings.com

ACL 2025

The 7th Workshop on Narrative Understanding

Proceedings of the Workshop

May 4, 2025

Order copies of this and other ACL proceedings from:

Association for Computational Linguistics (ACL)
317 Sidney Baker St. S
Suite 400 - 134
Kerrville, TX 78028
USA
Tel: +1-855-225-1962
acl@aclweb.org

Introduction

Welcome to the 7th Workshop on Narrative Understanding!
This is the 7th iteration of the workshop, which brings together an interdisciplinary group of researchers to discuss methods to improve automatic narrative understanding capabilities. We are happy to present both archival and non-archival papers on this topic (non-archival papers to be presented only at the workshop).
We would like to thank everyone who submitted their work to the workshop and the program committee for their helpful feedback. We would also like to thank our invited speakers for their participation in this workshop.
—Ashutosh, Anneliese, Khyathi, Snigdha, Elizabeth, Mohit, and Yash

Program Committee

Chairs

Anneliese Brei, University of North Carolina at Chapel Hill
Khyathi Raghavi Chandu, Allen Institute of AI
Snigdha Chaturvedi, University of North Carolina, Chapel Hill
Elizabeth Clark, Google Research
Mohit Iyyer, University of Massachusetts Amherst
Yash Kumar Lal, Stony Brook University
Ashutosh Modi, Indian Institute of Technology Kanpur

Program Committee

Rajeev Ambati, University of North Carolina Chapel Hill
Maria Antoniak, Pioneer Centre for AI, University of Copenhagen
Kent Chang, UC Berkeley
Hans Ole Hatzel, Universität Hamburg
Junbo Huang, University of Hamburg
Abhinav Joshi, Indian Institute of Technology Kanpur
Haoyuan Li, University of North Carolina at Chapel Hill
Kawshik Manikantan, International Institute of Information Technology Hyderabad
Vishakh Padmakumar, New York University
Vahid Sadiri Javadi, University of Bonn (CAISA Lab)
Esther Shizgal, The Hebrew University of Jerusalem
Li Siyan, Columbia University
Sai Vallurupalli, University of Maryland at Baltimore County
Anvesh Rao Vijjini, UNC Chapel Hill
Chao Zhao, Google

Table of Contents

Program

Sunday, May 4, 2025

10:15 - 10:00	*Opening Remarks*
10:15 - 11:00	*Talk 1*
11:00 - 11:45	*Talk 2*
11:45 - 12:30	*Talk 3*
12:30 - 13:45	*Lunch*
13:45 - 14:30	*Talk 4*
14:30 - 15:15	*Talk 5*
15:15 - 15:30	*Break and poster setup*
15:30 - 16:30	*Poster session*

NarraDetect: An annotated dataset for the task of narrative detection

Andrew Piper
Languages, Literatures, and Cultures
McGill University

Sunyam Bagga
School of Computer Science
McGill University

Abstract

Narrative detection is an important task across diverse research domains where storytelling serves as a key mechanism for explaining human beliefs and behavior. However, the task faces three significant challenges: (1) inter-narrative heterogeneity, or the variation in narrative communication across social contexts; (2) intra-narrative heterogeneity, or the dynamic variation of narrative features within a single text over time; and (3) the lack of theoretical consensus regarding the concept of narrative. This paper introduces the NarraDetect dataset, a comprehensive resource comprising over 13,000 passages from 18 distinct narrative and non-narrative genres. Through a manually annotated subset of 400 passages, we also introduce a novel theoretical framework for annotating for a scalar concept of "narrativity." Our findings indicate that while supervised models outperform large language models (LLMs) on this dataset, LLMs exhibit stronger generalization and alignment with the scalar concept of narrativity.

1 Introduction

Narrative detection is an essential task in NLP and the subfield of computational narrative understanding (Bamman et al., 2019; Zhu et al., 2023; Piper, 2023; Antoniak et al., 2023; Abdessamed et al., 2024). A growing body of research is developing across a variety of domains that focus on storytelling as a key mechanism for explaining human beliefs and behavior (Gottschall, 2012). Being able to detect where, when and to what degree the act of narration is taking place among textual outputs will support research into the function of narration across a range of fields.

We see three core challenges facing the task of narrative detection. First is the high degree of variety surrounding the social contexts of storytelling. This is called "situatedness" by Herman (2009) and is one of the four essential elements of narrative in his scheme. Stories can appear in the news media, on social media, in both fiction and non-fiction books, online fan writing sites, scattered throughout large cultural heritage archives, and multi-modally as well (graphic novels, comic books, and children's books) to name a few. While certain components of narrative behavior will likely change across contexts, we also expect some core behavior should remain consistent. We call this the problem of "inter-narrative" heterogeneity.

The second main challenge is what we call "intra-narrative" heterogeneity, i.e. the degree to which narrative communication can differ over narrative time. Narrative practices do not consist of a single, fixed set of behaviors that occur always and everywhere in a story, but rather a dynamic combination of features that may wax and wane.

One of the principal theoretical shifts to occur in the field of narratology over the past few decades has been this shift from understanding narrative as a matter of kind to one of degree (Herman, 2009; Giora and Shen, 1994; Pianzola, 2018). "Narrativity" according to this theoretical framework is a quality that can best be understood not as a global binary class (a document either is or is not a narrative), but as a local, multi-dimensional scalar property (Ochs et al., 2009). A narrative document, such as a novel, may exhibit greater or lesser degrees of narrativity at different moments in the text, just as ostensibly non-narrative documents, such as scientific reports, may also exhibit degrees of narrativity and in different ways.

This stylistic heterogeneity introduces the third challenge facing the task of narrative detection, which is the theoretical heterogeneity underlying the task. The concept of "narrative" consists of a complex set of dimensions and different sources have proposed different frameworks for its study. Not surprisingly, narrative continues to be understood and operationalized in different ways. A key goal for the field moving forward will be the devel-

Proceedings of the The 7th Workshop on Narrative Understanding, pages 1–7
May 4, 2025 ©2025 Association for Computational Linguistics

opment of more standardized narrative models.

In this paper, we introduce the *NarraDetect* dataset, which aims to make the following contributions:

1. Address the social diversity of narrative communication by compiling a large collection of over 13,000 passages from 18 different narrative and non-narrative genres. This dataset captures a wide variety of narrative communication from significantly different social contexts.
2. Address intra-narrative diversity by introducing a novel theoretical framework for the annotation of a scalar concept of "narrativity." This framework is then used for the manual annotation of a subset of ca. 400 passages from the large corpus.
3. Validate our data on the task of narrative detection using both supervised and unsupervised models. We show that supervised models outperform LLMs on our data but generalize less well on other data. LLMs also illustrate solid understanding of our scalar concept of narrativity, suggesting good calibration with our theoretical framework.

We make all of our data and annotations available in a long-term repository following the best practices of open science (Collaboration, 2015).[1]

2 Prior Work

The creation of narrative datasets within the field can be divided into two principal areas: the first is the development of domain specific collections of stories or story dimensions for the purposes of narrative understanding. These include news stories (Chambers and Jurafsky, 2008), cultural heritage material (Underwood et al., 2020; Bagga and Piper, 2022; Hamilton and Piper, 2023), novels (Brahman et al., 2021; Iyyer et al., 2016), birth stories (Antoniak et al., 2019), and artificial stories (Mostafazadeh et al., 2016), to name but a few.

Datasets for the task of narrative detection are far more scarce and rely on both positive and negative examples. Antoniak et al. (2023) have created one of the few publicly available narrative detection datasets. The *StorySeeker* corpus consists of an annotated dataset of narratives at the sentence level on a set of 502 Reddit posts and comments drawn from over 100 different subreddits from the Webis-TLDR-17 dataset (Völske et al., 2017). They use a binary model of annotation applied to sentence spans and following Sims et al. (2019) define a narrative as "a sequence of events involving one or more people."

Doyle et al. (2024) have created a collection of 750 manually annotated Reddit posts for the presence of narrative from the *r/SuicideBereavement* subreddit. Following (Smith, 2001), they annotate posts based on the following categories: the presence of a plot, characters, the author as a character, and a clear beginning, middle, and end.

Ganti et al. (2022) annotated a collection of 849 Facebook posts related to the topic of breast cancer for the presence of narratives. In a follow-up study, Ganti et al. (2023) annotated a collection of 3,000 tweets drawn from the *ANTiVax* (Hayawi et al., 2022) and *CMU-MisCov19* (Memon and Carley, 2020) datasets respectively. They annotate tweets for the presence of "narrative style," which they define as: "the presentation of a sequence of events experienced by a character or characters" following (Dahlstrom, 2021).

Narrative detection datasets to date can thus be characterized by the following qualities: narrative has only been operationalized as a binary category; annotation has largely been undertaken with respect to a specific domain (social media); and different theoretical constructs have been used to inform annotation, with events and event sequences being the most predominant category.

3 The NarraDetect Dataset

3.1 Large Corpus: Binary genre-labeled collection

We introduce two corpora to support the task of narrative detection. The first is a large collection of 13,543 text passages drawn from 18 different genres as described in Table A2 in the Appendix. Genres are labeled according to a binary scheme of narrative or non-narrative. Narratives consist of both fictional and non-fictional stories from different social contexts (social media, contemporary publishing, cultural heritage material, and online experimental writing like flash fiction). Non-narrative passages are drawn from a range of informational documents such as Supreme Court decisions, academic articles and abstracts, book reviews, and legal contracts. All passages are randomly sampled from respective documents and consist of five sentences in length.

While this collection has the advantage of size

[1] https://doi.org/10.5683/SP3/HEEEKN

and diversity compared to other manually annotated datasets, it still utilizes a binary conception of narrative. Additionally, because we are sampling passages rather than full documents (to align with our interest in "narrativity") it is possible that passages in the narrative genres may exhibit low-levels of narrativity and vice versa. For this reason, we recommend using the scalar corpus in the next section as the test set. We observe that 6% of passages in the manually annotated scalar corpus are misaligned with their categorical labels, giving users some sense of the possible mislabel rate in the large corpus. Despite these limitations, the large corpus provides researchers with a diverse cross-section of storytelling behavior for the purposes of model training and narrative understanding.

3.2 Scalar Corpus: Human Annotated Collection

As mentioned above, narrative theorists have emphasized the concept of "narrativity" to capture the idea of narrative as one of degree rather than kind. Such a scalar concept is one way of capturing the intra-narrative stylistic diversity that attends narrative communication, though others may be proposed. We develop our annotation framework from one of the foundational handbooks in narrative theory (Herman, 2009). While we do not directly annotate passages over narrative time, our passage-level annotations can be used for estimating changes in narrativity over narrative time.

We utilize the following three categories:

Agency. Narrative is first and foremost language addressing individual experience (Fludernik, 2002). As Herman (2009) writes, "Narrative roots itself in the lived, felt experience of human or human-like agents interacting in an ongoing way with their surrounding environment" (21). Narrativity thus depends on the prominence of a few distinct agents actively experiencing events in the passage.

Event Sequencing. Narrative is about time and process (Ricoeur, 2012). As Herman (2009) writes, "Narrative is a basic human strategy for coming to terms with time, process, and change." One of the principal ways this can occur is through the sequencing of events. Narrativity thus depends on the clarity with which sequences of events are presented.

World Building. Narratives are not just about individuals and events, but as Herman (2009) argues they are also about *lived experience*. Narrativity thus depends on the extent to which an experiencable world is constructed, one that can be clearly seen and felt by the reader.

We trained three undergraduate literature students to code passages using a detailed codebook. After multiple training rounds, they rated each passage on a 5-point Likert scale. In the final round, they annotated 394 passages representing approximately 20 documents per genre.

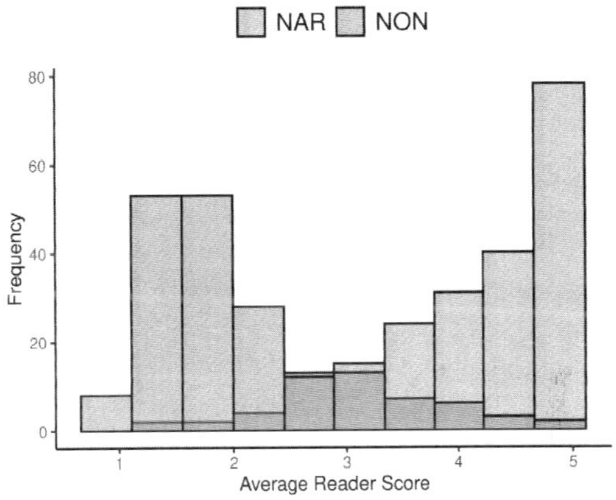

Figure 1: Histogram of average reader narrativity scores across all three categories by positive and negative labels for the scalar corpus.

Figure 1 shows a bimodal distribution of reader scores, clustering below 2 and above 4. Inter-rater agreement, measured using the average deviation index (O'Neill, 2017), yielded a median of 0.37 and a mean of 0.41 (+/- 0.31), indicating strong consistency within half a Likert point. We found no association between narrativity score and agreement levels. Table A3 provides examples of passages rated for high, medium, and low narrativity, while Figure A4 shows the full distribution of reader scores across our three narrative dimensions.

4 Evaluating the NarraDetect Corpus for Narrative Detection

We evaluate the utility of the NarraDetect dataset using both supervised and unsupervised methods. For supervised models, we experiment with two feature representations: (1) a semantically neutral feature space derived from part-of-speech (POS) tags excluding punctuation and (2) contextual embeddings obtained from the BERT large cased model. An SVM with a Gaussian kernel serves as the classifier in both cases.

In order to disentangle narrativity-related features from genre-specific signals, we employ an adversarial learning approach. A shared feature extractor, implemented as a feedforward neural network, generates input representations optimized for narrativity classification. The primary narrativity classifier predicts whether a passage is narrative or non-narrative, while an auxiliary genre predictor identifies the passage's genre. A gradient reversal layer between the extractor and genre predictor suppresses genre-specific signals, with a combined loss function balancing narrativity and genre prediction using a trade-off parameter λ. This approach enables the model to learn features capturing narrativity independently of genre.

The adversarial learning process achieves an F1 score of 0.87 / 0.97 for narrativity classification using POS / BERT features, while keeping genre prediction accuracy low at 0.18 / 0.19 on our manually annotated test set. These results demonstrate the model's ability to extract narrativity-relevant features with minimal genre interference.

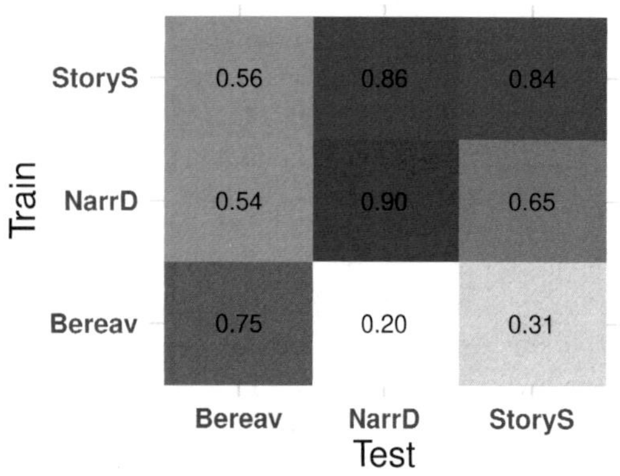

Figure 2: Heatmap of F1 scores using different train and test set combinations using the BERT feature space.

Next we test our data alongside two other datasets discussed in prior work: StorySeeker (Antoniak et al., 2023) and the r/Bereavement data (Doyle et al., 2024). Once again using our SVM classifier and two feature representations, we rotate through all train / test splits and measure F1 scores for each scenario. As shown in Figure 2, there is high within-group accuracy, coupled with considerable decline on out-of-domain data. The exception is the StorySeeker data which generalizes well to our data though the reverse is not the case. The r/Bereavement data shows the lowest generalizability of all sets.

For our unsupervised training, we employ GPT-4 (`gpt-4-0613`) as our frontier model and Llama3.1:8B as our open-weight model. We use a zero shot prompting framework: "Is this passage from a story? Answer only with a number: 1 if yes, 0 if no." For the scalar task, we use similar prompts to what our human annotators received (e.g. "How strongly do you agree with this statement: This passage is organized around sequences of events that occur over time"). Table 1 shows the performance of our two models on the different datasets in both the binary task (F1) and correlation with the scalar task (ρ) as illustrated in Figure A3.

	GPT-4		**Llama3.1**	
Dataset	F1	ρ	F1	ρ
NarraDetect	0.87	0.81	0.89	0.78
StorySeeker	0.84	-	0.74	-
Bereavement	0.58	-	0.59	-

Table 1: F1 scores for our two candidate LLMs for binary classification and Spearman's ρ for our scalar model comparing LLMs to human annotations.

5 Conclusion

To advance the goal of narrative detection, we introduce the *NarraDetect* dataset, which formalizes "narrativity" theoretically and includes two sub-corpora. The large corpus captures diverse narrative practices across contexts, while the smaller, manually annotated dataset provides a novel scalar framework to address intra-narrative heterogeneity, grounded in foundational narrative theory (Herman, 2009).

Our models achieve high predictive accuracy, though supervised models show performance drops on out-of-domain data, warranting further investigation. Unsupervised LLMs, however, demonstrate robustness across narrative datasets and align well with human annotations, reinforcing the validity of our framework.

We hope *NarraDetect* enriches existing resources and aids in benchmarking LLMs for narrative understanding.

Limitations

Despite our data being drawn from numerous genres and social situations, the cultural contexts of storytelling are vast. Future work will want to continue to expand the number of situations, genres, and languages to facilitate the benchmarking of narrative detection at broader scales and in more domains. As noted in the paper, researchers need to use caution in supervised learning scenarios both to control for genre effects and also on the appropriateness of out of domain data for the task.

One further limitation of this project is the limited amount of comparative data. We were only able to surface two other data sets for comparison, one of which appears to be not well aligned with the task of narrative detection given its low performance across models. The field will benefit from the creation of further manually annotated narrative datasets.

Finally, our work on unsupervised approaches was limited to two LLMs. Future work will want to do a cross-model assessment on all available models to assess the trade-offs between size and performance on this task. We also look forward to future iterations that are able to perform multilingual narrative detection.

Acknowledgements

We wish to thank the Social Sciences and Humanities Research Council of Canada (435-2022-089) for funding to support this research.

References

Yosra Abdessamed, Shadi Rezapour, and Steven Wilson. 2024. Identifying narrative content in podcast transcripts. In *Proceedings of the 18th Conference of the European Chapter of the Association for Computational Linguistics (Volume 1: Long Papers)*, pages 2631–2643, St. Julian's, Malta. Association for Computational Linguistics.

Maria Antoniak, David Mimno, and Karen Levy. 2019. Narrative paths and negotiation of power in birth stories. *Proceedings of the ACM on Human-Computer Interaction*, 3(CSCW):1–27.

Maria Antoniak, Joel Mire, Maarten Sap, Elliott Ash, and Andrew Piper. 2023. Where do people tell stories online? story detection across online communities. *arXiv preprint arXiv:2311.09675*.

Sunyam Bagga and Andrew Piper. 2022. Hathi 1m: Introducing a million page historical prose dataset in english from the hathi trust. *Journal of Open Humanities Data*, 8.

David Bamman, Snigdha Chaturvedi, Elizabeth Clark, Madalina Fiterau, and Mohit Iyyer. 2019. Proceedings of the first workshop on narrative understanding. In *Proceedings of the First Workshop on Narrative Understanding*.

Faeze Brahman, Meng Huang, Oyvind Tafjord, Chao Zhao, Mrinmaya Sachan, and Snigdha Chaturvedi. 2021. "let your characters tell their story": A dataset for character-centric narrative understanding. In *Findings of the Association for Computational Linguistics: EMNLP 2021*, pages 1734–1752.

Nathanael Chambers and Dan Jurafsky. 2008. Unsupervised learning of narrative event chains. In *Proceedings of ACL-08: HLT*, pages 789–797, Columbus, Ohio. Association for Computational Linguistics.

Open Science Collaboration. 2015. Estimating the reproducibility of psychological science. *Science*, 349(6251):aac4716.

Michael F Dahlstrom. 2021. The narrative truth about scientific misinformation. *Proceedings of the National Academy of Sciences*, 118(15):e1914085117.

Dylan Thomas Doyle, Jay K Ghosh, Reece Suchocki, Brian C Keegan, Stephen Voida, and Jed R Brubaker. 2024. Stories that heal: Characterizing and supporting narrative for suicide bereavement. In *Proceedings of the International AAAI Conference on Web and Social Media*, volume 18, pages 354–366.

Monika Fludernik. 2002. *Towards a 'Natural' Narratology*. Routledge.

Achyutarama Ganti, Eslam Ali Hassan Hussein, Steven Wilson, Zexin Ma, and Xinyan Zhao. 2023. Narrative style and the spread of health misinformation on twitter. In *Findings of the Association for Computational Linguistics: EMNLP 2023*, pages 4266–4282.

Achyutarama Ganti, Steven Wilson, Zexin Ma, Xinyan Zhao, and Rong Ma. 2022. Narrative detection and feature analysis in online health communities. In *Proceedings of the 4th Workshop of Narrative Understanding (WNU2022)*, pages 57–65, Seattle, United States. Association for Computational Linguistics.

Rachel Giora and Yeshayahu Shen. 1994. Degrees of narrativity and strategies of semantic reduction. *Poetics*, 22(6):447–458.

Jonathan Gottschall. 2012. *The storytelling animal: How stories make us human*. Houghton Mifflin Harcourt.

Sil Hamilton and Andrew Piper. 2023. Multihathi: A complete collection of multilingual prose fiction in the hathitrust digital library. *Journal of Open Humanities Data*, 9.

Kadhim Hayawi, Sakib Shahriar, Mohamed Adel Serhani, Ikbal Taleb, and Sujith Samuel Mathew. 2022. Anti-vax: a novel twitter dataset for covid-19 vaccine misinformation detection. *Public health*, 203:23–30.

David Herman. 2009. *Basic elements of narrative*. John Wiley & Sons.

Mohit Iyyer, Anupam Guha, Snigdha Chaturvedi, Jordan Boyd-Graber, and Hal Daumé III. 2016. Feuding families and former friends: Unsupervised learning for dynamic fictional relationships. In *Proceedings of the 2016 Conference of the North American Chapter of the Association for Computational Linguistics: Human Language Technologies*, pages 1534–1544.

Shahan Ali Memon and Kathleen M Carley. 2020. Characterizing covid-19 misinformation communities using a novel twitter dataset. *arXiv preprint arXiv:2008.00791*.

Nasrin Mostafazadeh, Nathanael Chambers, Xiaodong He, Devi Parikh, Dhruv Batra, Lucy Vanderwende, Pushmeet Kohli, and James Allen. 2016. A corpus and cloze evaluation for deeper understanding of commonsense stories. In *Proceedings of the 2016 Conference of the North American Chapter of the Association for Computational Linguistics: Human Language Technologies*, pages 839–849.

Elinor Ochs, Lisa Capps, et al. 2009. *Living narrative: Creating lives in everyday storytelling*. Harvard University Press.

Thomas A O'Neill. 2017. An overview of interrater agreement on likert scales for researchers and practitioners. *Frontiers in psychology*, 8:264983.

Federico Pianzola. 2018. Looking at narrative as a complex system: The proteus principle. In *Narrating complexity*, pages 101–122. Springer.

Andrew Piper. 2023. Computational narrative understanding: A big picture analysis. In *Proceedings of the Big Picture Workshop*, pages 28–39.

Paul Ricoeur. 2012. *Time and Narrative, Volume 1*. University of Chicago press.

Matthew Sims, Jong Ho Park, and David Bamman. 2019. Literary event detection. In *Proceedings of the 57th Annual Meeting of the Association for Computational Linguistics*, pages 3623–3634, Florence, Italy. Association for Computational Linguistics.

Carlota S Smith. 2001. Discourse modes: aspectual entities and tense interpretation. *Cahiers de grammaire*, 26(1):183–206.

Ted Underwood, Patrick Kimutis, and Jessica Witte. 2020. Noveltm datasets for english-language fiction, 1700-2009. *Journal of Cultural Analytics*, 5(2).

Michael Völske, Martin Potthast, Shahbaz Syed, and Benno Stein. 2017. Tl; dr: Mining reddit to learn automatic summarization. In *Proceedings of the Workshop on New Frontiers in Summarization*, pages 59–63.

Lixing Zhu, Runcong Zhao, Lin Gui, and Yulan He. 2023. Are NLP models good at tracing thoughts: An overview of narrative understanding. In *Findings of the Association for Computational Linguistics: EMNLP 2023*, pages 10098–10121, Singapore. Association for Computational Linguistics.

Appendix

Narrative	# Docs
Artificial Stories (ROC)	976
AskReddit	971
Biographies	898
Fables	258
Fairy tales	740
Flash fiction	390
Histories	979
Memoirs	935
Novels (19C)	998
Novels (Contemporary)	776
Short Stories	451
Non-narrative	
Academic Articles (Phil)	519
Academic Articles (Lit)	468
Aphorisms	462
Book reviews	776
Contracts	1054
Scientific Abstracts	950
U.S. Supreme Court Decisions	942

Table 2: Table of narrative and non-narrative genres in the Large Corpus.

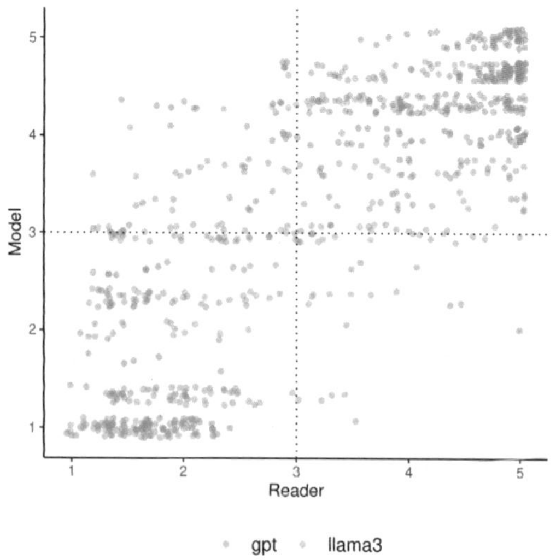

Figure 3: Correlation between average reader scores and GPT and Llama3.1:8B scores on the scalar task.

Score 5.0 / Deviation = 0.0 *In the center of the town, the Mercedes stopped a second time, outside a charcuterie and an adjoining boulangerie. Again Keller sped past, but Gabriel managed to conceal himself in the lee of an ancient church. There he watched as the woman climbed out of the car and entered the shops alone, emerging a few minutes later with several plastic sacks filled with food.*
Score = 3.0 / Deviation = 0.84 *There were other dramatic glitches, too. Despite Cornell's love for the part, she was not suited to it. While Anouilh's Antigone epitomized the enfant terrible, Cornell was in her early fifties and brought to the role a calm, dignified strength, making it harder for the audience to feel that she was imperiled. Photographs of the production reveal her imposing, statuesque presence, precisely the opposite of "la petite maigre" called for by Anouilh.*
Score = 1.2 / Deviation = 0.38 *To understand a thing is to discover how it operates. The eternal forms of things are laws of natural action. Such are the law of gravitation, the laws of optics or of chemical combination. A static picture unless so interpreted must be at once valueless and meaningless. It follows that Thought and Discourse, in furnishing us with Knowledge, must themselves be active, and must in some way or other reproduce the activity of Nature.*

Table 3: Examples of passages with high, medium, and low ratings for narrativity.

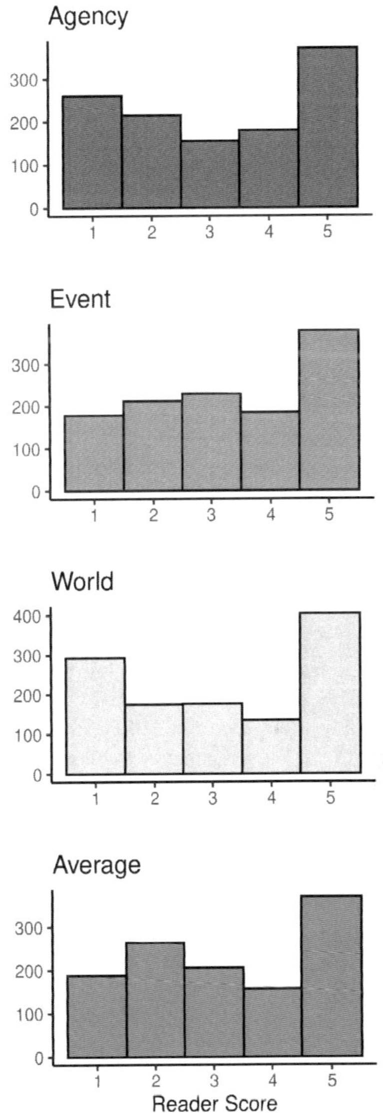

Figure 4: Distribution of reader scores across our three primary narrativity dimensions along with the average of all scores.

On the Transferability of Causal Knowledge for Language Models

Gourab Dey
Stony Brook University
gdey@cs.stonybrook.edu

Yash Kumar Lal
Stony Brook University
ylal@cs.stonybrook.edu

Abstract

Language understanding includes identifying causal connections between events in a discourse, such as news and instructional text. We study the transferability of causal knowledge across these two domains by analyzing the extent to which understanding preconditions in narratives such as news articles can help models reason about plans such as cooking recipes, and vice-versa. Our experiments show that using instructions to pretrain small models on one domain before similarly finetuning it on the other shows a slight improvement over just finetuning it. We also find that finetuning the models on a mix of both types of data is better ($\sim$3-7% absolute) for understanding causal relations in instructional text. While we find that the improvements do not translate to larger or already instruction tuned models, our analysis highlights the aspects of a plan that are better captured through the interoperability of causal knowledge.

1 Introduction

Understanding underlying causal relationships is an important component of understanding narratives such as news articles. These causal relationships often show up as implicit preconditions and effects of the described events or actions. Preconditions provide a form of logical connection between events that explains why they occur together. They include background information and provide the glue to reason about chains of events common in narratives.

Preconditions also form the base for reasoning about other forms of text. Instructional texts such as how-to procedures often contain prerequisites and details about world states. Recognizing the causal elements in a story aids in identifying prerequisites in instructional text, while grasping procedural preconditions can enhance one's ability to track news events. Humans use a shared framework to comprehend preconditions and other causal relations regardless of the type of text they are reading. In this paper, we aim to study whether understanding aspects of causal knowledge about narratives can help models better understand instructional text and vice versa.

We use PEKO (Kwon et al., 2020), a dataset of annotated preconditions between event pairs in news articles, and CAT-BENCH (Lal et al., 2024a), a benchmark testing step order prediction in cooking recipes. First, we establish the performance of different T5 (Raffel et al., 2020) and FLANT5 (Wei et al., 2021) models by finetuning them on each dataset individually. Next, we study how much understanding causal relations within one domain helps understand those in the other. This is done through causal pretraining, i.e., pretraining models on the first domain, finetuning on the second as well as evaluating on it. Finally, we study whether models are able to capture different types of causal knowledge when trained on a data mix from both domains.

Our experiments show that learning various types of causal relations impacts models differently. Base models benefit from training over such knowledge in different domains while larger models already contain it through their pretraining. Our analysis finds that causal pretraining and multi-task finetuning help understand long range relations in plans and cases where two steps in the plan are not dependendent on each other, and highlights areas to better use different types of causal knowledge together.

2 Related Work

There is a vast body of research on extracting different types of relations between events including temporal (Pustejovsky et al., 2003), causal (Girju, 2003), paraphrasal (Lin and Pantel, 2001), and precondition relationships (Kwon et al., 2020, 2021).

Proceedings of the The 7th Workshop on Narrative Understanding, pages 8–14
May 4, 2025 ©2025 Association for Computational Linguistics

ATOMIC (Sap et al., 2019) is a crowd-sourced dataset of event-event relations, where given a simple target event (verb phrase and its arguments), crowd workers provided various types of commonsense knowledge. The Rich Event Description (RED) dataset (O'Gorman et al., 2016) was created to model a broad set of event-event relations in news. CaTeRS (Mostafazadeh et al., 2016) contains data similar to preconditions captured through just one causal relation but focuses on 5 sentence short stories and only contains ~400 data points. EventStoryLine (Caselli and Vossen, 2017) is also small in size and further does not explicitly capture preconditions. The Precondition Knowledge (PEKO) dataset (Kwon et al., 2020) contains large-scale crowdsourced annotations about precondition relations between event pairs in news stories.

Understanding instructional text involves multiple aspects such as tracking entity states (Bosselut et al., 2018; Henaff et al., 2017), linking actions (Pareti et al., 2014; Lin et al., 2020; Donatelli et al., 2021), next event prediction (Nguyen et al., 2017; Zellers et al., 2019; Zhang et al., 2020a) and more. Zhang et al. (2020b) formalize several multiple-choice tasks related to step- and goal- relations in procedures. Kiddon et al. (2015) explore predicting dependencies in cooking recipes and related tasks. Similar work has been done on identifying dependencies in multimodal instructions with images and text (Pan et al., 2020; Wu et al., 2024). CAT-BENCH (Lal et al., 2024b) clearly studies the prediction and explanation of temporal ordering constraints on the steps of an instructional plan.

Humans have the ability to utilize knowledge from previous experiences when learning a new task. Prior work has explored techniques of transfer learning and domain adaptation to learn skills in various contexts. Zoph et al. (2016); Kocmi and Bojar (2018) explored using parallel data from high resource languages to improve translation in low resource languages. Gururangan et al. (2020); Han and Eisenstein (2019) use domain adaptation techniques for models to learn new tasks. Similar to these, we investigate whether understanding causal knowledge in one domain helps with another.

3 Data

To study the transferability of causal knowledge, we use CAT-BENCH and PEKO, which contain information about dependencies between a plan's steps and preconditions about events respectively.

CAT-BENCH (Lal et al., 2024b) is a dataset of causal dependency questions defined on cooking recipes to evaluate the causal and temporal reasoning abilities of models over instructional plans. Specifically, it focuses on the ability to recognize temporal dependencies between steps i.e., deciding if one step must happen before or after another. For a recipe in the dataset, containing an ordered number of steps, the dataset contains either of two binary questions: (1) Must $step_i$ happen before $step_j$? and (2) Must $step_j$ happen after $step_i$? We pool questions from dependent pairs of steps into DEP, and the rest into NONDEP[1].

PEKO is a dataset consisting of crowdsourced annotations of preconditions between event pairs in news articles. Kwon et al. (2020) first subsample events and their temporal relations using CAEVO (Chambers et al., 2014) from the New York Times Annotated Corpus (Sandhaus, 2008). The resultant set was then filtered to retain only pairs of events that have a "before" or "after" temporal relation between them. These were further sampled and given to annotators who evaluated whether or not the candidate precondition event was an actual precondition for the target event resulting in 30k annotations.

4 Experiment Details

We provide critical information about the models and training regimes we use for our experiments.

4.1 Models

We conduct our experiments with the base and large models of the T5 and FLANT5 model family.

T5 reframes all text-based language problems into a text-to-text format. It is based on the encoder-decoder transformer architecture and is fine-tuned across a wide range of tasks by converting inputs and outputs into text strings. This unified approach allows T5 to effectively transfer learned knowledge from one task to another, achieving then state-of-the-art results across a wide range of benchmarks.

FLANT5 involves fine-tuning a T5 model with a diverse set of task-specific instructions before applying it to downstream tasks. Different from previous standard pretraining and finetuning methods, this approach enhances the model's ability to generalize across different tasks by explicitly teaching it to follow instructions during the finetuning

[1]Note that the answers to all the questions in the DEP set are 'yes', and the answers to NONDEP questions are 'no'.

	T5-B	T5-L	FLAN-B	FLAN-L
PEKO / PEKO (FT)	0.76	0.80	0.78	0.80
CAT-BENCH → PEKO / PEKO (CP)	0.78	0.80	0.78	0.80
BOTH / PEKO (MFT)	0.79	0.80	0.79	0.81
CAT-BENCH / CAT-BENCH (FT)	0.8	0.92	0.91	0.95
PEKO → CAT-BENCH / CAT-BENCH (CP)	0.82	0.89	0.91	0.92
BOTH / CAT-BENCH (MFT)	0.87	0.91	0.90	0.93

Table 1: Macro F1 of different T5 and FLANT5 trained models on PEKO and CAT-BENCH. The dataset listed in red denote the data the model was trained on, and the dataset listed in green denotes the benchmark on which the F1 score is calculated. B represents base sized models and L represents the large sized models. → denotes that the model has been sequentially trained on the dataset before → first and then on the dataset listed after it.

phase.

4.2 Experiments

We first manually craft an instruction for the task corresponding to each dataset and prepend[2] it to all data points. We then follow three distinct training regimes as described below.

Finetuning (FT) In this regime, we finetune a model on the corresponding dataset to establish its performance on the task.

Causal Pretraining (CP) We first pretrain a model on one dataset before finetuning on the other. To do so, for instance, we first pretrain a model on PEKO and then finetune on CAT-BENCH to study whether learning preconditions about real world events in news helps better understand aspects of causal knowledge within plans. Theoretically, the model learns to detect causal dependencies from the first stage before adapting to the target dataset. This is aimed to test the transferability of causal knowledge between narratives such as news and instruction following content such as recipes.

Multi-Task Finetuning (MTF) We combine the corresponding splits of both instruction prepended datasets, shuffle them and finetune a model on it. This setting studies whether a model can learn different aspects of causal knowledge when given data from varying domains.

5 Results

Table 1 shows the performance of different models trained using the various training regimes described above. First, we find that all the FT models for PEKO achieve better performance than the best finetuned models reported in Kwon et al. (2020). Particularly, comparing models of the same size, T5 and FLANT5 are better on this binary classification task than the reported BERT model even though they are generative models. FT models for CAT-BENCH show improved performance over any of the reported baselines, which is expected as the baselines are only zero- and few-shot settings.

We observe mixed results when using the causal pretraining regime (CP). It is clear that first learning about preconditions from news events helps T5-BASE understand cause and effect relations implicitly encoded within the steps of a plan. We hypothesize that larger models already encode such knowledge in their parameters and such pretraining does not affect downstream performance. These findings also hold when first learning about plans followed by news events. Clearly, transferring causal knowledge between generic news events and highly specific actions in a plan lead to improved reasoning across both.

Multi-task training (MFT) over both datasets together improves T5-BASE performance over finetuning (FT) regardless of the target task. In fact, there is a large improvement (~7%) on CAT-BENCH in this regime, and a small improvement in understanding news events in PEKO. However, while the opposite is true for T5-LARGE, the drop is negligible. This training paradigm does not impact FLANT5 performance on PEKO but mixing causal information in news with that in plans leads to slight decrease in understanding the latter.

Overall, we find that the training regime heavily impacts a model's performance on a causal understanding task. Simply following one regime will not lead to improvements across all tasks, and it is

[2] We also experiment with no prefix and an alternate prefix.

important to explore the different options.

6 Analysis

Having established the differences in training regimes across different settings, we investigate the abilities T5-BASE on CAT-BENCH to better understand our results.

6.1 Reasoning as a function of Step Distance

We study how the distance between the steps in question impacts model performance across training regimes. A question is said to be about *close* steps $(step_i, step_j)$ if $(j - i) < 3$, and *distant* otherwise. For CP and MFT, we calculate the number of cases where the corresponding regime corrects an error found in FT.

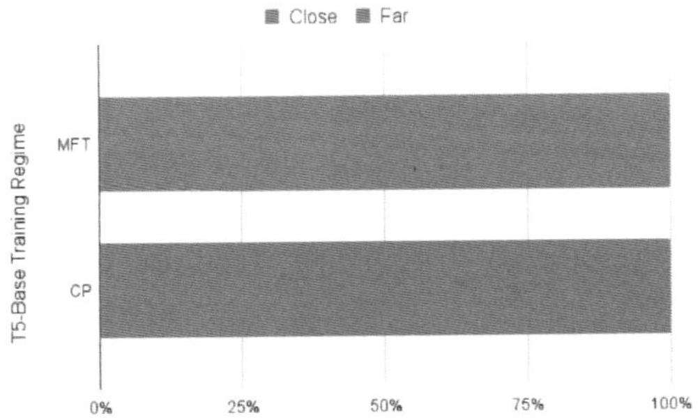

Figure 1: Distribution of improvements produced due to different T5-BASE training regimes for CAT-BENCH as a function of distance between the steps being asked about.

Figure 1 shows the distribution of these corrections as divided by the distance between the pair of steps in question. We hypothesize that models are likely to predict a dependencies between steps that are distant from each other, since it is likely that steps towards the end depend on ones near the start. We find that both CP and MFT improve reasoning more for distant steps rather than closer ones, indicating that the extra data helps understand indirect connections, or lack thereof, between steps.

6.2 Reasoning over Directional Dependencies

We study how models handle questions about different aspects of the same pair of steps. Typically, questions about why a step must happen *before* another require reasoning about preconditions and causes, while answering why a step must happen *after* another requires understanding the effects of any performed actions.

Table 2 shows the performance of T5-BASE on questions testing the 'before' and 'after' order between steps. We find that causal pretraining (CP) helps the model for questions about both dependent and non-dependent pairs of steps. In fact, CP helps the most on the non-dependent subset which is harder to detect.

		Before	After
DEP	FT	0.82	0.82
	CP	0.84	0.83
NONDEP	FT	0.77	0.76
	CP	0.80	0.79

Table 2: Performance (macro F1) of T5-BASE on CAT-BENCH when just finetuned (FT) on the target dataset as compared to using causal pretraining (CP) split by the type of dependence relations between the plan steps.

We also use the dependency related annotations in CAT-BENCH to understand the types of improvements the different training setups brings over finetuning. To do so, we extract the cases where FT fails but CP or MFT fix that error.

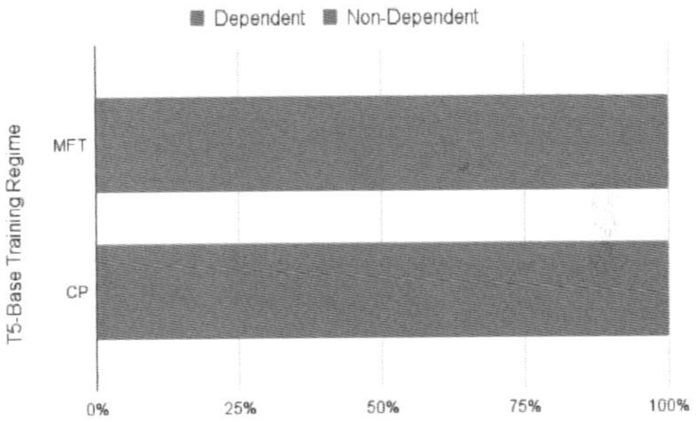

Figure 2: Distribution of improvements produced due to different T5-BASE training regimes for CAT-BENCH as a function of whether there is a dependency between within the pair of steps being asked about.

Figure 2 shows that the overwhelming majority of improvements are found for step pairs without a dependency. Detecting that two steps do not depend on each other is harder than the inverse since it involves eliminating all possibilities of there being a dependency between the steps.

7 Conclusion

With the ubiquity of causal relations, we study the transferability of such knowledge between critical, real-world domains. We investigate how learning about preconditions in news events impacts models' abilities to reason about causes and effects in plans and vice versa. Comparing different training setups reveals that, while different domains require varying finetuning strategies, transferring causal knowledge is helpful for smaller models. Larger models often already encode such information. Our error analysis reveals aspects of a plan that such regimes help with, highlighting areas of improvement for future research.

Limitations

We limit our investigation to two encoder-decoder pretrained models which are much smaller (in terms of number of parameters) than decoder-only large language models such as GPT-3 and others. Nonetheless, these small models are pretrained on large swathes of text and capture a model causal knowledge related to the world in their parameters. While we study such models as an artifact possibly reflecting a view of the world, we acknowledge that they don't capture all aspects of it. Even with our findings, they must be deployed only after extensive testing to study how they impact people. Finally, our work only investigates English-language documents and this limits the generalizability of our findings to other languages.

References

Antoine Bosselut, Omer Levy, Ari Holtzman, Corin Ennis, Dieter Fox, and Yejin Choi. 2018. Simulating action dynamics with neural process networks. *ICLR*.

Tommaso Caselli and Piek Vossen. 2017. The event StoryLine corpus: A new benchmark for causal and temporal relation extraction. In *Proceedings of the Events and Stories in the News Workshop*, pages 77–86, Vancouver, Canada. Association for Computational Linguistics.

Nathanael Chambers, Taylor Cassidy, Bill McDowell, and Steven Bethard. 2014. Dense event ordering with a multi-pass architecture. *Transactions of the Association for Computational Linguistics*, 2:273–284.

Lucia Donatelli, Theresa Schmidt, Debanjali Biswas, Arne Köhn, Fangzhou Zhai, and Alexander Koller. 2021. Aligning actions across recipe graphs. In *Proceedings of the 2021 Conference on Empirical Methods in Natural Language Processing*, pages 6930–6942, Online and Punta Cana, Dominican Republic. Association for Computational Linguistics.

Roxana Girju. 2003. Automatic detection of causal relations for question answering. In *Proceedings of the ACL 2003 Workshop on Multilingual Summarization and Question Answering*, pages 76–83, Sapporo, Japan. Association for Computational Linguistics.

Suchin Gururangan, Ana Marasović, Swabha Swayamdipta, Kyle Lo, Iz Beltagy, Doug Downey, and Noah A. Smith. 2020. Don't stop pretraining: Adapt language models to domains and tasks. In *Proceedings of the 58th Annual Meeting of the Association for Computational Linguistics*, pages 8342–8360, Online. Association for Computational Linguistics.

Xiaochuang Han and Jacob Eisenstein. 2019. Unsupervised domain adaptation of contextualized embeddings for sequence labeling. In *Proceedings of the 2019 Conference on Empirical Methods in Natural Language Processing and the 9th International Joint Conference on Natural Language Processing (EMNLP-IJCNLP)*, pages 4238–4248, Hong Kong, China. Association for Computational Linguistics.

Mikael Henaff, Jason Weston, Arthur Szlam, Antoine Bordes, and Yann LeCun. 2017. Tracking the world state with recurrent entity networks. *ICLR*.

Chloé Kiddon, Ganesa Thandavam Ponnuraj, Luke Zettlemoyer, and Yejin Choi. 2015. Mise en place: Unsupervised interpretation of instructional recipes. In *Proceedings of the 2015 Conference on Empirical Methods in Natural Language Processing*, pages 982–992, Lisbon, Portugal. Association for Computational Linguistics.

Tom Kocmi and Ondřej Bojar. 2018. Trivial transfer learning for low-resource neural machine translation. In *Proceedings of the Third Conference on Machine Translation: Research Papers*, pages 244–252, Brussels, Belgium. Association for Computational Linguistics.

Heeyoung Kwon, Nathanael Chambers, and Niranjan Balasubramanian. 2021. Toward diverse precondition generation. In *Proceedings of *SEM 2021: The Tenth Joint Conference on Lexical and Computational Semantics*, pages 160–172, Online. Association for Computational Linguistics.

Heeyoung Kwon, Mahnaz Koupaee, Pratyush Singh, Gargi Sawhney, Anmol Shukla, Keerthi Kumar Kallur, Nathanael Chambers, and Niranjan Balasubramanian. 2020. Modeling preconditions in text with a crowd-sourced dataset. In *Findings of the Association for Computational Linguistics: EMNLP 2020*, pages 3818–3828, Online. Association for Computational Linguistics.

Yash Kumar Lal, Vanya Cohen, Nathanael Chambers, Niranjan Balasubramanian, and Ray Mooney. 2024a. CaT-bench: Benchmarking language model understanding of causal and temporal dependencies in plans. In *Proceedings of the 2024 Conference on Empirical Methods in Natural Language Processing*, pages 19336–19354, Miami, Florida, USA. Association for Computational Linguistics.

Yash Kumar Lal, Vanya Cohen, Nathanael Chambers, Niranjan Balasubramanian, and Raymond Mooney. 2024b. Cat-bench: Benchmarking language model understanding of causal and temporal dependencies in plans. *Preprint*, arXiv:2406.15823.

Angela Lin, Sudha Rao, Asli Celikyilmaz, Elnaz Nouri, Chris Brockett, Debadeepta Dey, and Bill Dolan. 2020. A recipe for creating multimodal aligned datasets for sequential tasks. In *Proceedings of the 58th Annual Meeting of the Association for Computational Linguistics*, pages 4871–4884, Online. Association for Computational Linguistics.

Dekang Lin and Patrick Pantel. 2001. Dirt @sbt@discovery of inference rules from text. In *Proceedings of the Seventh ACM SIGKDD International Conference on Knowledge Discovery and Data Mining*, KDD '01, page 323–328, New York, NY, USA. Association for Computing Machinery.

Nasrin Mostafazadeh, Alyson Grealish, Nathanael Chambers, James Allen, and Lucy Vanderwende. 2016. CaTeRS: Causal and temporal relation scheme for semantic annotation of event structures. In *Proceedings of the Fourth Workshop on Events*, pages 51–61, San Diego, California. Association for Computational Linguistics.

Dai Quoc Nguyen, Dat Quoc Nguyen, Cuong Xuan Chu, Stefan Thater, and Manfred Pinkal. 2017. Sequence to sequence learning for event prediction. In *Proceedings of the Eighth International Joint Conference on Natural Language Processing (Volume 2: Short Papers)*, pages 37–42, Taipei, Taiwan. Asian Federation of Natural Language Processing.

Tim O'Gorman, Kristin Wright-Bettner, and Martha Palmer. 2016. Richer event description: Integrating event coreference with temporal, causal and bridging annotation. In *Proceedings of the 2nd Workshop on Computing News Storylines (CNS 2016)*, pages 47–56, Austin, Texas. Association for Computational Linguistics.

Liang-Ming Pan, Jingjing Chen, Jianlong Wu, Shaoteng Liu, Chong-Wah Ngo, Min-Yen Kan, Yugang Jiang, and Tat-Seng Chua. 2020. Multi-modal cooking workflow construction for food recipes. In *Proceedings of the 28th ACM International Conference on Multimedia*, MM '20, page 1132–1141, New York, NY, USA. Association for Computing Machinery.

Paolo Pareti, Benoit Testu, Ryutaro Ichise, Ewan Klein, and Adam Barker. 2014. Integrating know-how into the linked data cloud. In *International Conference on Knowledge Engineering and Knowledge Management*, pages 385–396. Springer.

James Pustejovsky, Patrick Hanks, Roser Sauri, Andrew See, Robert Gaizauskas, Andrea Setzer, Dragomir Radev, Beth Sundheim, David Day, Lisa Ferro, et al. 2003. The timebank corpus. In *Corpus linguistics*, volume 2003, page 40. Lancaster, UK.

Colin Raffel, Noam Shazeer, Adam Roberts, Katherine Lee, Sharan Narang, Michael Matena, Yanqi Zhou, Wei Li, and Peter J. Liu. 2020. Exploring the limits of transfer learning with a unified text-to-text transformer. *Journal of Machine Learning Research*, 21(140):1–67.

Evan Sandhaus. 2008. The New York Times Annotated Corpus. Abacus Data Network.

Maarten Sap, Ronan Le Bras, Emily Allaway, Chandra Bhagavatula, Nicholas Lourie, Hannah Rashkin, Brendan Roof, Noah A. Smith, and Yejin Choi. 2019. Atomic: An atlas of machine commonsense for if-then reasoning. *Proceedings of the AAAI Conference on Artificial Intelligence*, 33(01):3027–3035.

Jason Wei, Maarten Bosma, Vincent Zhao, Kelvin Guu, Adams Wei Yu, Brian Lester, Nan Du, Andrew M Dai, and Quoc V Le. 2021. Finetuned language models are zero-shot learners. In *International Conference on Learning Representations*.

Te-Lin Wu, Alex Spangher, Pegah Alipoormolabashi, Marjorie Freedman, Ralph Weischedel, and Nanyun Peng. 2024. Understanding multimodal procedural knowledge by sequencing multimodal instructional manuals. *Preprint*, arXiv:2110.08486.

Rowan Zellers, Ari Holtzman, Yonatan Bisk, Ali Farhadi, and Yejin Choi. 2019. HellaSwag: Can a machine really finish your sentence? In *Proceedings of the 57th Annual Meeting of the Association for Computational Linguistics*, pages 4791–4800, Florence, Italy. Association for Computational Linguistics.

Hongming Zhang, Muhao Chen, Haoyu Wang, Yangqiu Song, and Dan Roth. 2020a. Analogous process structure induction for sub-event sequence prediction. In *Proceedings of the 2020 Conference on Empirical Methods in Natural Language Processing (EMNLP)*, pages 1541–1550, Online. Association for Computational Linguistics.

Li Zhang, Qing Lyu, and Chris Callison-Burch. 2020b. Reasoning about goals, steps, and temporal ordering with WikiHow. In *Proceedings of the 2020 Conference on Empirical Methods in Natural Language Processing (EMNLP)*, pages 4630–4639, Online. Association for Computational Linguistics.

Barret Zoph, Deniz Yuret, Jonathan May, and Kevin Knight. 2016. Transfer learning for low-resource neural machine translation. In *Proceedings of the 2016 Conference on Empirical Methods in Natural Language Processing*, pages 1568–1575, Austin, Texas. Association for Computational Linguistics.

A Experiment Details

A.1 Hyperparameters

Here, we describe the hyperparameters we use to train our models. For both T5-BASE and FLANT5-BASE, we use a learning rate of 3e-4 for FT and MTF. For transfer during the CP stage, we use a lower learning rate of 1e-4, specifically we find that using a higher learning rate leads to a degradation in performance here for the FLANT5-BASE models. For T5-LARGE and FLANT5-LARGE, we use a learning rate of 5e-5 for CAT-BENCH and 1e-4 for PEKO during FT, and a learning rate of 5e-5 for MTF. For the transfer stage, we use a learning rate of 1e-4, and surprisingly find that a lower learning rate here leads to poor performance in contrast to the base models. All models were trained with a batch size of 64 and for a maximum of 7 epochs with early stopping.

A.2 Dataset Details

	Train	Validation	Test
CAT-BENCH	13,868	1,616	2,840
PEKO	23,158	2,895	2,895

Table 3: Number of examples in different splits of each dataset

Table 3 presents statistics of the datasets - PEKO and CAT-BENCH - used for our experiments.

Finding Common Patterns in Domestic Violence Stories Posted on Reddit

Mohammad Shokri[1]**, Emily Klapper**[2]**, Jason Shan**[2]**, Sarah Ita Levitan**[2]

[1]The Graduate Center, CUNY
[2]Hunter College, CUNY

Abstract

Domestic violence survivors often share their experiences in online spaces, offering valuable insights into common abuse patterns. This study analyzes a dataset of personal narratives about domestic violence from Reddit, focusing on event extraction and topic modeling to uncover recurring themes. We evaluate GPT-4 and LLaMA-3.1 for extracting key sentences, finding that GPT-4 exhibits higher precision, while LLaMA-3.1 achieves better recall. Using LLM-based topic assignment, we identify dominant themes such as psychological aggression, financial abuse, and physical assault which align with previously published psychology findings. A co-occurrence and PMI analysis further reveals the interdependencies among different abuse types, emphasizing the multifaceted nature of domestic violence. Our findings provide a structured approach to analyzing survivor narratives, with implications for social support systems and policy interventions.

1 Introduction

Narratives are central to human communication, proven to foster empathy, shared beliefs, and persuasiveness. With the growth of internet use globally, individuals increasingly share personal stories online, seeking empathy and emotional support from the online community. Domestic violence stories are a striking example of this trend. The abundance of domestic violence stories on the internet provides a unique opportunity for computational analysis to identify commonalities and variations in how these experiences are narrated. By examining these stories at scale, we can uncover recurring patterns in them, such as how survivors describe the progression of abuse, the typology of abuse, the role of legal interventions, or the types of support they seek.

Identifying common patterns in domestic violence narratives opens the door to various applications, ranging from privacy protection to early intervention strategies. For instance, detecting outlier patterns could help develop systems that prevent individuals from sharing stories that might inadvertently reveal their identities. Additionally, recognizing progressions in abuse-related narratives could contribute to predictive models that identify when relationships are at risk of escalating into more severe abuse. Beyond these, computational insights from these stories could be applied to support systems, legal frameworks, and advocacy efforts, ultimately improving both understanding and response strategies for domestic violence cases.

To enable these potential applications, we first need to distinguish common patterns from unique details within domestic violence stories. This paper focuses on learning the recurring structures in these narratives by identifying the key events that define interactions between the victim and the perpetrator. Events are central to narrative structure, and understanding which events frequently co-occur allows us to detect broader storytelling patterns. We hypothesize that domestic violence stories share a high degree of similarity, particularly in the progression of events that characterize abusive relationships.

Leveraging recent advancements in natural language processing (NLP), we explore the ability of large language models (LLMs) to extract and analyze these key events. In this paper, we propose a fully LLM-based method for processing stories and attributing topics to the events, with the goal of clustering and finding similar patterns. Specifically, we use LLaMA-3.1 (Dubey et al., 2024) and GPT-4 (Achiam et al., 2023) to extract those sentences from a narrative that capture interactions between the victim and the perpetrator. We use these LLMs to assign topics to the extracted sentences, which facilitates learning topic progressions in the stories. We analyze topic co-occurrence and topic n-grams from the stories to find similar patterns between our

Proceedings of the The 7th Workshop on Narrative Understanding, pages 15–25
May 4, 2025

set of stories. We collected a large set of domestic violence stories from Reddit, consisting of more than 11,100 posts which we filtered for story-like posts, using a pre-trained classifier (Antoniak et al., 2023). Our dataset is available upon request.

2 Related Work

Narrative is commonly defined as a sequence of events that unfolds over time (Labov and Waletzky, 1997; Eisenberg and Finlayson, 2021). Events are the fundamental building blocks of narratives, providing structure and coherence by linking actions, participants, and consequences (Zhang et al., 2021). Earlier studies in the literature took a verb-based perspective on events, primarily focusing on extracting predicate-argument triples to represent narrative progression (Mousavi et al., 2023; Chaturvedi et al., 2017; Chambers and Jurafsky, 2008). More recent works have employed supervised learning, transfer learning, and sequence-to-sequence models for developing models that can extract events from a piece of text (Lu et al., 2021; Li et al., 2021; Sims et al., 2019; Uddin et al., 2024; Huang et al., 2017). Li et al. (2022) presents an extensive survey of deep learning-based methods for event extraction. Identifying recurring event structures allows researchers to analyze narrative evolution, uncover causal dependencies, and detect common thematic patterns across large story datasets.

While event extraction focuses on explicit actions, states, and participants, topic modeling provides a higher-level view of recurring themes within narratives, and it enables researchers to model narrative schema and arcs across large datasets (Min and Park, 2016; Schmidt, 2015; Boyd et al., 2020; Mathewson et al., 2020; Antoniak et al., 2023). As an example, Antoniak et al. (2019) used topic modeling to find clear patterns of events that occur in birth stories and used the learned topic transition probabilities to find outlier stories. Wagner et al. (2022) proposed a Point wise Mutual Information (PMI) based method to capture topic segmentation for Holocaust testimonies.

Recent advancements in Transformer-based language models (Vaswani, 2017) have enhanced computational narrative understanding. Piper and Bagga (2024) examined ways in which LLMs could contribute to understanding core narrative features. Wagner et al. (2024) used GPT-4 thanks to its long context window (128k tokens) to extract trajectory mappings from a set of Holocaust testimonies. Heddaya et al. (2024) fine-tuned LLaMA (Dubey et al., 2024) and used GPT-4 in few-shot and zero-shot settings for detecting causal micro-narratives within a sentence.

Despite their abundance and importance, domestic violence narratives have not been studied extensively in the NLP community. Schrading et al. (2015) developed classifiers using n-grams and semantic roles as features for detecting posts on reddit discussing domestic abuse. Karlekar and Bansal (2018) used CNN-RNN architectures to classify between narratives containing different forms of sexual harassment shared online through a forum called SafeCity. Calderwood et al. (2017) studies physiological responses of readers reacting to abuse survivors studies. Shokri et al. (2024) focused on extracting common events from a small set of domestic violence stories and developed a classifier to classify between domestic violence stories and non-domestic violence stories based on a vector distance metric. In this paper, we introduce a large set of personal domestic violence stories from Reddit, and use LLMs to extract the events from stories and identify their topics.

3 Dataset

To collect personal stories about domestic violence, we turned to Reddit, specifically the subreddit *r/domesticviolence*, where users share their experiences and receive support from others. This community provides information and emotional support for victims, with members offering insights based on their personal experiences rather than professional opinions. We scraped this publicly available subreddit and archived 11,176 posts spanning from 2005 to 2021 to construct our dataset. To ensure anonymity, we only keep the posts' text.

An initial exploration of the dataset revealed that not all posts contain personal experiences. Some posts are general discussions or rants about domestic violence and its effects, without explicitly describing eventful personal narratives. To filter out non-narrative posts, we use *StorySeeker* (Antoniak et al., 2023), a pretrained RoBERTa model (Liu, 2019) designed for binary classification of stories vs. non-stories. Applying this model to our dataset, we identified 9,872 posts as stories (see Table 1).

To understand the structure of the collected stories, we analyzed the distribution of sentence

Category	Count
Non-story posts	1,304
Posts classified as stories	9,872
Total posts collected	11,176

Table 1: Summary of collected Reddit posts and distribution of story vs. non-story labels based on StorySeeker classification output.

counts per post. As shown in Figure 1, the majority of stories are relatively short, with a steep drop-off in frequency as sentence count increases. The median story length is around 16 sentences, with 25% of stories having fewer than 9 sentences and 75% having fewer than 28 sentences. While most stories contain only a few sentences, there are outliers with significantly higher sentence counts, reflecting variations in detail and narrative style. The distribution suggests that while many users share brief experiences, others provide in-depth narratives describing complex events. After extracting events from the stories (see Section 4), we only keep stories with at least 5 sentences to ensure working with story-like posts.

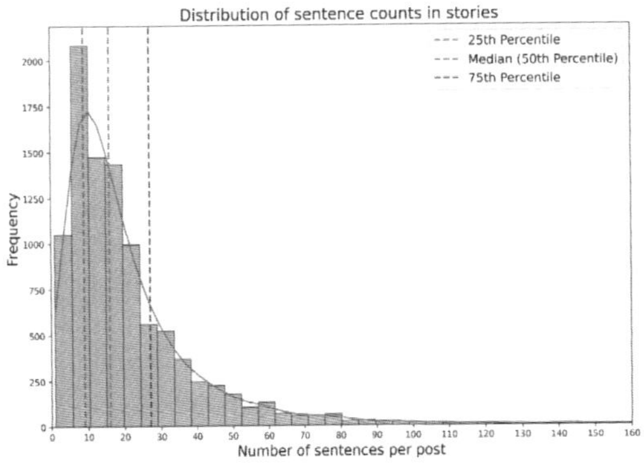

Figure 1: Distribution of sentence counts per post in the dataset. The majority of posts are short, with a few containing significantly more sentences. The x-axis is limited to 160 sentences to improve readability. The maximum number of sentences per post in our dataset is 477.

4 Extracting Events

After collecting the stories from Reddit, we aimed to extract events from them to enable an analysis of themes in the stories. Events are fundamental building blocks of a story, yet they are not unanimously and clearly defined in the literature. Most prevailing conceptions of events are based on changes in state (Vauth et al., 2021; Sims et al., 2019; Aguilar et al., 2014; Sims et al., 2019). Vendler (1957) categorized the relationship between verbs and time into four types: *activities*, *achievements*, *accomplishments*, and *states*. Sims et al. (2019) classifies activities, achievements, accomplishments, and changes of state as "events". Building on this, Antoniak et al. (2023) developed a more flexible event span annotation framework that includes not only real events but also hypothetical and recurring actions. We adopt the definition from Antoniak et al. (2023) and modify it to incorporate verbal interactions, as verbal abuse is a prevalent form of domestic abuse and we observed that it frequently appears in our dataset. The definition of event is provided in the Appendix section A.1.

People share their personal stories with varying levels of detail; some provide extensive background on their own or their partner's lives, while others narrate in detail the sequence of events leading up to instances of domestic violence. We focus on events involving both the victim and the perpetrator because we are most interested in uncovering patterns that characterize abusive relationships.

We do not assume all aspects of these stories are alike, given the numerous ways relationships start and people's diverse life backgrounds. Therefore, to identify the commonalities we believe exist in domestic violence narratives, we first extract sentences that describe events or actions that directly involve both the victim and the perpetrator. We prompt LLaMA-3.1 8B (`meta-llama/Llama-3.1-8B-Instruct`) and GPT-4 (`GPT-4-Turbo`) with the definition of events and a description of the task. We provide three examples in the prompt to clarify the task and serve as few-shot examples. The prompt we used for this task is available in the Appendix section (A.1). We set the temperature = 0.0 while prompting both models.

4.1 Annotation

In order to evaluate the LLM-based event extraction, we asked two members of our research team to read the stories and extract the sentences which *describe an event or action that happened in the story which involved the victim and the perpetrator.* We randomly selected 50 stories from our dataset and asked the annotators to find eventful sentences. The total number of sentences in the stories were 1587. In cases where the annotators' labels disagreed, we conducted a consolidation session, during which both annotators discussed their reasoning to resolve conflicts. Final labels were assigned based on mutual agreement, ensuring a consistent and high-quality labeled dataset. There were 431 sentences extracted as eventful sentences.

The inter-annotator agreement calculated as Cohen's kappa (Cohen, 1960) score was 0.67 which indicates substantial agreement. Although a high level of inter-annotator agreement was observed, certain disagreements arose during the classification of events. Variations in narrative styles across the stories contributed to ambiguity in identifying specific events. In numerous instances, the narrator's commentary implied an event without explicit mention, leading to interpretive differences. Additionally, disagreements emerged when analyzing sentences involving individuals beyond the victim and perpetrator (such as bystanders, law enforcement, etc.), as well as in cases where stories featured multiple victims or perpetrators. These complexities highlight the nuanced nature of event classification within this dataset.

4.2 Evaluation of Event Extraction

The results of our sentence extraction task are shown in Table 2. Our results highlight key differences between LLaMA-3.1 and GPT-4 in terms of precision, recall, and F1-score, both for eventful and non-eventful sentences.

For eventful sentences (positive class), GPT-4 achieves a slightly higher F1-score (0.5374) compared to LLaMA-3.1 (0.5355), despite having much lower recall (0.4084 vs. 0.6729). This indicates that GPT-4 is more selective, extracting fewer irrelevant sentences (higher precision: 0.7857 vs. 0.4448), but LLaMA-3.1 captures a broader range of eventful sentences due to its higher recall, though at the cost of more false positives.

For sentences not containing description of events (negative class), both models perform strongly, with GPT-4 achieving an F1-score of 0.8797 and LLaMA-3.1 scoring 0.7594. Notably, GPT-4 excels in recall (0.9585), identifying nearly all non-eventful sentences, while LLaMA-3.1 shows a better balance between precision (0.8492) and recall (0.6869).

Looking at the overall macro averages, GPT-4 outperforms LLaMA-3.1 with a higher F1-score (0.7086 vs. 0.6475), achieving better balance across both eventful and non-eventful classes. These results suggest that LLaMA-3.1 is better suited when comprehensive coverage (high recall) is essential, while GPT-4 is preferable when precision is critical, minimizing false positives and extracting more reliable eventful sentences.

	GPT-4			LLaMA-3.1		
	Precision	Recall	F1-Score	Precision	Recall	F1-Score
Event Class (Positive)	0.7857	0.4084	0.5374	0.4448	0.6729	0.5355
Non-Event Class (Negative)	0.8129	0.9585	0.8797	0.8492	0.6869	0.7594
Macro Average	0.7993	0.6834	0.7086	0.6470	0.6799	0.6475

Table 2: Comparison of GPT-4 and LLaMA-3.1 Performance on Event Sentence Extraction

Figure 2 presents the distribution of the number of sentences extracted by GPT-4 and LLaMA-3.1 for our dataset. Consistent with the performance metrics discussed earlier in this section, we observe a key difference in the extraction tendencies of the two models. GPT-4 produces a more concentrated distribution, with a median of 3 extracted sentences per story and a mean of 3.4, suggesting that the model is more selective in identifying eventful sentences. This aligns with its higher precision (0.79), as it extracts fewer sentences overall, reducing false positives but potentially missing relevant details.

On the other hand, LLaMA-3.1 demonstrates a much broader distribution, with a median of 7 extracted sentences per story and a mean of 10.9. This reinforces the previously observed higher recall (0.68) of LLaMA-3.1, indicating that it tends to classifies a larger number sentences as relevant, even at the cost of lower precision. The figure suggests that using the same prompt, LLaMA-3.1 often extracts significantly more sentences per story, capturing a wider range of contextual information, albeit with more noise.

We filter our dataset to retain only stories with at least five sentences extracted by GPT-4 to ensure that there are sufficient descriptions of events between a victim and perpetrator so we can identify patterns of such events in a meaningful way. This resulted in 1576 stories. The remaining analysis in this paper considers only this set of stories.

5 Generating Topics for Sentences

After extracting sentences containing events, we generated topics for those sentences in order to uncover patterns in topics across stories.

5.1 TopicGPT

We use TopicGPT (Pham et al., 2023) to generate topics for the sentences extracted from stories. TopicGPT is a prompt-based framework that uses LLMs to uncover latent topics in a text collection

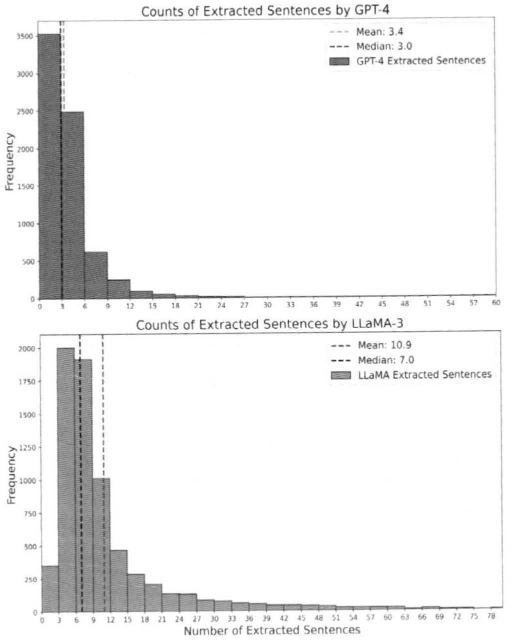

Figure 2: Distribution of the number of extracted sentences per story by GPT-4 and LLaMA-3 in our dataset.

(Pham et al., 2023). Given a corpus and some manually-curated example topics, TopicGPT identifies additional topics in each corpus document. For each document, the model is instructed to either assign a document to an existing topic or generate a new topic that better describes the document and add it to the list of topics. The framework then refines the list by merging repeated topics and removing infrequent topics. Once the set of topics are established, given the generated topics, an LLM assigns the most relevant topic to each document.

Previous studies have utilized dependency parsing to capture the main verb of the sentence to represent as the main event (Chaturvedi et al., 2017). However, with this approach, some contextual and useful information is lost in complex sentences which contain more than one verb. The advantage of using TopicGPT is that it assigns topics to sentences which are closely aligned with human categorizations and this approach sustains more context (Pham et al., 2023). Additionally, it allows us to inject our prior knowledge about topics that are extremely likely to be seen in the documents. To craft the initial set of topics which will improve TopicGPT's performance, we look at scientific works on domestic violence.

5.2 Initial Set of Topics

Intimate partner violence and its typologies have been studied extensively (Ali et al., 2016; Chapman and Gillespie, 2019; Krebs et al., 2011). The world health organization defines IPV as "behavior within an intimate relationship that causes physical, sexual or psychological harm, including acts of physical aggression, sexual coercion, psychological abuse and controlling behaviors" (Organization et al., 2010). One of the most commonly used measures of IPV is the revised conflict tactics scale (CTS2) (Straus et al., 1996). These scales were created to objectively measure the prevalence and frequency of tactics used by partners to resolve conflicts in dating, cohabiting, or marital relationships (Chapman and Gillespie, 2019). The CTS2 includes scales to measure four conflict tactics: *physical assault*, *psychological aggression*, *negotiation*, and *sexual coercion*. Each scale is divided into two subscales—*minor* and *severe*—with negotiation further including emotional and cognitive components. These eight high-level topics form our initial set of topics which we pass to the model as part of our topic generation process.

5.3 Generating Topics

To generate topics for the sentences which were extracted in the previous section, we used a slightly modified version of TopicGPT. The prompt we used is available in the Appendix section (A.2).

First, we passed the extracted sentences to the LLM individually. Next, instead of running the framework in two separate phases (generation and assignment), we provided the model with a predefined set of initial topics and instructions to assign one of the provided topic(s) or generate a topic for the sentence if there is no topic to which the model belongs. At each iteration, a newly generated topic is retained only if it is not too similar to an existing topic. To measure topic similarity, we use Sentence-BERT (Reimers, 2019) to capture topic embeddings. Figure 3 summarizes the the number of unique topics found after processing all 1576 stories with different similarity thresholds. As seen in Figure 3, using similarity thresholds in the set {0.5, 0.6, 0.7} will lead to a stable number of unique topics after processing around 300-600 stories for both models, whereas setting the similarity threshold to higher values generates unbounded number of topics as the number of stories grows. We set the similarity threshold to 0.7 to limit the

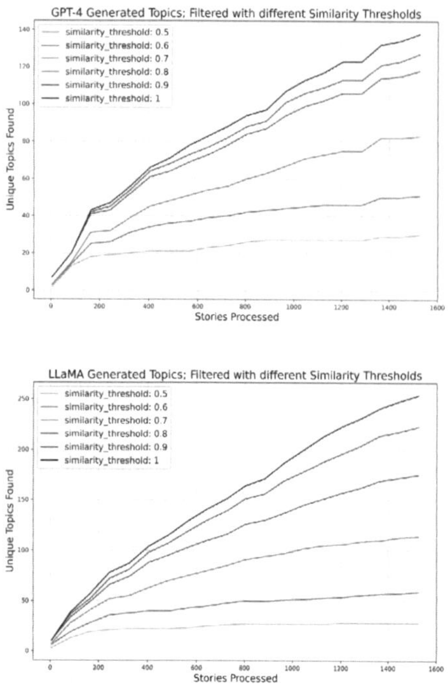

Figure 3: Number of unique topics found using different similarity thresholds.

number of generated topics but also to allow for more nuance in the generated topics. This resulted in 83 different topics.

6 Analysis

After identifying eventful sentences and generating topics for them, we then aimed to identify patterns of topics across stories.

6.1 Topic Co-occurrence

To find patterns within the stories, we investigate the topics that co-occur most frequently together within a story. Figure 5 presents a Pointwise Positive Mutual Information (PPMI) heatmap, capturing the relationships between the top 10 most frequent topics in the stories.

A notable pattern is the strong connection between "emotional manipulation" and "financial neglect", suggesting that financial and emotional control often co-occur within survivor narratives. Similarly, "economic abuse" frequently appears alongside "minor psychological aggression". The association between "substance use" and "legal protections" suggests that intoxication often precipitates conflicts or incidents that result in legal interventions, such as protective orders or law enforcement

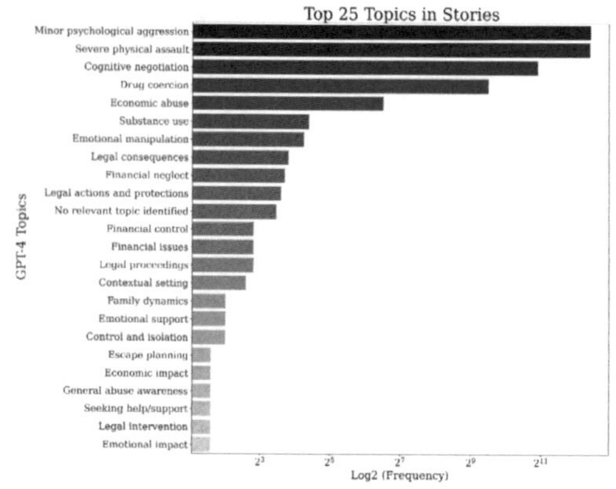

Figure 4: The top 25 most frequent topics generated by GPT-4. The x-axis represents the log_2-transformed frequency of each topic.

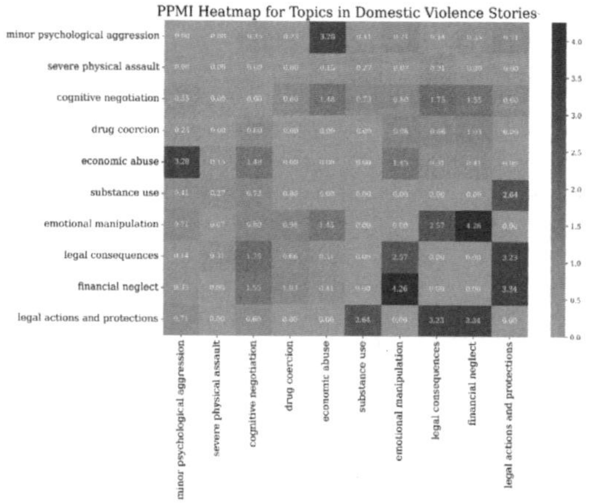

Figure 5: PPMI heatmap showing the relationships between the top 10 most frequent topics assigned to extracted sentences. Darker shades indicate stronger-than-expected associations between topics.

involvement.

Interestingly, some topics have low or zero co-occurrence with others, such as "severe physical assault", which does not show strong connections with many of the top topics. This suggests that descriptions of physical violence may often appear in isolation, rather than alongside financial or psychological abuse in the same sentence-level context.

Overall, this heatmap highlights the interconnected nature of abuse forms, showing how certain patterns of violence, manipulation, and financial control frequently emerge together in survivor accounts. The strong positive PMI values for certain topic pairs reinforce the idea that domestic abuse is often multidimensional, rather than consisting of isolated forms of harm.

6.2 Topic N-grams and Sequential Patterns

To identify meaningful topic patterns beyond simple frequency biases, we employed a Monte Carlo-based significance analysis (Robert et al., 1999). In our data so far, we have reduced each story into its eventful constituent sentences and each sentence into its dominant topic(s), constructing a set of topic sequences. In this section, we construct topic sequences with lengths of two, three, four, and five, and we refer to them as "topic n-grams". Since certain topics occur more frequently overall (see Figure 4), raw frequency counts of topic n-grams are insufficient for detecting meaningful patterns. To account for this, we generated a null distribution by randomly shuffling topics across sentences and stories while preserving the original dataset's structure. To preserve the dataset's structure, we maintain the number of stories, the number of sentences per story, and the occurrences of each topic within a sentence. By running multiple Monte Carlo simulations under these constraints, we computed the expected frequency of each topic n-gram under random shuffles within each sentence. The most distinctive topic n-grams were identified as those whose observed frequency in the real dataset was significantly greater than their expected frequency under the null distribution, as determined by statistical significance testing. Statistical significance was determined using Z-scores and one-tailed p-values from a normal approximation, ensuring that the extracted patterns reflect genuine structural relationships in the data rather than simple topic frequency effects.

N-gram	Total N-grams	Statistically Significant N-grams
3-grams	540	213
4-grams	934	484
5-grams	1511	737

Table 3: Number of statistically significant n-grams in the dataset based on Monte Carlo simulations (α = 0.05, one-tailed test with Z > 1.645).

The results presented in Table 3 indicate that a substantial proportion of topic n-grams exhibit statistically significant deviations from the null distribution, suggesting the presence of structured topic sequences in the dataset. The relatively high proportion of significant topic n-grams across all levels reinforces the idea that topic transitions are not random, but rather follow discernible patterns, reflecting underlying thematic structures in the stories.

Table 4 and Table 5 present the top tri-grams and four-grams respectively. The tables highlight the key narrative structures that emerge across stories, reinforcing the presence of natural topic progressions that differ from random assignment of topics. Many of these statistically significant n-grams encapsulate intuitive thematic patterns that summarize recurring story structures at an abstract level. As an example, in the Table 4, the sequence *"seeking help/support $\rightarrow$ emotional support $\rightarrow$ preparation for emergencies"* represent coherent progressions of events that naturally align with real-world experiences.

Tri-gram	Z-score
Seeking help/support - Emotional support - Preparation for emergencies	23.42
Legal and custodial actions - Legal consequences - Severe physical assault	10.40
Emotional support - Preparation for emergencies - Minor psychological aggression	10.10
Minor psychological aggression - Legal and custodial actions - Legal consequences	8.37
Cognitive negotiation - Legal actions and protections - Economic impact	7.50

Table 4: Top statistically significant trigrams based on Monte Carlo simulations ($\alpha = 0.05$, one-tailed test with $Z > 1.645$).

Four-gram	Z-score
Drug coercion - Economic abuse - Drug coercion - Severe physical assault	7.85
Financial neglect - Minor psychological aggression - Severe physical assault - Minor psychological aggression	4.64
Severe physical assault - Drug coercion - Cognitive negotiation - Cognitive negotiation	4.17
Severe physical assault - Emotional manipulation - Cognitive negotiation - Minor psychological aggression	4.08
Minor psychological aggression - Severe physical assault - Emotional manipulation - Cognitive negotiation	4.06

Table 5: Top statistically significant four-grams based on Monte Carlo simulations ($\alpha = 0.05$, one-tailed test with $Z > 1.645$).

Overall, these results indicate that topic sequences in the dataset are not merely driven by individual topic frequencies, but rather follow predictable, structured progressions that characterize different forms of conflict, abuse, and crisis response.

7 Conclusion

In this paper, we analyzed a large dataset of domestic violence stories posted on Reddit. We investigate LLMs' ability to extract events which involve main characters of the story. Our findings suggest that despite LLMs showing remarkable performance across various NLP tasks, they still fall short of human-level performance for extracting events that meet specific conditions. We used a modern LLM-based topic modeling approach, TopicGPT, and find it suits our task well, as is able to assign coherent and interpretable topics to sentences in the story. Our proposed method, an LLM based pipeline for extracting sentences and assigning topics to them, reduces each story into a structured topic sequence, facilitating narrative analysis. Using Monte Carlo simulations, we examined the topic sequences generated by our method, and found them to contain meaningful structures which are significantly different than any random assignment of the assigned topics. The results validate that our pipeline extracts structural patterns that are highly interpretable. In future work, we will analyze the stories with a generative approach and develop techniques for identifying narratives that deviate from predominant topic progression patterns.

Limitations

Despite the valuable insights gained from our analysis of domestic violence narratives, our approach has several limitations. First, the limited number of human-annotated examples for event extraction constrains the quality of model supervision, potentially affecting the accuracy of both tasks. Expanding the annotation set could lead to better understanding of LLMs' performance for event extraction. Second, our approach is susceptible to error propagation, as inaccuracies in event extraction directly impact the quality of topic assignments. For instance, if the LLM fails to identify a key event, the resulting topic sequence may misrepresent the narrative's structure, leading to misleading conclusions about topic progression patterns. Lastly, while we modeled topic transitions using a sequence-based approach, other methods of sequential analysis, such as Hidden Markov Models (HMMs), Recurrent Neural Networks (RNNs) could provide alternative perspectives on narrative structures. Exploring these methods in future work could enhance our understanding of how domestic violence narratives evolve over time.

Ethical Considerations

We use publicly available Reddit posts while adhering to the platform's terms of service, but we recognize the sensitive nature of the content. To protect individuals' anonymity, we do not disclose usernames, personal identifiers, or specific excerpts that could lead to the identification of survivors.

Our findings highlight common patterns in domestic violence narratives based on event and topic analysis. However, we stress that these patterns should not be used to invalidate or discredit stories that deviate from them, as every survivor's experience is unique. A story that does not follow the typical narrative structure identified in our study is not inherently inaccurate or less credible. Our analysis aims to provide insights into common themes, not to impose a rigid framework for assessing narrative authenticity.

References

Josh Achiam, Steven Adler, Sandhini Agarwal, Lama Ahmad, Ilge Akkaya, Florencia Leoni Aleman, Diogo Almeida, Janko Altenschmidt, Sam Altman, Shyamal Anadkat, et al. 2023. Gpt-4 technical report. *arXiv preprint arXiv:2303.08774*.

Jacqueline Aguilar, Charley Beller, Paul McNamee, Benjamin Van Durme, Stephanie Strassel, Zhiyi Song, and Joe Ellis. 2014. A comparison of the events and relations across ace, ere, tac-kbp, and framenet annotation standards. In *Proceedings of the second workshop on EVENTS: Definition, detection, coreference, and representation*, pages 45–53.

Parveen Azam Ali, Katie Dhingra, and Julie McGarry. 2016. A literature review of intimate partner violence and its classifications. *Aggression and violent behavior*, 31:16–25.

Maria Antoniak, David Mimno, and Karen Levy. 2019. Narrative paths and negotiation of power in birth stories. *Proceedings of the ACM on Human-Computer Interaction*, 3(CSCW):1–27.

Maria Antoniak, Joel Mire, Maarten Sap, Elliott Ash, and Andrew Piper. 2023. Where do people tell stories online? story detection across online communities. *arXiv preprint arXiv:2311.09675*.

Ryan L Boyd, Kate G Blackburn, and James W Pennebaker. 2020. The narrative arc: Revealing core narrative structures through text analysis. *Science advances*, 6(32):eaba2196.

Alexander Calderwood, Elizabeth A Pruett, Raymond Ptucha, Christopher Homan, and Cecilia Ovesdotter Alm. 2017. Understanding the semantics of narratives of interpersonal violence through reader annotations and physiological reactions. In *Proceedings of the Workshop Computational Semantics Beyond Events and Roles*, pages 1–9.

Nathanael Chambers and Dan Jurafsky. 2008. Unsupervised learning of narrative event chains. In *Proceedings of ACL-08: HLT*, pages 789–797.

Harriet Chapman and Steven M Gillespie. 2019. The revised conflict tactics scales (cts2): A review of the properties, reliability, and validity of the cts2 as a measure of partner abuse in community and clinical samples. *Aggression and violent behavior*, 44:27–35.

Snigdha Chaturvedi, Mohit Iyyer, and Hal Daume III. 2017. Unsupervised learning of evolving relationships between literary characters. In *Proceedings of the AAAI Conference on Artificial Intelligence*, volume 31.

Jacob Cohen. 1960. A coefficient of agreement for nominal scales. *Educational and psychological measurement*, 20(1):37–46.

Abhimanyu Dubey, Abhinav Jauhri, Abhinav Pandey, Abhishek Kadian, Ahmad Al-Dahle, Aiesha Letman, Akhil Mathur, Alan Schelten, Amy Yang, Angela Fan, et al. 2024. The llama 3 herd of models. *arXiv preprint arXiv:2407.21783*.

Joshua D Eisenberg and Mark Finlayson. 2021. Narrative boundaries annotation guide. *Journal of Cultural Analytics*, 6(4).

Mourad Heddaya, Qingcheng Zeng, Chenhao Tan, Rob Voigt, and Alexander Zentefis. 2024. Causal micronarratives. *arXiv preprint arXiv:2410.05252*.

Lifu Huang, Heng Ji, Kyunghyun Cho, and Clare R Voss. 2017. Zero-shot transfer learning for event extraction. *arXiv preprint arXiv:1707.01066*.

Sweta Karlekar and Mohit Bansal. 2018. Safecity: Understanding diverse forms of sexual harassment personal stories. *arXiv preprint arXiv:1809.04739*.

Christopher Krebs, Matthew J Breiding, Angela Browne, and Tara Warner. 2011. The association between different types of intimate partner violence experienced by women. *Journal of Family Violence*, 26:487–500.

William Labov and Joshua Waletzky. 1997. Narrative analysis: Oral versions of personal experience.

Qian Li, Jianxin Li, Jiawei Sheng, Shiyao Cui, Jia Wu, Yiming Hei, Hao Peng, Shu Guo, Lihong Wang, Amin Beheshti, et al. 2022. A survey on deep learning event extraction: Approaches and applications. *IEEE Transactions on Neural Networks and Learning Systems*.

Sha Li, Heng Ji, and Jiawei Han. 2021. Document-level event argument extraction by conditional generation. *arXiv preprint arXiv:2104.05919*.

Yinhan Liu. 2019. Roberta: A robustly optimized bert pretraining approach. *arXiv preprint arXiv:1907.11692*, 364.

Yaojie Lu, Hongyu Lin, Jin Xu, Xianpei Han, Jialong Tang, Annan Li, Le Sun, Meng Liao, and Shaoyi Chen. 2021. Text2event: Controllable sequence-to-structure generation for end-to-end event extraction. *arXiv preprint arXiv:2106.09232*.

Kory Wallace Mathewson, Pablo Samuel Castro, Colin Cherry, George Foster, and Marc G Bellemare. 2020. Shaping the narrative arc: Information-theoretic collaborative dialogue. In *Proceedings of the 11th International Conference on Computational Creativity*, pages 9–16.

Semi Min and Juyong Park. 2016. Mapping out narrative structures and dynamics using networks and textual information. *arXiv preprint arXiv:1604.03029*.

Seyed Mahed Mousavi, Shohei Tanaka, Gabriel Roccabruna, Koichiro Yoshino, Satoshi Nakamura, and Giuseppe Riccardi. 2023. Whats new? identifying the unfolding of new events in narratives. *arXiv preprint arXiv:2302.07748*.

World Health Organization et al. 2010. *Preventing intimate partner and sexual violence against women: Taking action and generating evidence*. World Health Organization.

Chau Minh Pham, Alexander Hoyle, Simeng Sun, Philip Resnik, and Mohit Iyyer. 2023. Topicgpt: A prompt-based topic modeling framework. *arXiv preprint arXiv:2311.01449*.

Andrew Piper and Sunyam Bagga. 2024. Using large language models for understanding narrative discourse. In *Proceedings of the The 6th Workshop on Narrative Understanding*, pages 37–46.

N Reimers. 2019. Sentence-bert: Sentence embeddings using siamese bert-networks. *arXiv preprint arXiv:1908.10084*.

Christian P Robert, George Casella, and George Casella. 1999. *Monte Carlo statistical methods*, volume 2. Springer.

Benjamin M Schmidt. 2015. Plot arceology: A vector-space model of narrative structure. In *2015 IEEE International Conference on Big Data (Big Data)*, pages 1667–1672. IEEE.

Nicolas Schrading, Cecilia Ovesdotter Alm, Raymond Ptucha, and Christopher Homan. 2015. An analysis of domestic abuse discourse on reddit. In *Proceedings of the 2015 conference on empirical methods in natural language processing*, pages 2577–2583.

Mohammad Shokri, Allison Bishop, and Sarah Ita Levitan. 2024. Is it safe to tell your story? towards achieving privacy for sensitive narratives. In *The 6th Workshop on Narrative Understanding*, page 47.

Matthew Sims, Jong Ho Park, and David Bamman. 2019. Literary event detection. In *Proceedings of the 57th annual meeting of the association for computational linguistics*, pages 3623–3634.

Murray A Straus, Sherry L Hamby, SUE Boney-McCoy, and David B Sugarman. 1996. The revised conflict tactics scales (cts2) development and preliminary psychometric data. *Journal of family issues*, 17(3):283–316.

Md Nayem Uddin, Enfa Rose George, Eduardo Blanco, and Steven Corman. 2024. Asking and answering questions to extract event-argument structures. *arXiv preprint arXiv:2404.16413*.

A Vaswani. 2017. Attention is all you need. *Advances in Neural Information Processing Systems*.

Michael Vauth, Hans Ole Hatzel, Evelyn Gius, and Chris Biemann. 2021. Automated event annotation in literary texts. In *CHR*, pages 333–345.

Zeno Vendler. 1957. Verbs and times. *The philosophical review*, 66(2):143–160.

Eitan Wagner, Renana Keydar, and Omri Abend. 2024. Zero-shot trajectory mapping in holocaust testimonies. In *Proceedings of the First Workshop on Holocaust Testimonies as Language Resources (HTRes)@ LREC-COLING 2024*, pages 63–70.

Eitan Wagner, Renana Keydar, Amit Pinchevski, and Omri Abend. 2022. Topical segmentation of spoken narratives: A test case on holocaust survivor testimonies. *arXiv preprint arXiv:2210.13783*.

Xiyang Zhang, Muhao Chen, and Jonathan May. 2021. Salience-aware event chain modeling for narrative understanding. *arXiv preprint arXiv:2109.10475*.

A Prompts

We include the exact prompts used for LLaMA-3.1 and GPT-4 during event extraction and topic assignment to ensure the reproducibility of our experiments. These prompts guided the models to extract sentences involving specific characters and to assign topics to narrative segments. Below are the prompts we used.

A.1 Prompts Used for Event Extraction

Following is the prompt we used for the event extraction task with both our models:

```
[Event Definition]
Events are “a singular occurrence at a particular place and time.” General, repeating, isolated, or hypothetical situations, states, and actions are usually not events.
Most stories are told in the past tense. Present and future tense can also be used, but the bar is higher and the narrated events need to be strongly story-like.
Most events are positively asserted as occurring, but depending on the context, negative verbs can also be events when occurring at a specific time and place.
Verbal interactions could be events too.
Events are usually verbs but can also be nouns and adjectives.


Read the story below and extract ALL the sentences that describe an event which only involves both the victim and the perpetrator in the story.


[few-shot examples]
.
.
.


[Story]
{}


Please ONLY return the extracted sentences.

[Your output]
Extracted sentences:
```

We provided three examples in the prompt for event extraction task. Due to space limitations, we didn't write them in the above prompt. We chose three of the annotated stories as few-shot examples and provided as few-shot examples in the prompt.

A.2 Prompts Used for Topic Generation

Following is the prompt we used for topic generation for both models:

```
You will receive a sentence from a domestic violence story posted on reddit and a set of topics. Your task is to identify topics within the sentence which describe the sentence best. If any relevant topics are missing from the provided set, please add them. Otherwise, output the existing topic as identified in the sentence.

[Topics]
{}

[Instructions]
Step 1: Determine topics mentioned in the sentence which describe the sentence best. - The topics must reflect a SINGLE topic instead of a combination of topics. - The new topics must have a short general label. - The topics must be broad enough to accommodate future subtopics.

[Example]
Sentence: He strangled me and told me he is going to kill me next time.
Topics:
1. Severe physical assault
2. Severe psychological agression

[Sentence]
{}

Please ONLY return the relevant or modified topics.

[Your response]
Topics:
```

A.3 Example Output

Here we show an example from GPT-4's output for both tasks related to the following story.
Content Warning: The following story contains language that may be offensive or disturbing to some readers.

```
Female, 19.dated my now ex-boyfriend (who is 20, turns 21 in a month) for a year and seven months. After we broke up in October of 2010, I was devastated. A lot of my friends didn't really understand why. They knew that he had been emotionally/verbally abusive and of course knew I was better off, but I never really came to that conclusion until many, many months later. He'd never outright call me fat or ugly, but he definitely found indirect ways to tell me. He even told me, after we'd been broken up for a couple of months, that if I were to have sex with anyone else but him, I'd be a slut. He's the only person I've ever slept with, and we were in a committed relationship for awhile before we started having sex.struggled with my self-esteem a lot before I started dating him, but now it's at all all-time low. Everything he used to say burns in the back of my mind. I go to the gym and work out three days a week and do pilates twice a week and try to eat healthy, but I feel like it will never be enough. I'm 5'2" and 135 pounds. I'm a size 4-6. But it's become an unhealthy obsession to win his approval even though I know I'm never going to get it. I want to be smaller. Lighter. Thinner.called me the other day and wanted to talk with me, so we hung out for a bit. He again found ways to call me a slut, and tell me that I'm still not as thin as I could be. I don't understand why I need his approval so badly. Other guys have told me that I have a great body and I'm pretty, but it holds absolutely no weight.do I stop this madness? I feel like I'm on a one-way path to self-destruction and I don't know how to stop, only how to slow down or speed up. Please help.

GPT-4 extracted sentences:

1. He even told me, after we'd been broken up for a couple of months, that if I were to have sex with anyone else but him, I'd be a slut.
2. He called me the other day and wanted to talk with me, so we hung out for a bit.
3. He again found ways to call me a slut, and tell me that I'm still not as thin as I could be.

GPT-4 assigned topics:

1. minor psychological aggression
2. Cognitive negotiation
3. Minor psychological aggression
```

A Theoretical Framework for Evaluating Narrative Surprise in Large Language Models

Annaliese Bissell [1]
McGill University

Ella Paulin [1]
McGill University

Andrew Piper
McGill University

Abstract

Narrative surprise is a core element of storytelling for engaging audiences, and yet it remains underexplored in the context of large language models (LLMs) and narrative generation. While surprise arises from events that deviate from expectations while maintaining retrospective coherence, current computational approaches lack comprehensive frameworks to evaluate this phenomenon. This paper presents a novel framework for assessing narrative surprise, drawing on psychological theories of narrative comprehension and surprise intensity. We operationalize six criteria—initiatoriness, immutability violation, predictability, post-dictability, importance, and valence—to measure narrative surprise in story endings. Our study evaluates 120 story endings, generated by both human authors and LLMs, across 30 mystery narratives. Through a ranked-choice voting methodology, we identify significant correlations between reader preferences and four of the six criteria. Results underscore the continuing advantage of human-authored endings in achieving compelling narrative surprise, while also revealing significant progress in LLM-generated narratives.

1 Introduction

Narrative surprise represents a fundamental mechanism through which stories engage and captivate audiences, yet our understanding of how to systematically measure this phenomenon in large language models (LLMs) remains limited. While traditional narratology has long recognized surprise as one of three key components of narrative tension alongside suspense and curiosity (Brewer and Lichtenstein, 1980; Sternberg, 1990; Hoeken and Van Vliet, 2000; Bermejo-Berros et al., 2022), the emergence of LLMs as storytelling agents presents novel challenges in quantifying their ability to generate genuine narrative surprise.

Recent work in computational story generation has focused on two key challenges relevant to this area that have nevertheless remained distinct from one another. Narrative *coherence* is essential for establishing narrative meaning by ensuring continuity among multiple narrative elements such as setting, characters, and events (Guan et al., 2019; Gupta et al., 2019). Narrative *surprise*, on the other hand, depends on the introduction of novel information while also maintaining narrative coherence. As Sternberg (1990) argues, for surprise to be effective, the unexpected turn of events must be *retrospectively coherent*.

From this perspective, recent approaches to evaluating narrative surprise in computational storytelling have important limitations. While researchers have made progress in developing word-level surprise metrics (Huang et al., 2023; Wilmot and Keller, 2020) and tracking narrative turning points through sentiment analysis (Tian et al., 2024; Knight et al., 2024; Elkins, 2022), these methods do not capture the complex temporal relationships that make stories coherent and meaningful. Specifically, they do not address how surprising events must deviate from expectations while remaining logically consistent within the broader narrative framework. This disconnect between the evaluation of local surprise and global coherence represents a significant gap in the field, underscoring the need for a more comprehensive theoretical framework that can assess both the unexpectedness of generated story elements and the success of their narrative integration.

In this paper, we present a novel theoretical framework for evaluating narrative surprise, grounded in psychological research on narrative comprehension and evaluation. Our framework introduces six key metrics that capture different dimensions of cognitive surprise in narrative understanding. To validate this framework, we conduct an analysis of 120 story endings, generated by both

[1]These authors contributed equally to the paper.

Proceedings of the The 7th Workshop on Narrative Understanding, pages 26–35
May 4, 2025 ©2025 Association for Computational Linguistics

human authors and LLMs, focusing on 30 mystery stories sourced from the Reedsy fiction platform. These stories are manually truncated before their pivotal revelations to enable controlled testing of ending generation. Using a ranked-choice voting methodology, we assess the relative quality of different endings and examine how our proposed metrics correlate with reader preferences.

Our analysis reveals that four of our six variables demonstrate significant associations with reader preferences, providing initial validation of our theoretical framework. We compare LLM and human performance using both voting data and our six-metric framework. We conclude by discussing future directions for enhancing narrative surprise evaluation in computational storytelling and share our underlying data.[2]

2 Prior Work

2.1 Theories of Narrative Surprise

Contemporary theoretical frameworks consistently identify cognitive surprise as an emotion triggered by the disparity between expected and actual events or information revelation (Ortony and Partridge, 1987; Brewer and Lichtenstein, 1980; Celle et al., 2017). In the context of narrative comprehension, Structural Affect Theory (SAT) provides a theoretical foundation for understanding surprise generation (Brewer and Lichtenstein, 1980). SAT posits that presentation of a *surprise event* (SE) without the presentation of its corresponding *initiating events* (IE) or causal antecedents can provoke surprise. Thus, in order to provoke *surprise* as defined in SAT, the initiating event (IE) or "expository information" must be withheld, while maintaining readers' unawareness of this omission. It is this lack of awareness of the omission that distinguishes surprise from curiosity, which arises when readers consciously perceive an information gap (Brewer and Lichtenstein, 1980).

Moreover, Ortony and Partridge (1987) propose that the intensity of the surprise is contingent on the type of expectation subverted. They categorize propositions into two types: *immutable* (fixed within the story's universe) and *mutable* (which can change without breaking the story's logic). In a murder mystery, for example, an immutable element is that the victim is dead—this is a real-world condition of the story's universe. Changing this would break the internal logic of the mystery. A mutable element is how the detective solves the case—whether uncovering a hidden letter, analyzing forensic evidence, or interrogating suspects, the path to the solution can vary without altering the story's basic premises. (Ortony and Partridge, 1987).

The framework also differentiates between *deducible* outcomes—which the reader would have been able to predict given a combination of evidence presented in the story and general world knowledge—and non-deducible outcomes, which could not have been predicted. The latter are often outcomes that lack a clear antecedent, e.g. a rock flying through a window without warning (Ortony and Partridge, 1987). They posit that a contradiction of an immutable expectation will elicit maximal surprise, while contradiction of a mutable expectation may elicit high but not maximal surprise.

Bae and Young (2013) provide a concrete set of criteria to check whether a story provokes surprise in the reader. Their Prevoyant story plan generation architecture implements a reader-modeling evaluator that assesses story plans across four dimensions: expectation failure, importance, emotional valence, and incongruity resolution. They posit that emotional valence (positive or negative) influences surprise quality, with higher surprise provoked by an outcome with negative valence than that of one with positive valence. They define incongruity resolution as the presentation of events or information that resolves any apparent contradictions in the story.

These works and concepts will function as the foundation of our annotation framework described in Section 3.

2.2 Language Model Narrative Generation

Prior work has identified significant limitations in LLM-generated narratives, particularly regarding narrative coherence and plot development. Tian et al. (2024) demonstrate that while readers appreciate logical and well-motivated plot developments, LLM outputs frequently default to simplistic positive trajectories or miraculous twists and may suffer from a lack of coherence.

Several methods have been proposed to provide coherent and surprising output. Huang et al. (2023) developed the Affective Story Generator (AffGen), which implements two key mechanisms to enhance narrative engagement: favouring less predictable words and using an Affective Reranking system

[2] https://doi.org/10.5683/SP3/TOXZSQ

that prioritizes heightened emotional intensity in generated content.

See et al. (2019) demonstrated that while GPT2-117 outperformed neural story generation systems in awareness of story context and lexical diversity, it produced similarly repetitive narratives. Building on this work, Akoury et al. (2020) explored domain adaptation through fine-tuning GPT-2 on data from the online storytelling platform STORIUM. They found that while the model achieved linguistic fluency, it struggled with maintaining narrative coherence, frequently introducing inconsistent story events or characters.

Although contemporary LLMs are more fluent and coherent, they continue to lack the ability to generate well-paced and diverse narratives. Tian et al. (2024) investigate the narrative generation ability of commercially available LLMs, finding that despite recent advances in LLM capabilities, story arcs in LLM output are more poorly paced than human narratives. Moreover, LLMs' tendencies toward homogeneous, positive plot trajectories lead to less suspenseful output.

Chakrabarty et al. (2024) find that LLM-generated narratives achieve only 10-33% of human-level performance across four dimensions of creativity. LLMs perform badly on tasks related to narrative surprise, containing "turns that are both surprising and appropriate" only between 22% and 34% as often as human narratives (Chakrabarty et al., 2024). Specific narrative surprise-related problems identified by Chakrabarty et al. (2024)'s annotators include illogical events, inconsistent characterization, clichés, unrealistic happy endings, unexpected surreal elements and failure to deliver on potential of a premise. However, when basing their analysis on amateur short stories on Reddit Zhou et al. (2024) show that GPT-4 rivals human ability to produce engaging, provocative and narratively complex short stories, which suggests model performance may vary based on the specific narrative generation task and evaluation context.

3 A Theoretical Framework for Measuring Narrative Surprise

We evaluate six criteria for narrative surprise, drawing from foundational work on story comprehension and narrative affect discussed above (see Table 1 for an overview). Our framework integrates Bae and Young (2013)'s work on computational models for generating surprising narratives and Ortony and Partridge (1987)'s framework for surprise intensity. The framework relies on narratives segmented into two structural components: the 'stem,' encompassing the beginning and middle of the narrative, and the 'ending,' which resolves earlier narrative events, often in the form of a 'big reveal'. Note that we assume the surprising event with unknown causes (SE) is presented in the 'stem,' while its initiating events (IEs), i.e. causes, are presented in the 'ending.'

Category	Description
Initiatory	Ending describes a novel event that temporally precedes and causes the SE.
Immutability Violation	Ending contradicts an immutable fact of the story world.
Predictable	A typical reader could have predicted the ending given the stem.
Post-dictable	Looking backwards at the whole story, the events are explainable, i.e. there are neither loose ends nor contradictions.
Important	Events of the ending meaningfully impact the protagonist.
Valence	Events of the ending are positive for the protagonist.

Table 1: Definitions of Surprise Criteria

The first criterion, *initiatoriness*, which operationalizes Brewer and Lichtenstein (1980)'s surprise generation hypothesis, examines whether initiatory events are presented in the ending which offer a causal explanation for the SE that occurred in the stem. A highly initiatory narrative ending will provide key initiating events that explain how the surprising event(s) of the narrative stem occurred.

The second criterion, *immutability violation*, builds on Ortony and Partridge (1987) theoretical framework concerning proposition violation. This dimension assesses the degree to which narrative events challenge established axioms within the story world's logical framework. Immutability violations occur when narratives contradict fundamental beliefs about the world (such as the absence of flying pigs). Narratives contradicting more flexible beliefs, such as the belief that employers always hire by merit, are less *immutability violating* and easier to accept as plausible.

The third criterion, *predictability*, builds on the observation of Ortony and Partridge (1987) that an expectation-reality discrepancy is required to elicit surprise. Our framework posits outcome predictability to be inversely related to surprise magnitude, while acknowledging that to ensure reader satisfaction, narrative surprises must not be totally impossible to predict. This suggests an optimal zone of moderate predictability.

The fourth dimension, *post-dictability*, is drawn from Bae and Young (2013). It measures the degree to which the narrative maintains internal consistency and fully explains plot events in order to leave readers with the feeling that the story makes sense in retrospect. This aligns with Sternberg (1990)'s argument that surprise necessitates events to be *retrospectively coherent*.

The final two criteria, *valence* and *importance*, are taken directly from the framework of Bae and Young (2013), where negativity and importance are hypothesized to be positively correlated with surprise.

4 Methods

4.1 Dataset

We construct a dataset of 30 mystery short stories drawn from the story prompt website Reedsy, written after October 2023. We choose this date as it post-dates our selected models' training period, ensuring that the LLMs are evaluated on new data. We use mysteries because surprisingness is both inherent to the genre and also highly structured. Each narrative begins with an unexplained event, followed by a systematic revelation of details that lead readers to the ultimate solution, i.e. all necessary information has been revealed.

Mysteries thus provide a controlled pattern for the study of narrative surprise, one that aligns with prior work on story ending generation (Guan et al., 2019). However, whereas prior work on story ending generation has typically focused on very short sequences–Zhou et al. (2024) focus on stories with an average length of 450 words, while Mostafazadeh et al. (2016) look at stories of 6 sentences in length–our stories are considerably longer by comparison posing a more challenging task (Table 2).

To prepare our data for evaluation, we manually divide each story into a "stem" and "ending," truncating the story at the point where the author begins to answer the central question posed at the beginning by the unexplained event (e.g. "who killed the protagonist's brother," "why is food going missing from the kitchen when nobody in the family is touching it," etc.), which we hypothesize to be where the "big reveal" happens. As can be seen in Table 2, stem and ending lengths are not only of considerably different lengths, but the two categories themselves contain considerable variance.

Story Portion	Mean	SD
Stem	2056	511
Human Ending	339	220
GPT Zero Shot Ending	447	82
GPT Few Shot Ending	577	144
Phi3 Zero Shot Ending	424	186

Table 2: Stem and Ending Lengths

4.2 Story Ending Generation

We then prompt two language models, one large frontier model, gpt-4o-2024-08-06, and one small open-weight model with a large-enough context window to handle our texts, Phi3-mini-128k-instruct. Both models were trained prior to our cut-off date for our stories. In order to generate an ending given a stem, we use two prompting strategies:

1. Zero Shot: "Your task is to write a surprising twist ending for a given incomplete mystery short story. The story does not need to have a moral, and the ending should be about 300 words. Here is the story: ..."

2. Few Shot: the same prompt as above was used, with the addition of "When writing your ending, follow these examples: ..." and 2 example stem/ending pairs.

We found that using a chain of thought approach, where the model was prompted to analyze the characters and plot points and brainstorm possible twist endings before generating a final ending, provided no improvement over the outputs of the zero shot or few shot approaches. We also found that the few shot approach diminished the quality of endings for our Phi3 model. Thus our final dataset consisted of 120 story endings, consisting of endings generated by GPT4 (Zero Shot), GPT4 (Few Shot), and Phi3 (Zero Shot) along with the original human-authored ending.

4.3 Narrative Surprise Annotation

A team of four undergraduate student annotators were assembled, all of whom have prior experience in literary studies and text annotation. They were given a codebook, included in the data repository, with explicit descriptions for each criterion and instructions for rating endings on a 5-point Likert scale. This approach follows Chhun et al. (2022)'s recommendations for using human annotations in automatic story generation evaluation, while the explicit scale descriptions help reduce subjectivity in the labeling process. Students were then asked to identify the ending that they felt was the "most" and "least" surprising.

5 Results

5.1 Inter-Annotator Agreement

To measure inter-annotator agreement on our Likert scale annotations, we use the average deviation index (ADI) as suggested by O'Neill (2017). As can be seen in Table 3, for all criteria the ADI is < 1 on a five-point scale suggesting good levels of agreement.

Category	ADI
Predictable	0.715
Post-Dictable	0.639
Immutability Violation	0.598
Initiatory	0.559
Important	0.466
Valence	0.459

Table 3: Average Deviation Index across all surprise criteria.

We analyzed inter-annotator agreement on story-ending preferences using Kendall's W, a non-parametric statistic particularly suited for ranked ordinal data. The analysis revealed moderate consensus among the four raters ($W = 0.552$, $\chi^2(119) = 263$, $p < 0.001$). This coefficient, ranging from 0 to 1, indicates reliable but subjective judgments in evaluating ending quality, with the highly significant p-value confirming non-random agreement.

Given prior research on the variation of the experience of surprise (Juergensen et al., 2014), a medium degree of agreement is expected. To address this, we add random effects to the regression model discussed in Section 5.3 to control for annotator variability when analyzing correlations between surprise criteria ratings and reader preferences.

5.2 Model Preference

To assess the performance of the generated endings, we compare the number of most/least surprising votes each model received across all annotators and endings along with the odds ratio of observed voting behaviour relative to a random baseline of equal votes across all models.

Model	Most	OR	Least	OR
Phi3	4	0.13	87	2.90
GPT4 (Zero)	24	0.80	10	0.33
GPT4 (Few)	34	1.13	8	0.27
Human	58	1.93	15	0.50

Table 4: Counts of reader preferences with accompanying odds ratio of observed votes relative to a random baseline of expected votes for each model.

As can be seen in Table 4, our analysis reveals clear preferences among story endings. Human-authored endings were most preferred, selected at nearly twice the random baseline rate. Combined GPT-4 endings received comparable preference (58 selections total), though few-shot prompting proved more effective than zero-shot generation. In contrast, Phi3-generated endings were rarely preferred, suggesting significant quality differences between large and small language models for this task. Mixed-effects logistic regression confirmed these patterns, showing human-authored endings were 2.94 times more likely to be chosen than GPT-4 endings ($p < 0.001$), while Phi3 endings were significantly less preferred ($OR = 0.11$, $p < 0.001$).

5.3 Correlation with Reader Annotations

As a first step, we analyze the relationship between the distribution of surprise criteria across endings for our different models versus human endings. Using Spearman correlation coefficients, which are appropriate for ordinal Likert scale data, we find correlations of 0.60, 0.49, and 0.03 for GPT4-Zero Shot, GPT4-Few Shot, and Phi3, respectively with human-authored endings.

Fig. 1 illustrates the specific levels of correlation for each criteria and model comparison, indicating some meaningful degree of variance. GPT achieved the highest correlation on the initiatoriness of story endings and the lowest on post-dictability, i.e. the ability to explain ending events given prior story elements.

As a way of further illustrating the degree of correlation between human ratings and our LLMs,

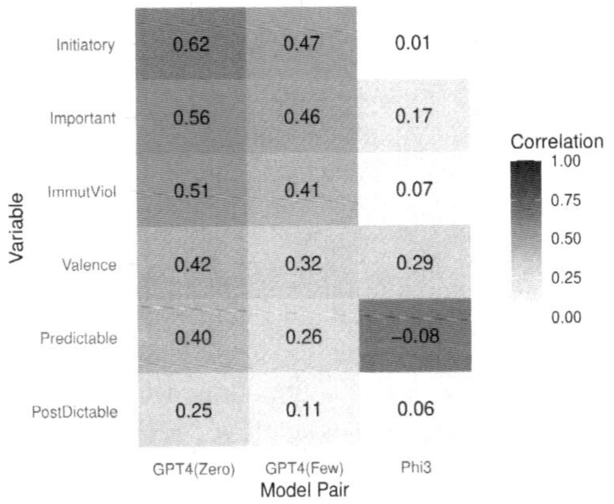

Figure 1: Spearman's correlation coefficient between human endings and each LLM.

Fig. 2 shows the distributions of annotator ratings across all six variables for human endings and GPT4 (Zero Shot), our highest correlated model.

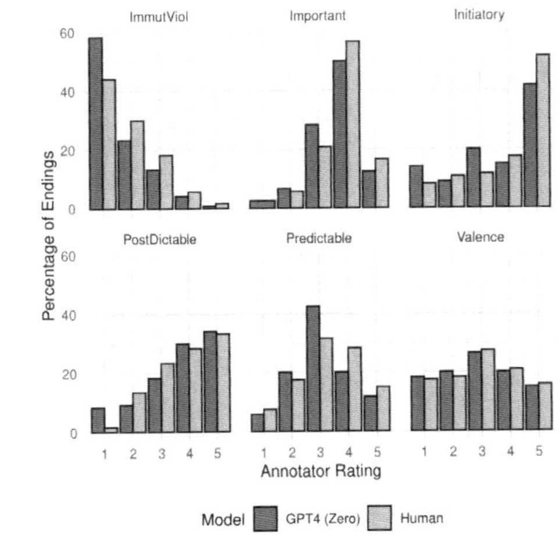

Figure 2: Distributions of annotator ratings for story endings authored by humans and GPT4 (Zero Shot) across all six variables.

We conducted a conditional logistic regression analysis to examine the relationship between our six predictor variables of surprise and the binary outcome of being the most preferred ending or not. We stratified the analysis by Stem to control for potential group-level effects. To assess model fit, we compared our model to a null model using likelihood ratio tests and evaluated the model's discriminative ability using the concordance index (C-index).

The conditional logistic regression model demonstrated strong overall fit (likelihood ratio test: $\chi^2(6) = 59.79$, $p < .001$). The model showed good discriminative ability with a C-index of 0.714 (SE = 0.028), indicating successful distinction between outcomes.

Bootstrap validation (100 resamples) suggested moderate model stability (SE = 9.81) with some potential for overfitting (bias = 14.88). We also compared our model to a random-effects model including annotator effects, but the lower AIC value for our primary model (AIC = 402.61 vs. 594.98) supported its selection as the final model.

As can be seen in Table 5, four predictors showed significant associations with being selected the most surprising ending, with two positively associated (Initiatory and Post-Dictable) and two negatively associated (Predictability and Valence). In Fig. 3, we illustrate the odds ratios and 95% confidence intervals showing how a one-unit increase in each variable affects the likelihood of being selected as winner.

	Dependent variable	
	Most Surprising	Odds-Ratio
ImmutViol	0.053 (0.133)	1.05
Important	0.256 (0.159)	1.30
Initiatory	0.352 (0.117)***	1.42
Post-Dictable	0.283 (0.133)**	1.33
Predictable	-0.496 (0.124)***	0.61
Valence	-0.263 (0.118)**	0.77

Note: *p<0.1; **p<0.05; ***p<0.01

Table 5: Logistic regression results analyzing the relationship between our surprise features and being selected the most surprising ending. We translate coefficients into the increased odds of winning with a one unit increase/decrease of a given variable.

Initiatoriness demonstrates the strongest positive influence, with each unit increase raising the odds of an ending being selected as most surprising by 42%. This effect is most pronounced when comparing extreme cases: endings with maximal initiatoriness were more than four times as likely to be chosen compared to those with minimal initiatoriness. Post-dictability shows a similar positive relationship, with each unit increase raising selection odds by 32%. At the extremes, maximally post-dictable endings were preferred over three times as often as minimally post-dictable ones.

On the other hand, both predictability and valence demonstrate significant negative relationships

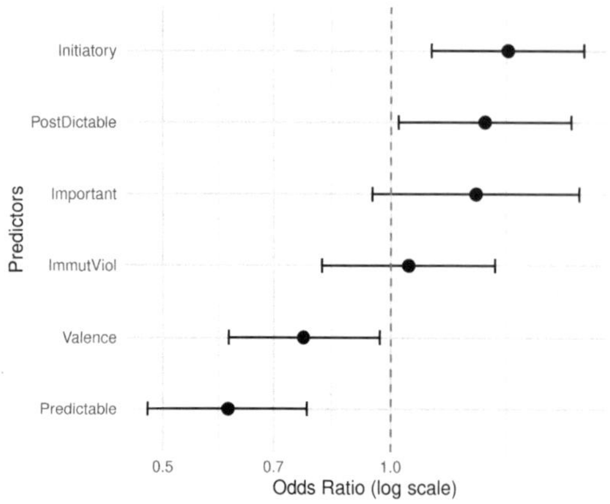

Figure 3: Odds-ratios with confidence intervals of being associated with the most surprising ending for our six surprise variables.

with surprise selection. Each unit increase in predictability reduces an ending's selection odds by 60%, with maximally predictable endings experiencing a sevenfold reduction in selection likelihood compared to minimally predictable ones. Valence shows a more moderate negative effect, with each unit increase (i.e., more positive outcomes) reducing selection odds by 24%. At the extremes, highly positive endings are 2.8 times less likely to be selected as surprising compared to highly negative ones.

6 Discussion

6.1 Understanding Narrative Surprise

Our analysis validates four of the six theoretically proposed criteria as significant predictors of narrative surprise intensity. These include endings with strong causal relationships to the main surprising event of the story (Initiatoriness); strong explanatory power of prior events (Post-Dictability); low predictability of reported events (Predictability); and negative valence (Valence).

In Story #10, for example, whose preferred ending was rated 4.75 (out of 5) for Initiatoriness, the story stem focuses on a protagonist who discovers a crumpled letter addressed to them. The preferred ending (human-authored) reveals that the protagonist had written and discarded the letter years prior. This demonstrates high initiatoriness by revealing a causal event that precedes the story stem's central surprising event.

Endings with high post-dictability are characterized by more complete and coherent resolution of narrative uncertainties from the story stem. Story #10's preferred ending was also rated highly for post-dictability by providing a coherent resolution that explains the letter's origin without contradicting established narrative elements.

Conversely, endings with higher predictability and more positive emotional valence had significantly reduced chances of being selected as the most surprising ending, in keeping with Bae and Young (2013) on the importance of negative valence for surprise intensity. Predictability had the strongest overall effect on reader preference, with each unit increase in predictability reducing an ending's odds of selection by 60%. As an example of this preference, consider story #6, which centres on an interaction between a menacing crime writer and his admiring fan during an alleged 'improv exercise.' When the writer lunges at the fan with a knife, claiming it's for creative inspiration, two possible endings emerge. Annotators consistently preferred the less predictable outcome—where the fan becomes the killer and achieves literary fame—over the more obvious ending where the writer kills his fan.

Interesting, immutability violations and event importance did not show meaningful associations with reader preferences. While most stories did not exhibit immutability violations (see Fig. 2), it is interesting and worth further consideration as to why this feature did not strongly factor into reader preferences. Although Ortony and Partridge (1987) hypothesized that more immutability-violating stories would provoke more surprise than less immutability-violating stories, we provide an initial hypothesis that there are two distinct pathways to narrative surprise: through immutability violations and through unexpected resolutions of mutable variables. We propose that readers can experience intense surprise when mutable variables—those naturally capable of taking different values—resolve to unexpected states. Consider a mystery narrative where evidence strongly implicates character A, but the ending reveals the seemingly innocent character B to be the perpetrator. The resulting surprise may derive not from violating any fundamental story-world constraints (immutable propositions) but from strategically subverting reader expectations about the specific value a mutable variable will resolve to, although future work is needed to evaluate this potential additional pathway by which a story without an immutability violation can produce intense narrative surprise.

6.2 Comparing LLM and Human Endings

When it comes to comparing model-generated and human endings, our analysis reveals significant preference disparities between human-authored endings and those generated by large language models. Human-authored endings were preferred almost three-times more often than even our best-performing model (GPT-4 Few-Shot). At the same time, GPT-4 generated endings were chosen about as often as human-authored endings, suggesting that the generation task is indeed feasible.

As an example of human/LLM differences, Story #30 provides a useful case. This story stem focuses on a British intelligence agent who follows a KGB spy who wears a red scarf. After learning of the double-agent's murder, the protagonist spots a red scarf in his colleague's car. The human ending reveals that the colleague, himself a double agent working for the KGB, killed the KGB spy with the red scarf because she had defected. In contrast, GPT-4's ending introduces unexplained elements—the double-agent is revealed to be alive, and she and the protagonist apparently have known each other the whole time.

This example illustrates a pattern with the GPT-4 endings where new details and backstory are often introduced which are not coherent with the existing story elements, potentially indicating the way the problem of hallucination infects narrative generation. In this ending, GPT-4 also fabricates details to create a more optimistic tone that deviates from the human version, a fact also noted by prior work (Tian et al., 2024).

In addition to these problems of positivity and coherence, GPT-4 endings were also on average more predictable than human-authored endings. For example, in Story #29, a man is trapped in a VR game show seeking funds for his son's medical treatment. When approached by a figure in white attempting to wake him, GPT-4's ending describes a straightforward rescue, while the human-authored ending reveals that the figure was the protagonist's son, producing significantly higher narrative surprise. This is a good example of the challenges of balancing novelty plus coherence that is the hallmark of successful narrative surprise. Too much new information risks damaging coherence (post-dictability), while too little risks being too predictable.

Future work will want to explore further prompt-engineering approaches to assess pathways towards more successful surprising narrative endings. It could also be the case that fine-tuning approaches might also facilitate a deeper understanding of the conditions of surprise. Given the small-scale of our evaluation experiment, further work exploring more diverse stories as well as larger evaluator pools will help solidify our understanding of the concept of narrative surprise.

7 Conclusion

This paper presents a novel theoretical framework for evaluating narrative surprise in stories generated by large language models (LLMs) and human authors. By integrating theoretical insights from narrative comprehension and cognitive surprise, we develop six key metrics to assess narrative surprise. Our analysis of mystery story endings highlights the value of these metrics in understanding reader preferences, with initiatoriness and post-dictability emerging as particularly significant factors in driving narrative surprise.

While our findings underscore the potential of LLMs to produce engaging narrative surprises, they also reveal limitations in their current ability to match the complexity and nuance of human-authored endings. The preference for human-authored stories suggests that LLMs need further advancements in generating unexpected yet coherent twists. In particular, enhancing the ability to generate causal relationships (Initiatoriness) and logically coherent endings (Post-dictability) and avoiding overly positive endings that are highly predictable offer promising avenues for improving the quality of machine-generated narratives.

Future research should go beyond the mystery genre to explore how narrative surprise varies across different storytelling traditions and audience expectations. Incorporating multilingual datasets will also be essential for understanding how cultural and linguistic factors shape perceptions of surprise, coherence, and narrative quality. Additionally, employing more diverse evaluation methodologies, such as real-time audience engagement tracking or large-scale reader surveys will help capture the multifaceted nature of narrative surprise. These efforts will not only refine our understanding of narrative dynamics but also advance the development of computational storytelling systems that are better equipped to create more nuanced and interesting stories.

Limitations

Limitations of our methodology include the inherent subjectivity of surprise assessment, which resulted in moderate inter-annotator agreement. Evaluating surprise, particularly in narrative contexts, is deeply influenced by individual differences in reader expectations, cultural backgrounds, and personal preferences, making it challenging to establish universally consistent criteria. While we employed a codebook and explicit descriptions to standardize the evaluation process, the inherently subjective nature of surprise likely contributed to the variability in ratings. Future work could explore ways to mitigate this limitation, such as integrating physiological measures of surprise (e.g., eye-tracking, galvanic skin response) or employing larger and more demographically diverse annotator pools to capture a broader range of reactions.

Second, our corpus composition—English-language mystery narratives from non-professional authors—may limit generalizability across different languages and literary traditions. Mystery stories, particularly those written in English, tend to follow culturally specific narrative structures and conventions that may not align with storytelling patterns in other languages or regions. Additionally, the use of non-professional authors introduces variability in narrative quality and style, which may not reflect the complexity and craftsmanship of professionally written texts. Expanding future datasets to include stories from diverse linguistic and cultural backgrounds, as well as works authored by professionals, would provide a richer foundation for analyzing narrative surprise and its universality.

Finally, our experimental design, focusing on ending completion, captures only a subset of the complex processes involved in constructing narrative surprise. While our approach allowed for controlled testing, it did not account for the broader aspects of storytelling and their relationship to surprise, such as plot architecture, pacing, or more local moments of surprise. These elements play a critical role in building tension, shaping expectations, and delivering impactful surprises. Future studies could incorporate a more holistic approach by analyzing full narratives, from their inception to resolution, and examining how surprise is cultivated across the entire arc of the story. Additionally, incorporating methods to evaluate narrative planning and the interplay of suspense, curiosity, and surprise could provide a more comprehensive understanding of the storytelling process.

Acknowledgements

We wish to thank the Social Sciences and Humanities Research Council of Canada (435-2022-089) for funding to support this research.

References

Nader Akoury, Shufan Wang, Josh Whiting, Stephen Hood, Nanyun Peng, and Mohit Iyyer. 2020. Storium: A dataset and evaluation platform for machine-in-the-loop story generation. *arXiv preprint arXiv:2010.01717*.

Byung-Chull Bae and R Michael Young. 2013. A computational model of narrative generation for surprise arousal. *IEEE Transactions on Computational Intelligence and AI in Games*, 6(2):131–143.

Jesús Bermejo-Berros, Jaime Lopez-Diez, and Miguel Angel Gil Martínez. 2022. Inducing narrative tension in the viewer through suspense, surprise, and curiosity. *Poetics*, 93:101664.

William F Brewer and Edward H Lichtenstein. 1980. Event schemas, story schemas, and story grammars. *Center for the Study of Reading Technical Report; no. 197*.

Agnès Celle, Anne Jugnet, Laure Lansari, and Emilie L'Hôte. 2017. *Expressing and describing surprise*. John Benjamins Amsterdam.

Tuhin Chakrabarty, Philippe Laban, Divyansh Agarwal, Smaranda Muresan, and Chien-Sheng Wu. 2024. Art or artifice? large language models and the false promise of creativity. In *Proceedings of the CHI Conference on Human Factors in Computing Systems*, pages 1–34.

Cyril Chhun, Pierre Colombo, Chloé Clavel, and Fabian M Suchanek. 2022. Of human criteria and automatic metrics: A benchmark of the evaluation of story generation. *arXiv preprint arXiv:2208.11646*.

Katherine Elkins. 2022. *The shapes of stories: sentiment analysis for narrative*. Cambridge University Press.

Jian Guan, Yansen Wang, and Minlie Huang. 2019. Story ending generation with incremental encoding and commonsense knowledge. In *Proceedings of the AAAI Conference on Artificial Intelligence*, volume 33, pages 6473–6480.

Prakhar Gupta, Vinayshekhar Bannihatti Kumar, Mukul Bhutani, and Alan W Black. 2019. Writerforcing: Generating more interesting story endings. *arXiv preprint arXiv:1907.08259*.

Hans Hoeken and Mario Van Vliet. 2000. Suspense, curiosity, and surprise: How discourse structure influences the affective and cognitive processing of a story. *Poetics*, 27(4):277–286.

Tenghao Huang, Ehsan Qasemi, Bangzheng Li, He Wang, Faeze Brahman, Muhao Chen, and Snigdha Chaturvedi. 2023. Affective and dynamic beam search for story generation. *arXiv preprint arXiv:2310.15079*.

James Juergensen, Joseph S Weaver, Kevin J Burns, Peter E Knutson, Jennifer L Butler, and Heath A Demaree. 2014. Surprise is predicted by event probability, outcome valence, outcome meaningfulness, and gender. *Motivation and Emotion*, 38:297–304.

Samsun Knight, Matthew D Rocklage, and Yakov Bart. 2024. Narrative reversals and story success. *Science Advances*, 10(34):eadl2013.

Nasrin Mostafazadeh, Nathanael Chambers, Xiaodong He, Devi Parikh, Dhruv Batra, Lucy Vanderwende, Pushmeet Kohli, and James Allen. 2016. A corpus and cloze evaluation for deeper understanding of commonsense stories. In *Proceedings of the 2016 Conference of the North American Chapter of the Association for Computational Linguistics: Human Language Technologies*, pages 839–849.

Thomas A O'Neill. 2017. An overview of interrater agreement on likert scales for researchers and practitioners. *Frontiers in psychology*, 8:777.

Andrew Ortony and Derek Partridge. 1987. Surprisingness and expectation failure: what's the difference? In *IJCAI*, volume 87, pages 106–108.

Abigail See, Aneesh Pappu, Rohun Saxena, Akhila Yerukola, and Christopher D Manning. 2019. Do massively pretrained language models make better storytellers? *arXiv preprint arXiv:1909.10705*.

Meir Sternberg. 1990. Telling in time (i): Chronology and narrative theory. *Poetics today*, 11(4):901–948.

Yufei Tian, Tenghao Huang, Miri Liu, Derek Jiang, Alexander Spangher, Muhao Chen, Jonathan May, and Nanyun Peng. 2024. Are large language models capable of generating human-level narratives? *arXiv preprint arXiv:2407.13248*.

David Wilmot and Frank Keller. 2020. Modelling suspense in short stories as uncertainty reduction over neural representation. *arXiv preprint arXiv:2004.14905*.

Hanyu Zhou, Sreya Muppalla, Zeynep Yildiz, Miryung Kim, Amit Sahai, Nanyun Peng, et al. 2024. Measuring psychological depth in language models. In *Proceedings of the 2024 Conference on Empirical Methods in Natural Language Processing*, pages 17162–17196.

Beyond LLMs: A Linguistic Approach to Causal Graph Generation from Narrative Texts

Zehan Li **Ruhua Pan** **Xinyu Pi**
University of California, San Diego
{zel025, r3pan, xpi}@ucsd.edu

Abstract

We propose a novel framework to generate causal graphs from narrative texts, bridging the gap between high-level causality and finer-grained event-specific relationships. Our approach first extracts concise, agent-centered "vertices" using an LLM-based summarization strategy. We then introduce an *Expert Index*—seven linguistically grounded features—and incorporate them into a **STAC** (Situation, Task, Action, Consequence) classification model. This hybrid system (RoBERTa embeddings + Expert Index) achieves superior precision in identifying causal links compared to LLM-only baselines. Finally, we apply a structured, five-iteration prompting process to refine and construct a connected causal graph. Experiments on 100 chapters and short stories show that our method consistently outperforms GPT-4o and Claude 3.5 across key dimensions of causal graph quality, while maintaining comparable readability. The resulting open-source tool offers an interpretable and efficient solution for capturing nuanced causal chains within narrative texts.

1 Introduction

Causal research has historically leveraged knowledge graphs to explore relationships between events (JM;, 1999). Modern approaches, such as AI-driven causal graph generation, have gained prominence for their ability to summarize causal events at scale (Jaimini and Sheth, 2022; Pieper et al., 2023). However, current AI models largely focus on high-level causality (e.g., "HIV leads to AIDS"), and they fall short in capturing nuanced causal relationships in specific narratives, such as political events or historical occurrences(Donnelly, 2025). Addressing this gap, we propose a method for generating causal graphs from texts that describe discrete, event-specific narratives.

Understanding these finer-grained causal relationships is crucial for researchers and practitioners who analyze how certain events lead to tangible outcomes in areas like social movements, policy-making, and historical trends. By capturing causal links from narrative texts, stakeholders can more accurately trace the chain of events that precipitate significant changes, enabling better decision-making, deeper historical insight, and more targeted interventions. Furthermore, automated causal graph generation facilitates scalable analysis of large document collections, providing structured representations that can be easily interpreted, queried, and expanded upon.

Most existing methods for generating causal graphs follow a two-stage pipeline: (1) a Causality Finder to detect causal relations, and (2) a graph Generator to construct knowledge graphs from these relations. While effective, these methods face limitations in interpretability and accuracy, particularly when dealing with complex sentence structures or implicit causal links(Kıcıman et al., 2024) (Kyono et al., 2024).

Causality finders have evolved through three phases: (1) early pattern-based models that learned causal relationships from fixed sentence structures (Hidey and McKeown, 2016) (Heindorf et al., 2020) , (2) BERT-based approaches that addressed issues in text training but failed to account for semantic context (Tan et al., 2023) (Dasgupta et al., 2018) (Li et al., 2020), and (3) LLMs, which improved contextual reasoning but struggled to distinguish intricate causal relationships (Kıcıman et al., 2024) (Shen et al., 2022) (Luo et al., 2024).

In this paper, we present a novel framework that leverages linguistic feature extraction to enhance causal graph generation from narrative texts. Our approach introduces a Quaternary Classification system to categorize sentences into four components: (1) Situation, (2) Task, (3) Action, and (4) Consequences. This structured decomposition allows for more precise identification of causal links. We also propose a Neural Network model trained

Proceedings of the The 7th Workshop on Narrative Understanding, pages 36–51
May 4, 2025 ©2025 Association for Computational Linguistics

on these linguistic features, achieving higher accuracy and interpretability compared to LLM-based methods, with lower computational costs.

Our contributions are twofold: (1) We develop an open-source, end-to-end causal graph generation model that significantly improves interpretability and accuracy. (2) We introduce a Linguistics Feature system, which efficiently classifies sentences for causal graph construction, validated through experiments on various narrative texts.

2 Problem Setting

This paper studies the problem of causal relationship graphs as follows. Given a narrative text, such as a story by O. Henry or a piece of narrative news, we can generate its causal relationship graph containing the main causal relationships. More specifically, when we input a set of narrative sentences $S = \{s_1, s_2, \ldots, s_n\}$, we aim to obtain a connected graph $G = (V, E)$ to represent the structure of the story, where:

- V is the set of vertices, each vertex representing a major event in the story.
- E is the set of edges, where each edge $(u, v) \in E$ represents the temporal or causal relationship from event u to event v.

For the definition of Edges E, We say Event A causes Event B if:

- (the multi-factorial definition): in combination with other factors, Event A is a necessary or a sufficient condition for Event B (Oppenheimer and Susser, 2007)
- (the probabilistic definition): the occurrence of Event A raises the probability of Event B occurring (Reichenbach, 1991).

3 Methodology

Our complete Causal graph Model is an End-to-End model. We hope to input any story and generate a Connected Graph G. This model contains four main parts:(1) Vertices Extraction, (2)Expert Index Extraction, (3) STAC Categorization, (4)Graph Construction.

3.1 Vertices Extraction

We define each vertex in our causal graph as a single event or state, represented by:

$$V = \{v_1, v_2, \ldots, v_n \mid v_i = \text{a single event/state}\}.$$

These vertices serve as Vertices capturing key information with causal relationships in the narrative. Our goal is to transform the original text into concise, event-specific sentences by leveraging a LLM and prompt engineering. In particular, we used the LangChain framework to guide the LLM in generating simple sentences that reflect core plot elements.

Requirements for Each Vertex

1. **Concise**: Each sentence must contain no more than two clauses.
2. **Agent-Centered**: The subject (or agent) of the action must be explicitly identified, with only one subject per sentence.
3. **Active Voice**: Each sentence should clearly convey an action initiated by its subject.

Extraction Procedure We applied a structured prompting workflow to simplify the text into short, self-contained sentences, each representing a single narrative event:

1. **Summarization**: The LLM receives a paragraph and generates a brief summary, ensuring each resulting sentence is as simple as possible.
2. **Pronoun Substitution**: All pronouns are replaced with explicit referents. For a first-person narrative, the speaker is replaced by a clear identifier, such as the speaker's name or "The Protagonist" if none is provided.
3. **Clause Simplification**: Complex or compound sentences are split into multiple simple sentences, each containing one core action or state. Unimportant details that do not affect the plot are removed.
4. **Continuous Flow**: The resulting sentences are checked to ensure they preserve a logical, causal flow of events, discarding irrelevant or tangential information.

By enforcing these requirements and following this workflow, we derive a set of concise, agent-specific sentences—each of which becomes a vertex in our causal graph. This method preserves the essential narrative structure while ensuring that each vertex encapsulates only a single event or state.

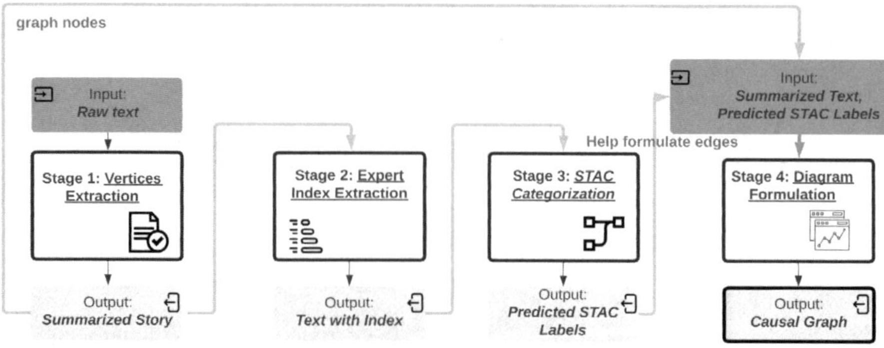

Figure 1: Overview of our framework. It is an end to end Model. First we input a Random Narrative Text. Then in Stage 1, we Contribute the Vertices of the Graph. And in Stage 2, we Use our Expert Index to indicate the Vertices. Next, In stage 3,we use a STAC system to label the Vertices. In STAGE 4, we use STAC Label + Vertices to complete the Causal Graph

3.2 Expert Index Extraction

This section describes our methodology for extracting the *Expert Index* features from each sentence and subsequently training a model to classify them. We adopt seven key features grounded in traditional and computational linguistics literature, the full description see table 3:

1. **Genericity**: Determines whether the sentence's subject is *specific* (e.g., a person, a dog) or *generic* (e.g., a season, an emotion) (Becker et al., 2017; Carlson, 1980).

2. **Eventivity**: Classifies the verb as *dynamic* (observable actions such as speaking or running) or *stative* (expressing states or non-action, such as deciding or thinking) (Becker et al., 2017; Vendler, 1967).

3. **Boundedness**: Identifies if a event is *episodic* (occurs at a specific time), *habitual* (recurring over time), or *static* (always true or in a state of being) (Becker et al., 2017; Smith, 1991).

4. **Initiativity**: Distinguishes whether the subject *initiates* the action (has agency) or *receives* it (lacks agency) (Dai and Huang, 2018; Comrie, 1976).

5. **Time Start**: Notes if the event begins in the *past* or the *present* relative to the narrative timeline (Dowty, 1979; Allen, 1983).

6. **Time End**: Determines if the event concludes in the *present* or the *future* (Dowty, 1979; Allen, 1983).

7. **Impact**: Indicates whether the event's effect persists (*impact*) or is entirely *resolved* by the time it ends (Dowty, 1979; Moens and Steedman, 1988).

Except for **Boundedness**, which has three categories, each feature has two categories, for a total of 192 possible combinations. We refer to each resulting combination as an *Expert Index*. Inspired by prior work that classified sentences as episodic, habitual, or static, we adopt a more granular approach to better capture distinctions relevant to our four main narrative labels: **Situation**, **Task**, **Action**, and **Consequence**.

To train a model for these features, we used RoBERTa, a robustly optimized variant of BERT(Liu et al., 2019). We prepared a dataset of 750 annotated sentences from 23 short stories and novel chapters, ensuring balanced coverage of tenses and narrative types. Human evaluations served as ground truth. The model was trained separately for each of the seven features and their respective categories, enabling transparent prediction of the *Expert Index* for every sentence.

3.3 STAC Categorization

We developed the STAC model to classify narrative sentences into four categories—**Situation**, **Task**, **Action**, and **Consequence**—based on structured thinking from business management. In practice, we observed that narrative events often follow a logical flow: a change in the environment (*Situation*) prompts a requirement (*Task*), leading to an activity (*Action*), which in turn yields a lasting result (*Consequence*)(Minto, 2009). Concretely:

1. **Situation**: Provides background context or

sets the stage for future events.

2. **Task**: States an explicit requirement or responsibility that must be fulfilled.

3. **Action**: Indicates an activity actively performed or just completed.

4. **Consequence**: Describes the outcome of a prior event that changes the state.

To automatically assign these four STAC labels, we trained a model using both RoBERTa embeddings and *Expert Index* features as inputs. Their relation is as follows: A.6. Specifically, we extracted each sentence's embedding from RoBERTa's default Autotokenizer (a 768-length array), capturing semantic and contextual meanings. We then one-hot encoded the *Expert Index* categories (non-ordinal attributes) to obtain binary vectors. By concatenating these embeddings and encoded features, we formed a comprehensive input array.

For classification, we used **XGBoost** due to its efficiency and robust performance relative to traditional models. The model was trained on human-labeled STAC categories and human-labeled *Expert Index* features as ground truth, with regularization techniques to avoid overfitting. Once trained, the model can predict a sentence's STAC category from its tokenized RoBERTa embedding and *Expert Index* attributes.

3.4 Graph Construction

After classifying all vertices using the STAC model—**Situation**, **Task**, **Action**, and **Consequence**—we aimed to build a causal diagram capturing the complexity of narrative events. Initially, we considered 16 possible bonds (i.e., relationships) between the four STAC categories; however, only 11 of these bonds were meaningful in the actual narrative context. Furthermore, we observed that real-world events often exhibit relationships such as *Action* $\rightarrow$ *Action* or *Situation* $\rightarrow$ *Situation*, underscoring the non-linear nature of storytelling.

To systematically determine the edges between vertices, we adopted a five-iteration LangChain-based prompting process. This approach refines causal relationships in stages, ensuring that each edge is relevant, logically consistent, and supported by the narrative.

Iteration 1: STAC Bond Learning We first prompted the LLM to internalize the STAC bonding schema, which outlines valid causal connections among **Situation**, **Task**, **Action**, and **Consequence**. By learning these inherent relationships, the model could more accurately propose potential edges in subsequent steps.

Iteration 2: Causal Relation Identification Next, the LLM evaluated pairs of vertices (in total $O(n^2/2)$ pairs) to propose potential causal links based on the STAC bonds. At this stage, the model only suggested edges that aligned with valid STAC relationships and logically connected one event's outcome or state to another event's occurrence.

Iteration 3: Logical Consistency and Pruning After generating an initial set of edges, the LLM applied counterfactual reasoning—asking, "If A did not occur, would B still happen?"—to filter out any bonds that did not have explicitly causal relationship. Non-causal or weakly supported edges were systematically pruned, leaving only robust causal connections.

Iteration 4: Isolated Vertices Refinement In the fourth step, the LLM revisited any vertices that remained isolated (i.e., lacking causal connections). By prompting the model with a "why" question, we explored whether there were overlooked causes or effects. If new connections surfaced, they were subjected to the same scrutiny and pruning as in Iterations 2 and 3, ensuring consistency and avoiding redundant links.

Iteration 5: Final Graph Construction Finally, the refined set of vertices and edges was compiled into a coherent graph that depicts the full range of causal relationships within the narrative. This final graph integrates all relevant Vertices and edges, with every link verified for logical soundness and alignment with the STAC bonding schema.

By iterating through these five steps, we resolved the complexities of linking narrative events—particularly cases where *Action* leads to another *Action* or *Situation* follows another *Situation*. The result is a structured causal diagram A.5 that accurately reflects the underlying relationships dictated by both the story and the STAC framework.

4 Experiment Setup

4.1 Corpus Collection

We hand-collected excerpts from 50 full-length novels and 50 short stories, covering works published between *1800 and 1950*. Each data selection features either one chapter from a novel or a complete short story, with lengths averaging 5,000 words. All narratives were sourced from various public domain web archives. These works were selected in part because our annotators were already familiar with the narratives, reducing ambiguity and enabling more consistent annotation.

The dataset incorporates both *complete story cycles* (e.g., short stories) and *fragmentary narratives* (e.g., chapters), allowing for comparative event-flow analysis (Sims and Bamman, 2019; Kirti et al., 2024). Thematically, it spans *fairy tales*, *stream-of-consciousness storytelling* (e.g., Poe's *Berenice* (Poe, 1835)), and *implied-content stories* (e.g., works by O. Henry (Henry, 1906)), ensuring a diverse testing ground for event-extraction models (Levi et al., 2022; Elson, 2012).

4.2 Summarization and Dataset Structuring

After selecting corpus material, we employ a multi-layered Large Language Model (LLM) pipeline to iteratively refine narrative content, forming our finalized corpus dataset. The pipeline extracts and refines key sentences and concepts based on the story's progression, creating a connected-event narrative structure. The input to the pipeline is a raw chapter or story from the gathered corpus material, and the output is a concise summarization where each sentence has a declarative, complete narrative structure (Goyal and Durrett, 2022; Lu et al., 2023).

After processing each piece in the corpus through the pipeline, we gather a dataset optimized for event flowchart mapping. The final summaries, averaging under 40 sentences for each short story or novel chapter, serve as standardized Vertices in the output graph. Details on the pipeline and prompt methodology are provided in the Appendix A.1.

4.3 Expert and STAC Labeling

To construct the event-flow graph, we apply a structured labeling process integrating *expert index* classification and *STAC labeling*. This ensures clear labeling of narrative components into actionable event Vertices (Barth, 2021).

We asked ten anonymous annotators to assign *expert index* and *STAC labeling* to every sentence in the dataset. When differences arose, the mode was used (Fleiss, 1971). Annotators assigned the *expert index* based on predefined criteria introduced earlier. They were then instructed to assign *STAC labeling* to the same sentences following a hierarchical rule set:

- An execution of an action verb solely defines an *action*.
- If no action verb is present, sentences implying an execution are labeled as *tasks*.
- If a description is shaped by the main flow of events and tasks, it is a *consequence*.
- Otherwise, it is classified as a *situation*.

This layered process ensures consistency across the dataset, aligning narrative progression with structured event representation for final graph construction.

We also explored generating STAC labels and Expert Index levels using a standardized prompt driven by a Large Language Model (LLM), detailed explicitly in the Appendix A.1. However, the resulting annotation performance was suboptimal. Specifically, after evaluation across 300 datasets compared to annotations produced by human annotators, the Cohen's Kappa (Cohen, 1960; Landis and Koch, 1977) for the Expert Index generated by the LLM was found to be 0.73, indicating good but not excellent agreement. In contrast, the Cohen's Kappa for STAC labels generated by the LLM fluctuated around 0.63, suggesting only moderate agreement and thus inadequate for reliable model training. Consequently, for all subsequent scenarios involving Expert Index and STAC labeling, we adopted human annotations exclusively as the ground truth.

5 Experiments

5.1 Vertices Extraction Result

We evaluate and compare the performance of different models by comparing and rating their performances on fifteen selected stories. Ten of these were short stories, and five were chapters from well-known novels: *The Giver* (Lowry, 1993), *The Great Gatsby* (Fitzgerald, 1925), and *Rebecca* (Du Maurier, 1938). For each story or chapter, three summaries were generated using the same prompt and parameter settings (detailed in the Appendix A.2, A.3) with no post-editing, following standard practices for comparative evaluation of summarization models (Goyal and Durrett, 2022; Lu et al., 2023).

To reflect the downstream goal of transforming summaries into structured event flowcharts, we defined a three-part evaluation rubric based on existing summarization literature (Kryscinski et al., 2019; Fabbri et al., 2021):

- **Conciseness and Sentence Structure:** Clean sentence flow, minimal subordination, and avoidance of redundancy.
- **Coverage and Coherence:** Inclusion of all key story events in proper logical order.
- **Information Span & Economy:** Avoidance of unnecessary elaboration or repeated ideas.

Each summary was scored across the three dimensions (0–5 scale per category, 15 max per summary) by three LLM models (GPT-4o, GPT-4 Turbo, Claude 3.5), and the mean was then taken. Two additional criteria, Agent-Centered and Active Voice, were achieved at 100% by all models and thus not considered further in our analysis.

Model	Concise	Cover	Info Span
GPT-4o	4.2	4.9	4.4
GPT-4 Turbo	3.9	4.7	4.5
GPT-o1	4.1	4.4	4.2

Table 1: GPT-4o demonstrates superior performance across all evaluated dimensions.

These results suggest that GPT-4o consistently demonstrates superior performance, producing efficient narrative compression while retaining complete event arcs—a critical capability for generating effective, structured flowchart-ready summaries (Li et al., 2022; Sims and Bamman, 2019). Consequently, GPT-4o was selected as our primary summarization model for dataset structuring.

5.2 Expert Index Result

We used a RoBERTa-based classifier fine-tuned on a custom-labeled dataset of 1,000 summary-extracted sentences annotated by humans. The dataset was split 80/20 into training and testing sets, with hyperparameters tuned via default cross-validation. Each trait was modeled independently as a multi-class classification task.

Performance scores for each trait dimension are shown in Table 5. Overall, the classifier exhibited strong performance on traits with more balanced or semantically distinct labels. *Genericity*, *Eventivity*, and *Initiativity* all yielded F1-scores above 0.85 on their dominant classes. *Boundedness* posed greater challenges due to conceptual overlap between the *habitual* and *static* classes, leading to reduced precision and recall.

The classifier achieved high overall accuracy across most traits, with particularly strong results for identifying Initiate vs. Receive references and dynamic event types. Errors in *Boundedness* are unsurprising given the theoretical overlap between habitual and static categories. For traits with label imbalance, such as retextitTime Start, outcome reveals minor reduced recall.

5.3 STAC Categorization Result

We conducted a series of experiments on a dataset of 1,000 ground-truth annotated sentences to evaluate the effectiveness of incorporating Expert Index features for STAC classification. Each sentence in the dataset is labeled with one of four STAC categories (Situation, Task, Action, or Consequence). We used a standard train/test split (e.g., 80/20) and report the F1-score for each category as well as the macro-averaged F1-score across all four labels. Six different classification models were compared to isolate the impact of the Expert Index (EI) features:

1. **RoBERTa (sentence only)** – A baseline model using only RoBERTa sentence embeddings (768-dimensional) with a linear classifier.
2. **RoBERTa + EI** – RoBERTa embeddings augmented with the 13-dimensional one-hot Expert Index vector (total 781 features) and classified by a linear layer.
3. **XGBoost (EI only)** – An XGBoost classifier using only the 13 Expert Index features.
4. **XGBoost (RoBERTa only)** – XGBoost using only 768-dim RoBERTa embedding as input.
5. **XGBoost (RoBERTa + EI)** – XGBoost using the combined feature set of RoBERTa embedding + EI (781 features).
6. **GPT-4 (prompt-based)** – Using GPT-4 directly for classification via prompt (zero-shot, without fine-tuning).

As shown in Figure 2, models that incorporate the Expert Index features consistently outperform their counterparts that use only the sentence embedding. For instance, augmenting RoBERTa with the EI features raises the F1-score score in each category by at least 5 percentage points compared to using RoBERTa alone. This improvement is

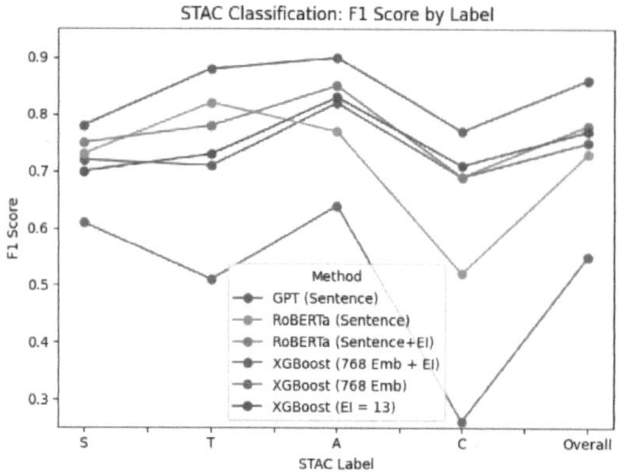

Figure 2: F1-score-score comparison across STAC labels for all six models. Each curve corresponds to a classification method, plotting F1-score for the four individual labels (S, T, A, C) and the overall macro-F1-score (rightmost point). The XGBoost model using both RoBERTa embeddings and Expert Index features (red curve) achieves the highest F1-score in every category.

most pronounced for the *Consequence* (C) category, where the RoBERTa+EI model achieves an F1-score of about 0.68 versus 0.55 with RoBERTa-only (a 13-point gain). Even the XGBoost classifier using only the 13 EI features (without any RoBERTa embedding) performs respectably across categories ($F_1 \approx 0.65$–0.80), underscoring that the Expert Index captures valuable signals for the STAC classification task.

Among all evaluated models, the XGBoost ensemble leveraging the combined RoBERTa + Expert Index features is the top performer. It attains the highest F1-score in each STAC category and the highest overall macro-F1-score. Notably, this model outperforms the GPT-4 classifier by approximately 10–15% (relative) in F1-score score, and yields about a 30% relative improvement over the baseline RoBERTa-only approach. These results demonstrate that incorporating the Expert Index not only consistently boosts classification accuracy for each STAC category, but that the combination of semantic embeddings with expert-driven features is especially powerful. The best model (XGBoost with RoBERTa+EI) provides a substantial performance margin over both a strong neural baseline and GPT-4, highlighting the benefit of hybridizing learned embeddings with expert knowledge.

5.4 Graph Formulation Result

We define eight key dimensions for evaluating the quality of a causal event graph. Each dimension captures a different aspect of how well the graph represents the narrative's causal structure:

Causality vs. Chronology – Does the graph emphasize true cause-effect relationships rather than merely the temporal order of events? Causal connectivity strongly shapes comprehension and recall of events (Trabasso and Van Den Broek, 1985).

Explicit Motivations/Intent – Are characters' goals and intentions explicitly represented as causes for their actions? Agents' motivations (the "why" for actions) reflects the intentional dimension of narratives (Zwaan and Radvansky, 1998) and ensures explanation on why events occur.

Granularity (Level of Detail) – Does the graph use an appropriate level of detail for events? A balanced level of detail enables both clarity and informativeness (Mulkar-Mehta et al., 2011).

Logical Completeness – Are all necessary causal steps and connections present to form a logically complete story? Missing links or unexplained leaps between events undermine narrative coherence (Brewer and Lichtenstein, 1982), undermining the logical soundness of the graph.

Hierarchy or Grouping – Does the graph organize events into higher-level groupings or hierarchical structures (e.g., subplots or phases)? A hierarchical organization (events grouped into episodes or goal-driven segments) improves understanding greatly (Mandler and Johnson, 1977).

Accuracy of Connections – Are the causal links in the graph correct and faithful to the story? Each connection should reflect a true causal or enabling relation in the narrative, and incorrect causal links can mislead reasoning (Pearl, 2009). Every link in the graph shall not be coincidental nor erroneous.

Decision Points as Branches – Does the graph explicitly show branching at decision points? Representing decision points as branch Vertices highlights the narrative's points of divergence (e.g., choices or hypothetical alternatives) and is important especially in interactive or non-linear narratives (Moser and Fang, 2012).

Ease of Reading – Is the graph easy to interpret visually, with a clear layout and labeling? Graph design principles (e.g., minimizing crossed links and clutter) improve human readability (Purchase, 1997), so a higher score means the graph is more reader-friendly.

Experimental Setup. We validated these evaluation dimensions by comparing our proposed method against strong baseline approaches, using large language models (LLMs) prompted to gener-

Dimension	Our Method vs GPT-4o	Our Method vs Claude 3.5
Causality vs. Chronology	100%	100%
Explicit Motivations/Intent	95%	92%
Granularity (Level of Detail)	86%	84%
Logical Completeness	100%	100%
Hierarchy or Grouping	94%	92%
Accuracy of Connections	100%	100%
Decision Points as Branches	97%	95%
Ease of Reading	52%	57%

Table 2: Win-rate of our model in pairwise comparisons against GPT-4o and Claude 3.5 on each dimension. Higher values indicate the percentage of cases where our model's graphs were preferred for that dimension.

ate causal graphs from the same narratives. In particular, we benchmarked our method against GPT-4o and against Claude 3.5, as representative state-of-the-art LLMs A.8. We also tested enhanced prompting with in-context examples: GPT-4o and Claude 3.5 denote prompting the LLM with 10 example narratives and their graphs (10-shot learning) to guide its generation. For each narrative text in our test set (100 narratives), both our method and a baseline LLM produced a causal graph. We then performed pairwise evaluations: for each narrative and each of the eight dimensions above, the graph from Method A was compared to the graph from Method B to decide which one was better along that specific dimension. This yields, per narrative, a binary win/loss outcome for each dimension. We conducted these pairwise comparisons for all relevant pairs: our method vs GPT-4o, our method and our method vs Claude 3.5,

To ensure the reliability of the evaluation, we used a panel of five human annotators to judge the graph pairs dimension-by-dimension. Additionally, we employed an LLM-based evaluator (GPT-4) to perform the same pairwise judgments. We found a very high agreement between the aggregate human decisions and the LLM judge's decisions: Cohen's $\kappa = 0.92$ for dimension-level agreement. This suggests that the LLM-based evaluation is largely consistent with human, validating its use for scaling up our evaluation. In the analysis that follows, we thus report results based on the LLM evaluator's judgments for all 100 narrative graph pairs, given the strong alignment with human annotators.

In Table 2, we report the win-rates of our approach's graphs compared to two baseline systems (GPT-4o and Claude 3.5) across the eight dimensions. The results show that our model substantially outperforms both baselines on almost all aspects of causal graph quality. Notably, it achieves near-100% win rates against GPT-4o and Claude in dimensions such as *Causality vs. Chronology*, *Logical Completeness*, and *Accuracy of Connections*, indicating that our graphs consistently capture causal structure, completeness, and correct links better than the baseline graphs. Similarly, high win-rate margins in *Explicit Motivations*, *Granularity*, and *Hierarchy/Grouping* demonstrate the model's strength in including character intents, appropriate detail, and structured organization of events. In contrast, for *Ease of Reading*, the advantage of our model is much smaller (around 52–57% win-rate), suggesting that the clarity and readability of our graphs are roughly on par with those generated by GPT-4o and Claude. Overall, these results highlight that our proposed graph formulation provides significant improvements in most qualitative dimensions of causal graph representation, while maintaining comparable readability.

6 Conclusion

We have introduced a linguistics-focused, end-to-end approach for building causal graphs from narrative texts. By leveraging a lightweight *Expert Index* to capture seven core linguistic traits, our STAC classifier improves both interpretability and accuracy in labeling events. A specialized, multi-step prompting strategy then constructs a logically consistent causal graph that outperforms GPT-4o and Claude 3.5 on most causal quality metrics. The results highlight the benefits of integrating interpretable feature engineering with modern language models for fine-grained causal reasoning. Our framework is open-source and readily adaptable for broader applications in summarization, discourse analysis, and knowledge graph construction.

Acknowledgments

We would thank all the anonymous reviewers for their constructive feedback and insightful comments.

References

James F. Allen. 1983. Maintaining knowledge about temporal intervals. *Communications of the ACM*, 26(11):832–843.

Florian Barth. 2021. Annotation guidelines for narrative levels and narrative acts v2. *Journal of Cultural Analytics*.

Maria Becker, Magdalena Staniek, Vivi Nastase, Alexis Palmer, and Anette Frank. 2017. Classifying semantic clause types: Modeling context and genre characteristics with recurrent neural networks and attention. In *Proceedings of the 6th Joint Conference on Lexical and Computational Semantics (*SEM 2017)*, pages 230–240.

William F. Brewer and Edward H. Lichtenstein. 1982. Stories are to entertain: a structural-affect theory of stories. *Journal of Pragmatics*, 6(5):473–486.

Gregory N. Carlson. 1980. *Reference to Kinds in English*. Garland Publishing.

Jacob Cohen. 1960. A coefficient of agreement for nominal scales. *Educational and Psychological Measurement*, 20(1):37–46.

Bernard Comrie. 1976. *Aspect: An Introduction to the Study of Verbal Aspect and Related Problems*. Cambridge University Press.

Zeyu Dai and Ruihong Huang. 2018. Building context-aware clause representations for situation entity type classification. In *Proceedings of the 2018 Conference on Empirical Methods in Natural Language Processing (EMNLP 2018)*, pages 3305–3315.

Tirthankar Dasgupta, Rupsa Saha, Lipika Dey, and Abir Naskar. 2018. Automatic extraction of causal relations from text using linguistically informed deep neural networks. In *Proceedings of the 19th Annual SIGdial Meeting on Discourse and Dialogue*, pages 306–316.

Shannon Donnelly. 2025. Ai still can't answer complex questions about history, study finds.

David R. Dowty. 1979. *Word Meaning and Montague Grammar*. Reidel Publishing Company.

Daphne Du Maurier. 1938. *Rebecca*. Victor Gollancz.

David K. Elson. 2012. Dramabank: Annotating agency in narrative discourse. In *Proceedings of the Eighth International Conference on Language Resources and Evaluation (LREC'12)*.

Alexander R Fabbri, Wojciech Kryscinski, Bryan McCann, Caiming Xiong, Richard Socher, and Dragomir Radev. 2021. Summeval: Re-evaluating summarization evaluation. In *Transactions of the ACL*, volume 9, pages 391–409.

F. Scott Fitzgerald. 1925. *The Great Gatsby*. Charles Scribner's Sons.

Joseph L Fleiss. 1971. Measuring nominal scale agreement among many raters. *Psychological Bulletin*, 76(5):378.

Tanishq Goyal and Greg Durrett. 2022. News summarization and evaluation in the era of gpt-3. In *Proceedings of EMNLP*, pages 4046–4059.

Stefan Heindorf, Yan Scholten, Henning Wachsmuth, Axel-Cyrille Ngonga Ngomo, and Martin Potthast. 2020. CauseNet: Towards a causality graph extracted from the web. In *Proceedings of the 29th ACM International Conference on Information and Knowledge Management (CIKM)*.

O. Henry. 1906. *The Four Million*. Doubleday, Page Company.

Christopher Hidey and Kathleen McKeown. 2016. Identifying causal relations using parallel wikipedia articles. In *Proceedings of the 54th Annual Meeting of the Association for Computational Linguistics (Volume 2: Short Papers)*, pages 1424–1433, Berlin, Germany.

Utkarshani Jaimini and Amit Sheth. 2022. Causalkg: Causal knowledge graph explainability using interventional and counterfactual reasoning. *Preprint*, arXiv:2201.03647.

Greenland S;Pearl J;Robins JM;. 1999. Causal diagrams for epidemiologic research.

Chaitanya Kirti, Ayon Chattopadhyay, Ashish Anand, and Prithwijit Guha. 2024. Enhancing event extraction from short stories through contextualized prompts. *arXiv preprint arXiv:2412.10745*.

Wojciech Kryscinski, Romain Paulus, Caiming Xiong, and Richard Socher. 2019. Neural text summarization: A critical evaluation. *arXiv preprint arXiv:1908.08960*.

Trent Kyono, Yao Zhang, and van der Schaar Mihaela. 2024. Neural causal graph for interpretable and intervenable classification. In *Proceedings of the Twelfth International Conference on Learning Representations (ICLR 2024)*.

Emre Kıcıman, Robert Ness, Amit Sharma, and Chenhao Tan. 2024. Causal reasoning and large language models: Opening a new frontier for causality. *Preprint*, arXiv:2305.00050.

J Richard Landis and Gary G Koch. 1977. The measurement of observer agreement for categorical data. *Biometrics*, pages 159–174.

Effi Levi, Guy Mor, Tamir Sheafer, and Shaul R. Shenhav. 2022. Detecting narrative elements in informational text. *arXiv preprint arXiv:2210.03028*.

Zhen Li, Yijia Liu, Yue Zhang, and Ting Liu. 2022. Title2event: Benchmarking open event extraction with a large-scale chinese title dataset. *arXiv preprint arXiv:2211.00869*.

Zhongyang Li, Xiao Ding, Ting Liu, J. Edward Hu, and Benjamin Van Durme. 2020. Guided generation of cause and effect. In *Proceedings of the 29th International Joint Conference on Artificial Intelligence (IJCAI)*.

Yinhan Liu, Myle Ott, Naman Goyal, Jingfei Du, Mandar Joshi, Danqi Chen, Omer Levy, Mike Lewis, Luke Zettlemoyer, and Veselin Stoyanov. 2019. Roberta: A robustly optimized bert pretraining approach. *arXiv preprint arXiv:1907.11692*.

Lois Lowry. 1993. *The Giver*. Houghton Mifflin Harcourt.

Xingxing Lu, Yuning Mao, and Jason Wei. 2023. Autoeval: Llm-based automatic evaluation framework for text summarization. In *Findings of ACL*.

Kun Luo, Tong Zhou, Yubo Chen, Jun Zhao, and Kang Liu. 2024. Open event causality extraction by the assistance of llm in task annotation, dataset, and method. In *Proceedings of the LREC 2024 Workshop on Bridging Neurons and Symbols for NLP and Knowledge Graphs Reasoning*, pages 33–44.

Jean M. Mandler and Nancy S. Johnson. 1977. Remembrance of things parsed: Story structure and recall. *Cognitive Psychology*, 9(1):111–151.

Barbara Minto. 2009. *The Pyramid Principle: Logic in Writing and Thinking*, 3rd edition. Pearson Education, London, UK.

Marc Moens and Mark Steedman. 1988. Temporal ontology and temporal reference. *Computational Linguistics*, 14(2):15–28.

Christopher Moser and Xiaowen Fang. 2012. Effects of narrative structure and salient decision points in role-playing games. In *Proceedings of the 18th Americas Conference on Information Systems (AMCIS)*, Seattle, WA.

Rutu Mulkar-Mehta, Jerry R. Hobbs, and Eduard Hovy. 2011. Granularity in natural language discourse. In *Proceedings of the 9th International Conference on Computational Semantics (IWCS)*, pages 195–199.

Gerald M. Oppenheimer and Ezra Susser. 2007. Invited commentary: The context and challenge of von pettenkofer's contributions to epidemiology.

Judea Pearl. 2009. *Causality: Models, Reasoning, and Inference*, 2nd edition. Cambridge University Press, Cambridge, UK.

Sven Pieper, Carl Willy Mehling, Dominik Hirsch, Tobias Lüke, and Steffen Ihlenfeldt. 2023. causalgraph: A python package for modeling, persisting and visualizing causal graphs embedded in knowledge graphs. *Preprint*, arXiv:2301.08490.

Edgar Allan Poe. 1835. *Berenice*. Southern Literary Messenger.

Helen C. Purchase. 1997. Which aesthetic has the greatest effect on human understanding? In *Graph Drawing (Proc. 5th Int. Symposium, GD '97)*, volume 1353 of *Lecture Notes in Computer Science*, pages 248–261, Berlin, Heidelberg. Springer.

Hans Reichenbach. 1991. *The Direction of Time*, volume 65. Univ of California Press.

Shirong Shen, Heng Zhou, Tongtong Wu, and Guilin Qi. 2022. Event causality identification via derivative prompt joint learning. In *Proceedings of the 29th International Conference on Computational Linguistics (COLING)*, pages 2288–2299.

Matthew Sims and David Bamman. 2019. Literary event detection. In *Proceedings of the 57th Annual Meeting of the Association for Computational Linguistics*.

Carlota S. Smith. 1991. *The Parameter of Aspect*. Kluwer Academic Publishers.

Fiona Anting Tan, Xinyu Zuo, and See-Kiong Ng. 2023. Unicausal: Unified benchmark and repository for causal text mining. *Preprint*, arXiv:2208.09163.

Tom Trabasso and Paul Van Den Broek. 1985. Causal thinking and the representation of narrative events. *Journal of Memory and Language*, 24(5):612–630.

Zeno Vendler. 1967. *Linguistics in Philosophy*. Cornell University Press.

Rolf A. Zwaan and Gabriel A. Radvansky. 1998. Situation models in language comprehension and memory. *Psychological Bulletin*, 123(2):162–185.

A Appendix

A.1 LLM Prompt for Vertices Extraction

1. I will input a paragraph to you and you need to do the following.
2. You should summarize the sentences. All sentences should be SIMPLE sentences.
3. If the story is told in first person POV, try to find out the speaker's name or something to refer to the speaker. If you really can't find anything, sub the speaker with 'The Protagonist'.
4. Then, sub ALL pronouns, including the ones in the sentence, with the thing that they refer to.
5. Then, Break ALL clauses into **SIMPLE SENTENCES**. Delete unimportant clause-level information. Be CONCISE.
6. Your output at this time shall have LITTLE TO NO clauses.
7. You need to check the sentences. If they contain clause, BREAK IT INTO TWO SENTENCES.
8. The sentences, in their order, should give a continuous flow. DO NOT eliminate any important information that shows causal relationship.
9. However, only information that pushes the plot/story is needed. Be concise and do not include ANY irrelevant information.
10. Eventually, give me a summarization that focuses on causal relationships for the story.

A.2 LLM Prompt for STAC Categorization (Unused)

The following is our perspective on prompting as described in Section 4, specifically in Subsection 4.3. We attempted direct prompting using the STAC Model as we understood it; however, it did not serve as a suitable baseline. Instead, we employed it solely for comparison purposes.

Classify each sentence in each chunk individually into either a situation, a task, an action or a consequence. Note that the sentences ARE NOT related. We do these as follows:
1. Situation: Something that sets the stage of the BACKGROUND, without implying a particular action or task. The sentence will typically set the stage for something that happens later. Generally, it focuses on things that already happened at a certain stage of the story or something that would impact stuff later.
2. Task: Describes an explicit requirement, want, or responsibility that needs to be fulfilled. The sentence would explicitly(the action's name shall be mentioned) mention some event that one subject would accomplish later, but hasn't accomplished yet. If the sentence implies an action due to outforce changes, it's categorized as a situation.
3. Action: This refers to an activity that is BEING or HAS JUST BEEN carried out by someone. It requires someone to ACTIVELY do the action. Otherwise, it shall be a situation or a consequence.
4. Consequence: Describes when something happens as a result of at least one thing prior AND has an everlasting impact. It's always an action that 'finishes' (the action changed some state and does not normally change back) or a straightforward state change. It's different from a situation by the fact that it should be a result of something mentioned before in the paragraph, whereas a situation happens spontaneously.

A.3 LLM Prompt for Expert Index Extraction (Unused)

The following is our perspective on prompting as described in Section 4, specifically in Subsection 4.3. We attempted direct prompting using the Expert Index Model as we understood it; however, it did not serve as a suitable baseline. So we used humans as the Baseline.

IMPACT: I would give you a bunch of sentences and I want you to tell if the main event in the sentence has a lasting impact or if the main event is already resolved. for instance: - the door is left opened - impactful, focuses on shifting of door's state -He opened the door. - resolved, focuses on the person Border cases: - If you cannot determine any main event from the sentence, mark it as resolved because of a lack of state of change.

BOUNDEDNESS: I would give you a bunch of sentences, not in any order, and i want you to tell if the sentence's time span, labeled as 'Episodic', 'Habitual', or "Static'.
They are defined as follows: - The event is Episodic if it happens only once And is at a specific time period (you may not know that period, but you know the period exists and has a bound) - The Event is Habitual if the event happens on a regular basis. (There isn't a bound. The event is constant with intervals). - The Event is Static if the Event describes a characteristic of the subject or if the event is constant and doesn't not have a clear bound. (Lacking Past OR future bound satisfies the category).

SPECIFICITY: I would give you a bunch of sentences, not in any order, and i want you to tell if the sentence has a proper noun or a common noun main subject, labeled as 'Specific' or 'Generic'. Define Strictly on the subject, not the implied subject.
They are defined as follows: - All proper nouns are Specific. We Treat 'The Protagonist' and Any type of PRONOUNS as proper nouns in this case and are therefore Specific. Anything in First person POV is Specific. - Anything you can point to as 'It is THE ONE thing that does it' is Specific and treated as a proper noun. In a fairy tale, The Duck or A Tiger would be Specific because though they are not given a name, they act like proper nouns. (Think it like how the tiger's name would be Tiger) - As an addition to 2, any live thing or personified thing the Starts with 'the' are treated as proper nouns and are thus Specific. - A common noun, when can STRICTLY trace back to proper noun

EVENTIVITY: I will give you a bunch of sentences. Classify each sentence in each chunk into either Stative, Dynamically Active or Mentally Active. Do these as follows: Check if the sentence describes a stative action (Labeled Stative). This includes possession(Have, consist, contain, etc.), thoughts(Think, remember, suspect, realize, etc.), senses(Feel, seem. etc.), and emotions that do not trigger an action (like, dislike, appreciate, etc.)
Or the sentence describes a dynamic action (Labeled Dynamically Active, which is characterized by more physical than mental movement). This includes the majority of the verbs(Jump, Walk, Suggest, Answer, etc.). Note that Talking or Expressing an opinion would be a dynamic action, because no mental action actually takes place.
Or a mental action (Labeled Mentally Active). This includes action that happens mentally rather than physically, like decide, want, desire, hope, etc.

TIME END: Classify each sentence in each chunk into either Time End Current (Label as C), Or Time End Future(Label as F).
We do these as follows: Check if the Events will be continue happened after the sentence end itslef (In this case we label F(Future)) Def of End Future: A conclusion about what is happening now (Things will continue [according to logic]) (Things will continue [for sure]) Things don't end with the statement.

TIME START: Classify each sentence in each chunk into either Time Start Past, Or Time Start Now. We do these as follows: Check if the Events happened as we stated (In this case we label C(Current)) or the events happened as the sentences happened before (In this case we label P(Past))
If you find the event being persistent or stative and therefore does not have an explicitly start time, treat its start time as infinitely in the past and therefore label it as P.

INITIATIVE: I would give you a bunch of sentences, not in any order, and i want you to tell if the sentence represents an action it initiates or Receives. Define the main action and the main target through common sense and content. (NOT the subject). Now, I want you to tell me whether the target actively does(initiate), or receives an action(Receive). If the sentence itself is in passive form, it's automatically Receive. If the sentence itself is in active form, think about if the subject is able to do the action out of CHOICE or the action spontaneously happens. If the subject consciously does the action, it's an Initiate action. If not so, the subject Receives the action.
app:STAC Categorization Unused

A.4 Table Description for the Expert Index

A.5 Example Graph of Our Method

A.6 Table Description for STAC Bonding

A.7 Expert Index Result

A.8 Evaluation of Causal Graph Prompt

Input Story: xxxxX Causal Graph 1: xxxxxx Causal Graph 2: xxxxxx
Your job is to make judgement for each of the Causal Graph, determine which one is better in each of the dimension, here is the dimension description:

1. Causality vs. Chronology: Does the diagram emphasize actual cause-and-effect rather than merely stringing events in time?

2. Explicit Motivations/Intent: Are the driving reasons (e.g., revenge, pride, fear) clearly shown so the reader sees why a character or force triggers the next event?

3. Accuracy of Connections: Do arrows represent

Features Name	**Categories**	**Detail**
Generality	Specific	Refers to a particular instance or individual (e.g., a person, a dog).
	Generic	Refers to a general class or category (e.g., seasons, emotions).
Eventivity	Dynamic	Involves an observable action or change (e.g., speaking, running).
	Stative	Describes a state of being or condition (e.g., deciding, thinking).
Boundness	Episodic	Refers to an event occurring at a specific time.
	Habitual	Refers to actions that recur over time.
	Static	Refers to something that is always true or a permanent state.
Time Start	Past	The event began in the past relative to the narrative moment.
	Current	The event begins in the present relative to the narrative moment.
Time End	Current	The event concludes in the present relative to the narrative moment.
	Future	The event will conclude in the future relative to the narrative moment.
Initiality	Initiate	The subject has agency and initiates the action.
	Receive	The subject passively receives the action, without agency.
Impact	Impactful	The event has a lasting or significant effect.
	Resolved	The event's effect diminishes or resolves once completed.

Table 3: Table Description for the Expert Index

genuine causal links (A enables or drives B), and are there any missing or spurious connections?

4. Clarity and Brevity of Nodes: Are node labels concise and unambiguous? Too much text can clutter the diagram and obscure the causal flow.

5. Granularity/Level of Detail:Is the diagram capturing just enough detail to show cause-effect without trivial or irrelevant steps?

6. Logical Completeness: Does it include all critical causes and effects for key outcomes, so nothing pivotal is left out?

Begin Vertices	End Vertices	Definition
Situation	Situation	The first situation may create a setting that directly influences or causes a change in another situation without any intermediate actions or tasks.
	Task	The current environment imposes certain responsibilities or actions on the agent.
	Action	The environment itself drives the behavior, without an explicit task being identified first.
	Consequence	The scenarios where background factors alone create significant changes in the state of affairs.
Task	Action	This bond is a direct relationship where the execution of a task leads to a specific action.
	Consequence	In this bond, task itself will make an environment change as a result.
Action	Task/Action	This bond describes a sequence where one action leads directly to another action. Represents chains of immediate, active responses.
	Consequence	This bond reflects a causal relationship where an act brings about a lasting change or outcome.
Consequence	Situation	The consequence of a previous action or event sets up a new situation.(Different environment change)
	Task/Action	The consequence directly drives the agent's next move.
	Consequence	This bond reflects a sequence of cascading outcomes, where one consequence leads to another.

Table 4: Table Description for STAC Bonding

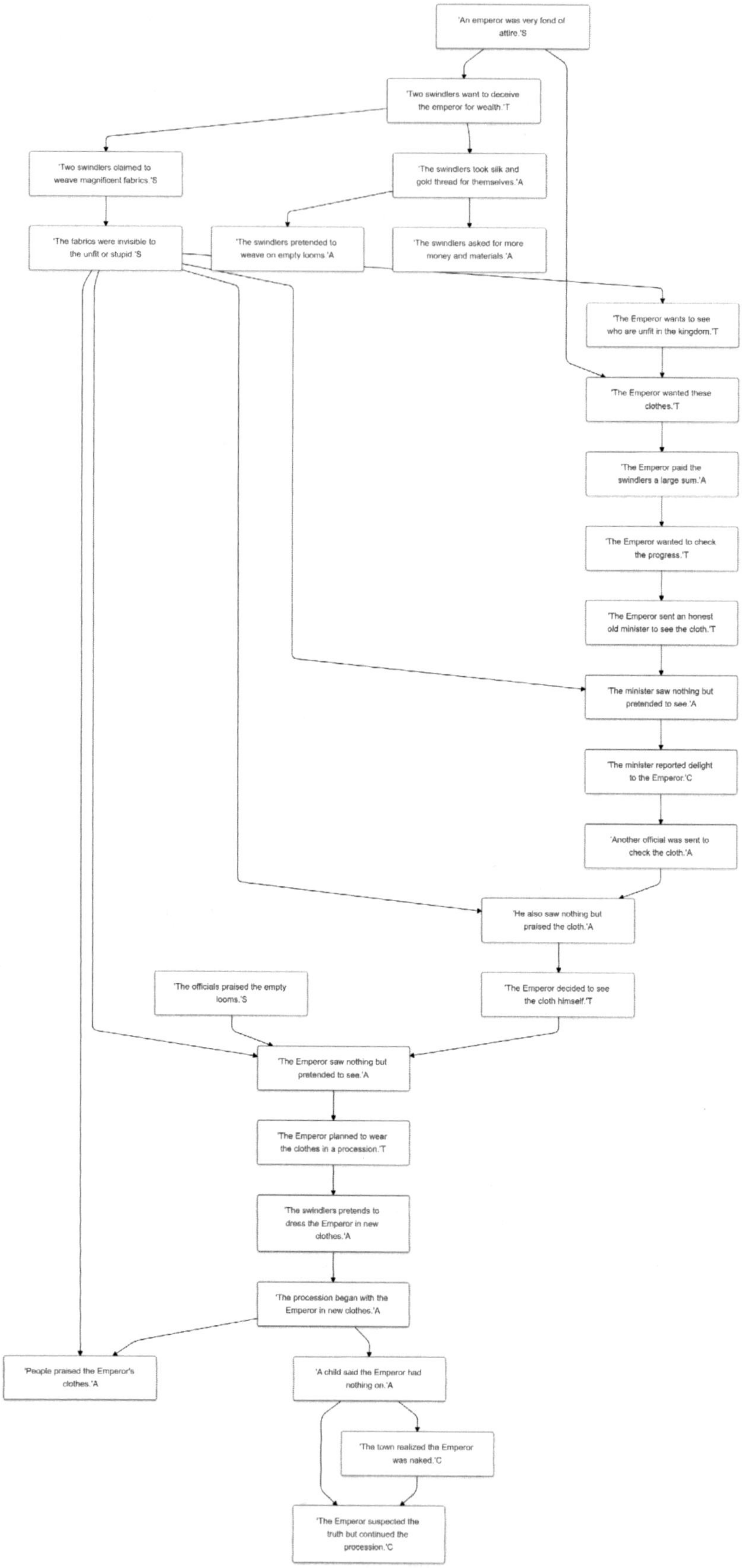

Figure 3: Example Graph Generation of Emperor's Cloth

Label	**Precision**	**Recall**	**F1**
Genericity (Generic)	0.72	0.58	0.64
Genericity (Specific)	0.93	0.96	0.94
Eventivity (D.Active)	0.94	0.93	0.93
Eventivity (M.Active)	0.68	0.92	0.7
Eventivity (Stative)	0.85	0.75	0.80
Boundedness (Ep.)	0.92	0.88	0.90
Boundedness (Hab.)	0.31	0.36	0.33
Boundedness (Static)	0.73	0.80	0.76
Initiativity (Initiate)	0.91	0.89	0.90
Initiativity (Receive)	0.84	0.86	0.85
Time End (Present)	0.92	0.86	0.89
Time End (Future)	0.63	0.78	0.69
Time Start (Past)	0.96	1.00	0.98
Time Start (Present)	1.00	0.60	0.73
Impact (Impactful)	0.88	0.76	0.82
Impact (Resolved)	0.84	0.89	0.87

Table 5: Classification results (test set, $n = 200$) for each trait and class label.

CHATTER: A Character Attribution Dataset for Narrative Understanding

Sabyasachee Baruah and **Shrikanth Narayanan**
Signal Analysis & Interpretation Laboratory
University of Southern California
sbaruah@usc.edu shri@usc.edu

Abstract

Computational narrative understanding studies the identification, description, and interaction of the elements of a narrative: characters, attributes, events, and relations. Narrative research has given considerable attention to defining and classifying character types. However, these character-type taxonomies do not generalize well because they are small, too simple, or specific to a domain. We require robust and reliable benchmarks to test whether narrative models truly understand the nuances of the character's development in the story. Our work addresses this by curating the CHATTER dataset that labels whether a character portrays some attribute for 88124 character-attribute pairs, encompassing 2998 characters, 12967 attributes and 660 movies. We validate a subset of CHATTER, called CHATTEREVAL, using human annotations to serve as a benchmark to evaluate the character attribution task in movie scripts. CHATTEREVAL also assesses narrative understanding and the long-context modeling capacity of language models.

1 Introduction

Narrativity occurs when characters interact with each other, triggering events that are temporally, spatially, and causally connected. This sequence of events forms the story. Piper et al. (2021) provided a symbolic definition of narrativity in which they asserted that narrativity occurs when the narrator $\mathcal{A}$ tells the perceiver $\mathcal{B}$ that some agent $\mathcal{C}$ performed the action $\mathcal{D}$ on another agent $\mathcal{E}$ at place $\mathcal{F}$ and time $\mathcal{G}$ for some reason $\mathcal{H}$. Baruah and Narayanan (2024) used this definition to identify four main elements of any narrative: characters, attributes, events, and relations. Labatut and Bost (2019) explored different types of character interactions and emphasized the central role characters play in narratives. Characters drive the plot forward through their actions, develop attributes, arouse tension and emotion in the story by creating conflicts or bonds with other characters, and embody tropes and stereotypes to relate to the audience. The vitality of characters in narratives makes character understanding an essential task in narrative research.

Dataset	Domain	Type	Size
Finlayson (2015)	Folklore	Archetype	282
Skowron et al. (2016)	Movies	Role	2010
Brahman et al. (2021)	Literature	Description	9499
Sang et al. (2022)	Movies	Personality	28653
Yu et al. (2023)	Literature	Traits	52002
CHATTER	Movies	Tropes	88124
CHATTEREVAL	Movies	Tropes	1061

Table 1: Comparison with other attribution datasets in terms of the attribute type and size. Size denotes the number of character-attribute pairs. CHATTER is the largest character attribution dataset collected so far.

Narratologists have explored various approaches to operationalize the character-understanding task. For example, Inoue et al. (2022) presented character understanding as a suite of document-level tasks that included gender and role identification of the character, *cloze* tasks, quote attribution, and question answering. Li et al. (2023) adopted coreference resolution, character linking, and speaker guessing tasks, and Azab et al. (2019) used character relationships and relatedness to evaluate character representations. We organized the character-understanding tasks into the following categories. **1) Identification** tasks find the unique set of characters and their mentions. It includes entity recognition, entity linking, and coreference resolution. The **2) Quotation** task maps utterances to characters. **3) Attribution** tasks, such as personality classification, persona modeling, and description generation, describe the character. The **4) *Cloze*** task asks the model to fill in the correct character name given an anonymized character description, story summary, or story excerpt. **5) Relation** tasks, such as relation classification, draw similarities between characters.

Among these tasks, character attribution is the

Proceedings of the The 7th Workshop on Narrative Understanding, pages 52–63
May 4, 2025 ©2025 Association for Computational Linguistics

most challenging because there exists a multitude of ways to qualify a character, such as personality (Sang et al., 2022), adjectives (Yu et al., 2023), persona (Bamman et al., 2013, 2014), archetypes (Finlayson, 2015), roles (Skowron et al., 2016), and descriptions (Brahman et al., 2021). Each of these approaches has drawbacks. For example, personality scales such as Big5 and MBTI cannot capture all the variation in characterization and can be difficult to interpret (Zillig et al., 2002). Adjective descriptors are too general and apply only to a limited context in the story. Persona roles are not explicitly defined. Archetypes (Propp, 1968; Jung, 2014) are abstract concepts specific to the domain of interest. Character descriptions are detailed, freeform, and scalable to any number of characters. However, we cannot factor them into simpler components or use them to compare between different characters.

We require a robust attribution taxonomy that can scale across different narratives, characters, and domains, is well-defined and discrete for effective character comparison, and necessitates document-level understanding to model them accurately. We developed the CHATTER dataset to fulfill this need. The CHATTER dataset uses tropes from the TVTropes website as the attribute type to describe characters. TVTropes editors and moderators comprehensively define every trope with illustrative examples from multiple media sources. Tropes cover a wider range of character descriptions than personality types and archetypes, and require longer context-understanding, compared to traits and adjectives, to accurately ascertain if a character portrays some trope. Unlike character descriptions, we can efficiently compare characters and their experiences using these well-defined tropes (Wang et al., 2021).

The CHATTER dataset contains labels indicating whether the character portrayed the trope in the movies they appeared in. It contains 88124 character-trope pairs. We drew our characters primarily from Hollywood movies across various genres. It also provides the full-length screenplays of the movies, averaging about 25K words per screenplay. We define the character attribution task as a **binary classification task** where, given a character-trope pair and the screenplays of the movies where the character appears, the model should predict whether the character portrayed the trope. We validate a subset of the CHATTER data, referred to as CHATTEREVAL, using human annotations to establish an evaluation benchmark for the character attribution task. We compared the zero-shot and few-shot performance of LLMs and CHATTER's labels to assess the suitability of using the CHATTER dataset as a training set for the attribution task. The dataset is available at `https://drive.google.com/drive/folders/11egMhs-zkWSASe7zJENwHg17-6VOeXDU?usp=sharing`.

2 Data

2.1 Tropes

Tropes are storytelling devices or conventions used by the writer to easily convey some story notion to the reader. They act like narrative motifs that readers can easily recognize, saving time and effort for the writer as they can omit details the readers can infer from the trope. For example, the *AntiHero* is a very popular trope that describes a protagonist who lacks traditional heroic qualities, often cynical and flawed, yet ultimately performs heroic actions. The character Severus Snape in the Harry Potter stories portrays the *AntiHero* trope as he gives Harry a hard time but stays loyal to Dumbledore (mentor) and works secretly to defeat Voldemort (antagonist).

Tropes can also relate to inanimate objects, events, locations or the environment. We focus only on character tropes in our work. The scope of a trope can vary greatly. Some tropes like *PetTheDog* (villain performing an act of kindness) are portrayed over short contexts, typically a single scene, whereas others like *HiddenDepths* (revealing unexpected talents as the story progresses) are portrayed over a longer context. The attribution model should be able to extract information from different points in the narrative and reason over it to identify the portrayed tropes.

We use the character trope labels of TVTropes[1]. TVTropes is a community-driven website, similar to Wikipedia, that catalogs tropes with definitions and examples. Fans of a creative work discuss and post tropes they identify in the narrative. Each trope has a dedicated page which contains its definition, illustrations, and portrayal examples from TV shows, movies, literature, animation, video games, and print media. TVTropes moderators ensure that the fan-edited content is correct. We collect the trope annotations from TVTropes to build the CHATTER dataset.

It is important to note that the character trope annotations we collect from TVTropes are those

[1] `https://tvtropes.org`

perceived by the reader. These might not align with the *actual* tropes intended by the creator. Since there is no quantifiable agreement on the published content, we treat the TVTropes data as a noisy source of character attribution.

2.2 Screenplays

We used movies as the source of our narratives. We chose the cinematic domain over the literary domain because it had more TVTropes labels, and we supposed it would be easier to find raters more knowledgeable about movies than books. Additionally, movies allow us to extend the attribution task to the multimodal domain, offering more opportunities for future research directions.

We used publicly available movie screenplays from the ScriptsonScreen[2] website. Each script is mapped to an IMDB[3] identifier so we can uniquely identify the movie. Most movies in our dataset are produced in the US or the UK after 1980. The average script size is about 25K words. We apply a named entity classifier and name alias generator to map the character names in the script to a unique character in the IMDB cast list. We preprocess the screenplays to find scenes, dialogues and descriptions using Baruah and Narayanan's (2023) screenplay parser. In total, our dataset contains screenplays of 660 movies.

2.3 CHATTER

We build the CHATTER dataset of character-trope pairs using the tropes of TVTropes and the screenplays of ScriptsonScreen. First, we download the movie screenplays from ScriptsonScreen, parse and map them to an IMDB page, and match the characters occurring in the document to a character in the IMDB cast list. Second, we search for the character in TVTropes and retrieve their character page. Third, we collect the tropes portrayed by the character from the character page, as labeled by the TVTropes community. Fourth, we search for the trope page and fetch its definition. We also summarize the definition using GPT-4 for the annotation task. The average size of the trope definition and its summary is 344 and 44 words, respectively.

We need good negative samples to evaluate the specificity of the attribution model. However, TVTropes does not provide this information because it does not label tropes *not* portrayed by the character. Instead, we analyze the trope definition to find antonym tropes and create the negative character-trope pairs. For example, the definition of the *AntiHero* trope contains the sentence –

`...Compare and contrast this trope with its antithesis, the AntiVillain...`

– which indicates that the *AntiVillain* trope is contrary to *AntiHero*. We search the trope definitions to retrieve opposing tropes by checking if negation words such as "contrast", "opposite" and "counterpart" exist within a five-word context window of the antonym trope mention[4]. For each positive character-trope pair, we create a negative pair by either – 1) selecting an antonym trope from the trope definition or 2) choosing a trope that is absent in any of the positive character-trope pairs for that character. It should be harder for the attribution model to distinguish antonym tropes from tropes portrayed by the character because they are much more closely related to the portrayed tropes than a trope randomly sampled with the second method. Therefore, the former method creates hard negatives and the latter method creates soft negatives. We randomly choose between the two methods with 50% probability to get a good mix of hard and soft negatives. We add the negative samples to complete the construction of the CHATTER dataset.

3 Evaluation Data

We can use CHATTER to train attribution models, but we require a more reliable dataset for evaluation. We annotate a subset of CHATTER using human raters and create the CHATTEREVAL dataset.

3.1 Annotation

We sampled movies from our dataset released after 2010 and collected the corresponding character-trope pairs for annotation. We employed workers on the Amazon MTurk[5] crowdsource annotation platform. We selected workers with high reputation and experience[6] and tested them on two separate qualification tasks, each containing five questions that asked them to decide whether the character portrayed the given trope. The task showed them the picture of the character, the movies that starred the character with Wikipedia links, a link to the fandom page[7] where the worker can read more about the

[2]https://scripts-onscreen.com

[3]https://imdb.com

[4]The full list of negation words is included in the dataset

[5]https://www.mturk.com

[6] >98% approval rate and worked on >5000 HITs

[7]https://www.fandom.com

character, and the summarized trope definition with a link to the trope's TVTropes page. Appendix A shows the annotation interface. We also surveyed the workers about the movies they had watched. We qualified 69 workers who correctly answered at least 80% of the questions and had watched at least ten movies out of the ones sampled for evaluation.

The qualified workers labeled whether the character portrayed the trope on a Likert scale: *no*, *maybe no*, *not sure*, *maybe yes* and *yes*. To reduce the cognitive load on the workers, they annotated the character-trope pairs in batches, each batch containing characters from at most ten movies. Before every batch, we inform the workers about the movies they will encounter to prepare them for the annotation task. After each batch, we estimate the worker's performance by calculating the accuracy of their ratings against the CHATTER labels and record how much time they spent on the task. We dropped workers whose accuracy dropped below 50% or those speeding through the samples, disqualifying them from working on future batches. Of the 69 workers, we disqualified 10 raters and were left with 59 reliable workers.

The annotation task ran for one month between August 11 to September 19 2024. Throughout the task, we maintained a communication channel for the workers in the TurkerNation Slack Workspace, where we responded to any questions the workers had about the task. We pay $1.5 for each question which turns out to be $18/hour because the workers spent an average of 5 minutes per question. The entire task cost us about $10K. We collected three annotations per character-trope pair, totaling 5683 annotations. The Krippendorff inter-rater reliability score is 0.448, indicating moderate agreement.

3.2 CHATTEREVAL

We aggregate the annotations to build the CHATTEREVAL dataset. The character-trope pairs do not all show clear agreement. Character attribution, like sentiment analysis, is a subjective task, and whether a character portrays some trope is perceived differently by people. We need to assign a definite binary label to each annotated sample for the character attribution task. We also need to drop the very ambiguous samples and those with insufficient reliable ratings to ensure high quality.

The MTurk workers answer *yes*, *maybe yes*, *not sure*, *maybe no* or *no* on each question. We map this ordinal scale to a numeric range by mapping the labels to 2, 1, 0, -1 and -2, respectively. Each character-trope pair is annotated by at most three reliable workers. We sum the label values for each sample to get an integer score s between -6 and 6. The higher the absolute score, the greater is the agreement among the raters. We drop samples whose absolute integer score falls below 3. For the remaining samples, we obtain the annotation confidence w by normalizing the integer score s between 0 and 1: $w = (|s| - 2)/4$. The confidence score takes values 0.25, 0.5, 0.75 and 1. Attribution models can use these scores to weigh their evaluation metrics. The sample gets the label 1 (character portrays the trope) if $s > 0$, else 0 (character does not portray the trope). We include the annotations of the individual raters in CHATTEREVAL to encourage multiannotator modeling.

Dataset	Characters	Tropes	Movies	Samples
CHATTER	2998	12967	660	88124
CHATTEREVAL	271	896	78	1061

Table 2: CHATTER and CHATTEREVAL's sizes

	Min	Max	Avg	95%tile
Movies/Character	1	5	1.04	1.0
Tropes/Character	1	1107	29.40	91.0
Words/Script	3051	87738	24614.98	34011.35
Tokens/Script	5149	158038	41952.05	58933.09
Words/Segment	3	28423	2981.28	9983.8
Tokens/Segment	4	43742	4350.89	14317.15

Table 3: CHATTER and CHATTEREVAL's statistics

4 Data Statistics

CHATTER contains 88124 character-trope pairs with an almost 50-50 split between positive and negative pairs. It covers 2998 unique characters from 660 movies and 12967 tropes. CHATTEREVAL contains 1061 human-annotated character-trope pairs, covering 271 characters, 896 tropes, and 78 movies. It contains 555 positive and 506 negative pairs. Tables 2 and 3 show some data statistics of CHATTER and CHATTEREVAL.

Most characters appear in a single movie script in our dataset. CHATTER contains attribution labels for about 30 tropes for each character. Segments indicate the portions of a movie script where a character speaks or is mentioned. As shown in Table 3, the maximum size of a movie script or a character segment can exceed 87K and 28K words, respectively. This corresponds to 158K and 43K tokens, respectively (We used the Llama3 (Dubey et al., 2024) tiktoken-based BPE tokenizer). There-

Character	Movies	Trope	Label
Benoit Blanc	*Knives Out (2019), Glass Onion (2022)*	The **NiceGuy** trope describes a character who is kind, friendly, morally good, and socially pleasant.	1
Mark Watney	*The Martian (2015)*	The **EarnYourHappyEnding** trope involves characters enduring significant hardship, anguish, and grief, but ultimately achieving a happy ending through hard work or love	1
Arthur Fleck	*Joker (2019)*	The **TheDogBitesBack** trope occurs when a villain is attacked or betrayed by an abused subordinate or victim who seizes the chance for revenge	0
Dr. King Schultz	*Django Unchained (2012)*	The **SoreLoser** trope describes a character who reacts to defeat with anger, accusations, and bad behavior	0

Table 4: Character-Trope examples from the CHATTEREVAL dataset

fore, we must use a model capable of handling long contexts for the attribution task.

Most movies in our dataset have been produced in the UK or the US after 1980. They cover a wide range of genres. The top five genres – *Action*, *Drama*, *Thriller*, *Adventure*, and *Comedy* – cover more than 50% of the movies. Table 4 shows qualitative examples from the CHATTEREVAL dataset. The tropes can relate to the character's attitude and personality (*NiceGuy*), some experience or incident (*SoreLoser*), or their overall story (*EarnYourHappyEnding*). The character attribution task entails that the model understands the trope definition, reads the scripts of the movies where the character appears, and, based on that, decides whether the character portrays the trope. Appendix D lists the most commonly occurring tropes and their definitions to visualize the trope space.

Our dataset does not contain scripts for all the movies where the character appears. For example, the character Arthur Fleck "Joker" has appeared in multiple movies, comics, and TV shows, but CHATTER only contains the movie script of the *Joker (2019)* movie. The TVTropes contributors and our raters draw their knowledge of the character from all sources. However, the attribution model predicts the attribute labels based only on the screenplay and its pretraining data. Therefore, intractable character-trope pairs could exist for which the model has insufficient information. In future work, we will investigate ways to find such intractable samples in our dataset.

5 Experiments

5.1 Models

We establish baselines on CHATTEREVAL using zero-shot and few-shot prompting. We used two closed-source models, Gemini-1.5-Flash (Reid et al., 2024) and GPT-4o-mini (Hurst et al., 2024), and three open-source models, Phi-3-small-7B-128k-Instruct (Abdin et al., 2024), Llama-3.1-8B-Instruct (Dubey et al., 2024) and Mistral-Nemo-Instruct-12B-2407 (Jiang et al., 2023), in our experiments. We selected these models because they can handle long contexts (128K tokens).

We experiment with four prompting strategies. **1) Priors** - We prompt the model with the character name, the list of movies where the character has appeared, and the trope definition. We do not include any screenplay content and ask the model to find the attribution label based solely on its prior knowledge about the character. **2) Script** - We include the full movie script in the prompt. **3) Segment (Zero-shot)** - We include the segments of the movie script where the character speaks or is mentioned. **4) Segment (Few-shot)** - We include the character segments and two examples from the CHATTEREVAL dataset. We select examples of the same trope. We also experimented with selecting random examples or examples of the same character, but they both performed worse than selecting same-trope examples. We do not apply few-shot prompting with movie scripts because the prompt size becomes too large. Appendix E describes the prompt template we used.

For the last three settings – **Script**, **Segment (Zero-shot)**, and **Segment (Few-shot)** – we replaced character names in the movie scripts or the character segments with random alphanumeric identifiers. We hypothesize that the LLM could be generating its response by recognizing the character name and using the knowledge it had accrued about the character from its pretraining datasets. The character-anonymization step possibly prevents the LLM from relying on its prior knowledge about the character and forces it to decide the attribution label based solely on the given movie script

Prompt	Model	Acc	P	R	F1
	Random	50.0	52.3	50.0	51.1
	CHATTER	*80.6*	*81.0*	*82.2*	*81.6*
Priors	Gemini-1.5	**81.9**	**91.4**	**72.2**	**80.7**
	GPT-4o	76.2	98.1	55.6	71.0
	Phi-7B	56.6	89.1	19.5	32.0
	Llama-8B	71.0	68.9	81.4	74.6
	Mistral-12B	73.1	83.0	61.3	70.5
Script	Gemini-1.5	72.4	83.1	59.4	69.3
	GPT-4o	**73.9**	**71.2**	**84.4**	**77.2**
	Phi-7B	65.5	77.4	48.1	59.3
	Llama-8B	61.4	61.4	70.7	65.7
	Mistral-12B	56.1	60.5	45.7	52.1
Segment (Zero-Shot)	Gemini-1.5	73.5	86.6	58.4	69.8
	GPT-4o	**78.5**	**77.4**	**83.3**	**80.3**
	Phi-7B	73.3	77.1	68.8	72.7
	Llama-8B	69.8	65.6	87.7	75.1
	Mistral-12B	69.3	81.4	53.2	64.3
Segment (Few-Shot)	Gemini-1.5	65.5	93.4	36.7	52.7
	GPT-4o	**74.5**	**79.5**	**69.2**	**74.0**
	Phi-7B	62.3	65.5	68.1	66.8
	Llama-8B	60.8	61.0	75.3	67.4
	Mistral-12B	62.0	62.0	73.6	67.3

Table 5: Prior, Zero-shot, and Few-shot performance on CHATTEREVAL for the character attribution binary classification task. The **CHATTER** row uses the CHATTER's labels as predictions. We bolden the model row with the best accuracy (or F1) for each prompting strategy.

or character segments. We observed that prompting with the non-anonymized documents produced better performance, validating our hypothesis. Future work should explore more effective prompting strategies to nullify the effect of the model's priors on the generated response.

We perform greedy decoding. We also evaluate CHATTER's labels against the annotations of CHATTEREVAL to assess its suitability as a training set for character attribution. We use permutation tests at $\alpha = 0.05$ to compare the performance of different prompting strategies and models. We apply Bonferroni correction to correct for multiple comparisons.

5.2 Results

Table 5 shows the performance of the different prompting strategies. The closed-sourced models were significantly more accurate than the open-sourced models for all strategies. This is expected because the closed-sourced models supposedly contain more parameters and have been trained on more extensive data. Gemini-1.5 has the strongest prior knowledge, followed by GPT-4o. They performed equally well when we prompted them on the full movie script. However, GPT-4o's zero-shot and few-shot accuracy on character segments was significantly better than Gemini's. There was no significant difference between the accuracy scores of Phi-7B, Llama-8B, and Mistral-12B for any of the prompting strategies, except for priors where Phi-7B performed worse than random.

Comparing the different prompting strategies, we observed that the zero-shot accuracy on character segments was significantly better than the few-shot accuracy across all the models. This discrepancy in performance is surprising because prompting models usually provide better results with exemplars in the prompt. A possible reason could be that the two examples in the prompt are insufficient to represent the task adequately. Increasing the number of prompts is not viable because of the context limit. A possible solution could be summarizing the character segments to fit more examples in the prompt.

Prompting the character segments usually performed as well or better than prompting the full movie scripts. However, in most cases, the model's prior performance already showed strong results. This confirms that these models were probably pretrained on the tropes data from TVTropes, making it harder to evaluate the true character attribution capability of the model. The huge gap in performance between the priors of the closed-source models and the zero-shot or few-shot prompting results of the open-sourced models shows that there is much scope for improvement for the open-sourced models. This is important because, given a movie script (or any other narrative document), we do not always want to prompt it using commercial APIs because they might contain private or unpublished information. Training local attribution models on the character-trope pairs of CHATTER should narrow this performance gap.

There is no significant difference between the results of the strongest-performing model and using the labels of the CHATTER dataset as predictions. Therefore, CHATTER can serve as a good training source for the character attribution task. The strong zero-shot performance of the closed-sourced models suggests that we can use them to create good-quality synthetic training data.

We also observe that the recall scores of the models are usually lower than their precision. A possible reason could be the sizeable prompt size, which makes it difficult for the model to pinpoint the relevant sections from the script or the character segments. While training character attribution models, we should further preprocess the data for more effective learning.

6 Related Work

Several past studies have curated character attribution datasets for narrative understanding. Finlayson (2015) annotated seven character archetypes in Russian folktales to create the ProppLearner corpus. Skowron et al. (2016) labeled hero, antagonist, sidekick, spouse and supporting roles in action-genre movies. Brahman et al. (2021) collected character descriptions from online study guides such as LitChart and Sparknotes, and created the LiSCU dataset for the character identification and description generation task. Sang et al. (2022) curated MBTI personality types from the personality database for movie characters. Yu et al. (2023) annotated reader's notes for character traits in Chinese-translated Gutenberg books. Baruah and Narayanan (2024) annotated screenplay excerpts for character attributes and evaluated in-context and chain-of-thought learning methods on the attribution task. Table 1 compares these datasets against CHATTER and CHATTEREVAL.

7 Conclusion

We proposed the CHATTER and CHATTEREVAL datasets for the narrative character attribution task. We addressed the limitations of previous datasets by curating a resource that is scalable, generalizable, well-defined and discrete. Experiments showed that CHATTER can serve as a reliable training set and CHATTEREVAL can be used as the evaluation benchmark for character attribution modeling. Future work includes developing character attribution models on our datasets to aid creators and writers in analyzing their narratives.

8 Limitations

We define the character attribution task as a binary classification task, where, given the character-trope pair and the screenplays of the movies in which the character appeared, the model should predict whether or not the character portrayed the trope. This formulation has some limitations. First, the screenplay's narrative may not exactly resemble the story told by the movie because of tweaks made during the filming process. Publicly available screenplays are rarely the final script but drafts from earlier in the production stage. Second, movies could have visual cues like the non-verbal behavior of the character that are missed by the screenplay text. Lastly, a character can appear in multiple movies, and our dataset does not contain scripts for all of them. These limitations have important implications because the TVTropes contributors and our raters draw their knowledge of the character from all sources. In contrast, the attribution model predicts the attribute labels based only on the screenplay. There could be character-attribute pairs for which the model has insufficient information and could lead to poor recall, as shown by the performance of the models in Table 5.

References

Marah Abdin, Jyoti Aneja, Hany Awadalla, Ahmed Awadallah, Ammar Ahmad Awan, Nguyen Bach, Amit Bahree, Arash Bakhtiari, Jianmin Bao, Harkirat Behl, et al. 2024. Phi-3 technical report: A highly capable language model locally on your phone. *arXiv preprint arXiv:2404.14219*.

Mahmoud Azab, Noriyuki Kojima, Jia Deng, and Rada Mihalcea. 2019. Representing movie characters in dialogues. In *Proceedings of the 23rd Conference on Computational Natural Language Learning (CoNLL)*, pages 99–109, Hong Kong, China. Association for Computational Linguistics.

David Bamman, Brendan O'Connor, and Noah A. Smith. 2013. Learning latent personas of film characters. In *Proceedings of the 51st Annual Meeting of the Association for Computational Linguistics (Volume 1: Long Papers)*, pages 352–361, Sofia, Bulgaria. Association for Computational Linguistics.

David Bamman, Ted Underwood, and Noah A. Smith. 2014. A Bayesian mixed effects model of literary character. In *Proceedings of the 52nd Annual Meeting of the Association for Computational Linguistics (Volume 1: Long Papers)*, pages 370–379, Baltimore, Maryland. Association for Computational Linguistics.

Sabyasachee Baruah and Shrikanth Narayanan. 2023. Character coreference resolution in movie screenplays. In *Findings of the Association for Computational Linguistics: ACL 2023*, pages 10300–10313, Toronto, Canada. Association for Computational Linguistics.

Sabyasachee Baruah and Shrikanth Narayanan. 2024. Character attribute extraction from movie scripts using llms. In *ICASSP 2024 - 2024 IEEE International Conference on Acoustics, Speech and Signal Processing (ICASSP)*, pages 8270–8275.

Faeze Brahman, Meng Huang, Oyvind Tafjord, Chao Zhao, Mrinmaya Sachan, and Snigdha Chaturvedi.

2021. "let your characters tell their story": A dataset for character-centric narrative understanding. In *Findings of the Association for Computational Linguistics: EMNLP 2021*, pages 1734–1752, Punta Cana, Dominican Republic. Association for Computational Linguistics.

Abhimanyu Dubey, Abhinav Jauhri, Abhinav Pandey, Abhishek Kadian, Ahmad Al-Dahle, Aiesha Letman, Akhil Mathur, Alan Schelten, Amy Yang, Angela Fan, et al. 2024. The llama 3 herd of models. *arXiv preprint arXiv:2407.21783*.

Mark A. Finlayson. 2015. ProppLearner: Deeply annotating a corpus of Russian folktales to enable the machine learning of a Russian formalist theory. *Digital Scholarship in the Humanities*, 32(2):284–300.

Aaron Hurst, Adam Lerer, Adam P Goucher, Adam Perelman, Aditya Ramesh, Aidan Clark, AJ Ostrow, Akila Welihinda, Alan Hayes, Alec Radford, et al. 2024. Gpt-4o system card. *arXiv preprint arXiv:2410.21276*.

Naoya Inoue, Charuta Pethe, Allen Kim, and Steven Skiena. 2022. Learning and evaluating character representations in novels. In *Findings of the Association for Computational Linguistics: ACL 2022*, pages 1008–1019, Dublin, Ireland. Association for Computational Linguistics.

Albert Q Jiang, Alexandre Sablayrolles, Arthur Mensch, Chris Bamford, Devendra Singh Chaplot, Diego de las Casas, Florian Bressand, Gianna Lengyel, Guillaume Lample, Lucile Saulnier, et al. 2023. Mistral 7b. *arXiv preprint arXiv:2310.06825*.

Carl Gustav Jung. 2014. *The archetypes and the collective unconscious*. Routledge.

Vincent Labatut and Xavier Bost. 2019. Extraction and analysis of fictional character networks: A survey. *ACM Computing Surveys (CSUR)*, 52(5):1–40.

Dawei Li, Hengyuan Zhang, Yanran Li, and Shiping Yang. 2023. Multi-level contrastive learning for script-based character understanding. In *Proceedings of the 2023 Conference on Empirical Methods in Natural Language Processing*, pages 5995–6013, Singapore. Association for Computational Linguistics.

Andrew Piper, Richard Jean So, and David Bamman. 2021. Narrative theory for computational narrative understanding. In *Proceedings of the 2021 Conference on Empirical Methods in Natural Language Processing*, pages 298–311, Online and Punta Cana, Dominican Republic. Association for Computational Linguistics.

Vladimir Propp. 1968. Morphology of the folktale. *U of Texas P*.

Machel Reid, Nikolay Savinov, Denis Teplyashin, Dmitry Lepikhin, Timothy Lillicrap, Jean-baptiste Alayrac, Radu Soricut, Angeliki Lazaridou, Orhan Firat, Julian Schrittwieser, et al. 2024. Gemini 1.5: Unlocking multimodal understanding across millions of tokens of context. *arXiv preprint arXiv:2403.05530*.

Yisi Sang, Xiangyang Mou, Mo Yu, Dakuo Wang, Jing Li, and Jeffrey Stanton. 2022. MBTI personality prediction for fictional characters using movie scripts. In *Findings of the Association for Computational Linguistics: EMNLP 2022*, pages 6715–6724, Abu Dhabi, United Arab Emirates. Association for Computational Linguistics.

Marcin Skowron, Martin Trapp, Sabine Payr, and Robert Trappl. 2016. Automatic identification of character types from film dialogs. *Applied Artificial Intelligence*, 30(10):942–973.

Zhilin Wang, Weizhe Lin, and Xiaodong Wu. 2021. Learning similarity between movie characters and its potential implications on understanding human experiences. In *Proceedings of the Third Workshop on Narrative Understanding*, pages 24–35, Virtual. Association for Computational Linguistics.

Mo Yu, Jiangnan Li, Shunyu Yao, Wenjie Pang, Xiaochen Zhou, Zhou Xiao, Fandong Meng, and Jie Zhou. 2023. Personality understanding of fictional characters during book reading. In *Proceedings of the 61st Annual Meeting of the Association for Computational Linguistics (Volume 1: Long Papers)*, pages 14784–14802, Toronto, Canada. Association for Computational Linguistics.

Lisa M Pytlik Zillig, Scott H Hemenover, and Richard A Dienstbier. 2002. What do we assess when we assess a big 5 trait? a content analysis of the affective, behavioral, and cognitive processes represented in big 5 personality inventories. *Personality and Social Psychology Bulletin*, 28(6):847–858.

A Annotation

We give the following annotation instructions to the Amazon MTurk workers.

A trope is a storytelling device or convention the storyteller uses to describe situations the audience can easily recognize, often used to stereotype characters. Think of them as character attributes.

Your task is as follows:

1. Identify the movie character from the pictures and the given movie(s). If you are having trouble recognizing the character, click on the Character Page link(s).

2. Read the definition of the character trope. You can open the link to know more.

3. Choose yes, maybe yes, not sure, maybe no, or no to answer whether the character portrays or is associated with the trope.

4. (Optional) Explain your choice in the provided text area or leave any other comment behind.

Figure 1 shows the annotation interface that the workers use to label character attribution.

B TVTropes

TVTropes is licensed under a Creative Commons Attribution-NonCommercial-ShareAlike 3.0 Unported License. This license allows for the copy and redistribution of the material in any medium or format for non-commercial purposes. CHATTER is published for academic research purposes and does not infringe the TVTropes license.

C ScriptsonScreen

ScriptsonScreen aggregates movie scripts from different websites such as IMSDB[8], Dailyscripts[9] and Script Slug[10]. All the movie scripts we use are licensed for fair use and available for public download.

D TROPES

There are 445 tropes in total that have at least one character portraying them in our dataset. We could not figure out a systematic way to cluster them because the tropes are very different from each other. Therefore, we simply list the most common tropes and their abbreviated definition. Tables 6 and 7 list the tropes that are portrayed by at least two characters in our dataset.

E Prompt

We used the following prompt template in our experiments.

```
A character trope is a story-telling
device used by the writer to describe
characters.

Given below is the definition of the
$TROPE$ trope enclosed between the
tags <TROPE> and </TROPE>.
Following that is a movie script
enclosed between the
tags <SCRIPT> and </SCRIPT>.
The character "$CHARACTER$" appears
in the movie script.

Read the movie script carefully
and based on that answer yes or no
if the character "$CHARACTER$"
portrays or is associated with the
$TROPE$ trope.
If yes, give a brief explanation.
Answer based only on the movie script.
Do not rely on your prior knowledge.

<TROPE>
$DEFINITION$
</TROPE>

<SCRIPT>
$SCRIPT$
</SCRIPT>

Does the character "$CHARACTER$"
portray or is associated with
the $TROPE$ trope in the above
movie script?
Answer yes or no.
```

[8]https:https://imsdb.com/

[9]https://www.dailyscript.com/

[10]https://www.scriptslug.com/

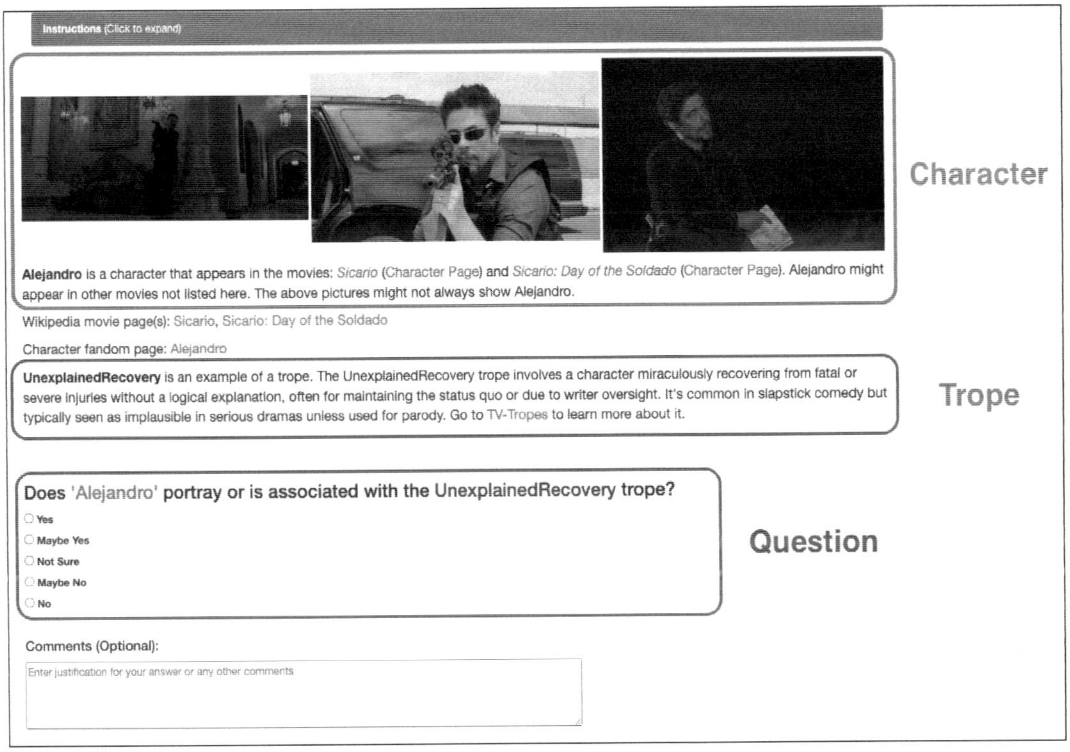

Figure 1: Interface of the annotation task.

```
If yes, give a brief explanation.
Do not use MarkDown.
```

We replace $CHARACTER$, $TROPE$, $DEFINITION$ and $SCRIPT$ with the character name, trope name, definition of the trope and the movie script during prompting.

	Trope	Definition
1.	AdaptationalAttractiveness	Plain characters are portrayed as attractive in adaptations
2.	AdaptationPersonalityChange	Character personality changes during medium adaptations
3.	AffablyEvil	Charming villain with kindness despite malevolent intentions
4.	AntiVillain	Heroic goals achieved through questionable or evil means
5.	AudienceSurrogate	Character audience identifies with for sympathy and relatability
6.	BadLiar	Character fails to lie convincingly; creates transparent falsehoods
7.	BerserkButton	Character's minor trigger causes explosive anger reaction
8.	BitchInSheepsClothing	Deceptive character appears kind but is secretly villainous
9.	BlueIsHeroic	Blue signifies heroism through calm, disciplined characters
10.	CatchPhrase	Repetitive distinctive phrase by a character or category
11.	ChildrenAreInnocent	Children embody innocence and purity, contrasting adult corruption
12.	Cloudcuckoolander	Cheerfully eccentric character, detached from reality, unexpectedly wise
13.	ControlFreak	Obsessively enforces rules, hindering effectiveness and dissent
14.	CynicismCatalyst	Trauma shifts idealistic character to cynicism and moral ambiguity
15.	DarkAndTroubledPast	Character's tragic past shapes their personality and behavior
16.	DeadpanSnarker	Sarcastic character who critiques and deflates others' egos
17.	Determinator	Unyielding persistence towards goals, regardless of challenges
18.	DramaQueen	Excessively dramatic characters who overreact and seek attention
19.	EvenEvilHasStandards	Villain shows moral boundaries despite overall remorselessness
20.	EveryoneHasStandards	Characters uphold personal standards despite their own flaws
21.	EvilWearsBlack	Villains wear black, symbolizing darkness and aggression
22.	FauxAffablyEvil	Polite villains hiding true cruelty for manipulation and enjoyment
23.	Gaslighting	Manipulating perception to induce doubt and confusion
24.	GentleGiant	Big, kind character defying intimidating appearance; gentle and reliable
25.	GoingNative	Character embraces new culture, rejects original society
26.	GrinOfRage	Smiling while angry, used for intimidation or provocation
27.	GuileHero	Cunning hero uses wit and charm for noble goals
28.	HairTriggerTemper	Explosive anger at minor irritations; unpredictable and dangerous
29.	HeroAntagonist	Good antagonist opposing protagonist for noble reasons
30.	HiddenDepths	Characters unveil unexpected talents, deepening their complexity
31.	Hypocrite	Authority figures failing to uphold their own ideals
32.	ItsAllAboutMe	Self-centered character believes world revolves around them
33.	Jerkass	Self-centered character creating conflict for comedic/dramatic effect
34.	JerkassHasAPoint	Morally flawed character speaks uncomfortable but true points
35.	KarmaHoudiniWarranty	Villain faces late justice, satisfying audience's desire for retribution
36.	KickTheDog	Character's cruel act establishes evil, shifts audience sympathy
37.	LackOfEmpathy	Characters recognize emotions but lack emotional connection
38.	LargeHam	Flamboyant, over-the-top character adding drama and charisma
39.	LaserGuidedKarma	Immediate consequences for characters' actions reinforce moral lessons
40.	LivingMacGuffin	Person drives quests due to intrinsic value or attributes
41.	LoveAtFirstSight	Instant deep love between characters upon first meeting
42.	LoveInterest	Romantic character involved with another, often archetypal roles
43.	ManlyTears	Stoic male character cries from strong, dignified emotions
44.	MeaningfulName	Character names reflect traits or roles meaningfully
45.	MoralityPet	Villain's bond with innocent character prompts redemption
46.	MorphicResonance	Characters retain recognizable traits across different forms
47.	MyGodWhatHaveIDone	Character regrets harmful actions, prompting remorse and conflict
48.	Narcissist	Character obsessed with self-admiration and validation, often hostile
49.	NeverBareheaded	Character always wears headgear, never seen bare-headed
50.	NiceGirl	Kind, friendly character contrasting cynical figures; endearing presence

Table 6: Tropes and their definitions (first part)

	Trope	Definition
51.	NiceGuy	Kind, morally good character contrasting with cynicism
52.	NiceJobBreakingItHero	Hero's victory causes unintended negative consequences
53.	NoCelebritiesWereHarmed	Parody characters resembling real celebrities, often with altered names
54.	NoSocialSkills	Characters lacking social awareness, often blunt but intelligent
55.	OhCrap	Character realizes impending disaster, leading to panic or horror
56.	OnlyOneName	Characters known by only one name, no identifiers
57.	OnlySaneWoman	Rational character amidst chaotic, irrational peers; often frustrated
58.	PayEvilUntoEvil	Revenge-driven morality blurs hero-villain boundaries
59.	PosthumousCharacter	Dead character influences plot through memories or narratives
60.	ReasonableAuthorityFigure	Open-minded leader who evaluates heroes' claims rationally
61.	RebelliousSpirit	Character defies norms, follows personal rules, often anti-heroic
62.	ShadowArchetype	Character reflecting protagonist's denied flaws, causing conflict and growth
63.	SirSwearsALot	Character known for excessive swearing, revealing deeper traits
64.	StepfordSmiler	Cheerful facade hides inner turmoil and psychological issues
65.	TheChessmaster	Cunning strategist who manipulates events for personal gain
66.	TheDon	Ruthless crime patriarch with moral codes, protective yet shrewd
67.	TheHeart	Caretaker and moral compass of the team
68.	TheImmune	Character immune to disease, pivotal for finding cure
69.	TheJerkIndex	Characters exhibiting rudeness contrasting with polite behavior
70.	TheSociopath	Character lacking empathy, manipulative, and morally ambiguous
71.	TopHeavyGuy	Exaggerated large upper body, skinny legs
72.	TragicVillain	Sympathetic villain regrets their actions, seeks redemption
73.	UncertainDoom	Ambiguous fate of a character, survival uncertain
74.	UndignifiedDeath	Ridiculous, embarrassing deaths blending humor and tragedy
75.	UnwittingInstigatorOfDoom	Unintentional catalyst for disaster, unaware of their role

Table 7: Tropes and their definitions (second part)

Tracking Evolving Relationship Between Characters in Books in the Era of Large Language Models

Abhilasha Sancheti **Rachel Rudinger**
University of Maryland, College Park
{sancheti, rudinger}@umd.edu

Abstract

This work aims to assess the zero-shot social reasoning capabilities of LLMs by proposing various strategies based on the granularity of information used to track the fine-grained evolution in the relationship between characters in a book. Without gold annotations, we thoroughly analyze the agreements between predictions from multiple LLMs and manually examine their consensus at a local and global level via the task of trope prediction. Our findings reveal low-to-moderate agreement among LLMs and humans, reflecting the complexity of the task. Analysis shows that LLMs are sensitive to subtle contextual changes and often rely on surface-level cues. Humans, too, may interpret relationships differently, leading to disagreements in annotations.

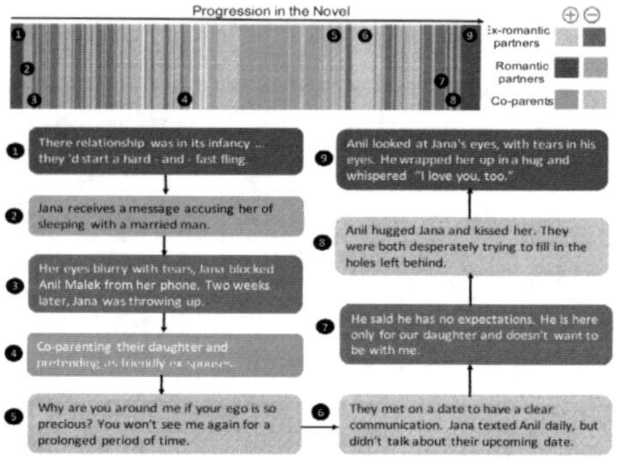

Figure 1: Sample trajectory of evolution in relationship between *Jana* and *Anil* in the book *Jana goes Wild*. Jana and Anil start as romantic partners followed by a tumultuous break-up but years later, co-parenting responsibilities of their daughter force them to confront lingering feelings, reevaluate their past, and rediscover love through shared growth and proximity. ⊕ (⊖) denote a positive (negative) evolution in the relationship.

1 Introduction

Plots and characters are the two key components of a narrative (among others) that contribute to a good piece of fiction (Kennedy and Gioia, 1983; McKee, 1997; Card, 1999). Character comprehension is key to understanding narratives in literary, and psychological research (Bower and Morrow, 1990; Paris and Paris, 2003; Currie, 2009; Kennedy et al., 2013). Particularly, characters and their relationships are one of the basic building blocks of narratives that make them engaging and interesting. Such relationships develop chapter-by-chapter in response to various events as the story progresses. For instance, Figure 1 depicts how Jana and Anil's relationship in *Jana Goes Wild* by Farah Heron, evolves from intense love to a painful breakup, followed by a separation and re-evaluation of their relationship to fall in love again.

Humans build mental models for characters and keep updating them as they read a narrative to explain such developing relationships, character's identity, their emotional status (Gernsbacher et al., 1998), and future behaviors (Fiske et al., 1979; Mead, 1990). However, a lot of manual hours are spent to obtain such insights. Having an automated system that can predict such insights has many practical applications that include book recommendation systems based on similar or diverse relation-archetype narratives, question-answering systems that can aid readers in recalling the relation-archetypes until a point in the book, and systems to predict character's personality or next action based on nature of the relationship.

While there exist works that predict static relationships from movie dialogues (Jia et al., 2021), TV series (Tigunova et al., 2021; Jurgens et al., 2023), or book summaries (Srivastava et al., 2016) and dynamic relationships from book summaries (Chaturvedi et al., 2016, 2017) or a sequence of passages from books (Iyyer et al., 2016), efforts are limited due to the modeling capacity, and unavailability of annotated datasets. With the advent of LLMs, known for their zero/few-shot reasoning capabilities (Brown et al., 2020; Touvron

Proceedings of the The 7th Workshop on Narrative Understanding, pages 64–82
May 4, 2025

et al., 2023; Jiang et al., 2023) and increased context window size (Team et al., 2023; Dubey et al., 2024), in this work, we ask how can we: (1) characterize evolution in the relationship between characters in book-length text? (2) use LLM's zero-shot reasoning capabilities (without gold labels) to track evolution in the relationship between characters?

We first characterize evolution in the relationship in terms of predefined relationship types and different ways (such as positive, negative, or stable) in which a relationship can evolve (§2). Then, we formally define the task of tracking evolution in the relationship (see Figure 1) between two characters (§3), and propose several strategies based on the granularity of information provided to LLMs to perform the task (§4). To address the issue of the unavailability of gold labels, we evaluate the predictions from the proposed strategies by analyzing the agreement between predictions from different families of LLMs (§7). Low-to-moderate agreement ($\alpha = 0.1 - 0.6$) between predictions from multiple LLMs suggests that the task is difficult even for LLMs with increased context window. To provide an upper bound on the performance achievable from the proposed strategies for this task, we manually examine the consensus predictions at both local and global-level (§8). Low-to-moderate agreement between humans reinforces the difficulty of the task. Finally, we present a quantitative (§9.1) and qualitative analysis (§9.2) of the predictions from LLMs and disagreement between humans to shed light on the challenging nature of this task.

2 Characterizing Evolution in Interpersonal Relationships

Prior works that model the evolution in the relationship between characters use an ontology of relationships that is either coarse-grained (cooperative vs non-cooperative) (Srivastava et al., 2016; Chaturvedi et al., 2016) or unsupervised (Chaturvedi et al., 2017; Iyyer et al., 2016) (such as topics from a topic model). However, relationships can be of various types such as familial (*e.g.*, parent and siblings), social (*e.g.*, friends and acquaintance), romantic (*e.g.*, married and engaged), and professional (*e.g.*, boss and colleague) (Rashid and Blanco, 2018; Tigunova et al., 2021; Jurgens et al., 2023). Following Jurgens et al. (2023), we use a subset of relationship types (see Table 1), that are observed in the most frequently used *tropes*[1] (*e.g.*, enemies-to-lovers, and friends-to-lovers) in romance novels where relationships evolve with time (Lissauer, 2014). Furthermore, relationships are defined by multiple interrelated *interactions* (Blumstein and Kollock, 1988), and the fine-grained characteristics of interactions are not necessarily the same as those of a relationship (*e.g.*, two friends can have a heated argument during an interaction but that does not affect the long-term friendship). Such fine-grained characteristics of interactions and relationships are called *dimensions* in social science (Wish et al., 1976; Deri et al., 2018; Qamar et al., 2021). Inspired by this, we define the interactions between characters using a set of dimensions (such as similarity, trust, romance, social support, identity, respect, knowledge exchange, power, fun, and conflict) proposed by Deri et al. (2018). We believe that change in the intensity of such dimensions determines the *fine-grained* evolution in relationships which can of three types: **positive**, **negative**, and **stable**. A positive evolution signifies deepening connection, increasing trust, support or respect, spending more time together, and sharing similar goals. Any tension in a relationship due to conflicts, arguments, distrust, disrespect, lack of support, or misunderstandings denotes negative evolution. A stable relationship neither evolves positively nor negatively.

Category	Relationship Types
Romantic	Engaged, Married, Romantic interest, Dating, One-sided romantic interest, Separated, Ex-romantic interest, Ex-engaged
Social	Stranger, Acquaintance, Friend, Best friend
Anti-Social	Competitor or Enemy

Table 1: The **ontology of relationships** used following prior work (Jurgens et al., 2023).

3 Task of Tracking Evolution in Relationship

We consider tracking evolution in the relationship between characters as a classification task formally defined as follows. Consider a book $B = \{P_1, P_2, \ldots P_n\}$ consisting of n chronologically ordered[2] (in book's passages) non-overlapping passages of a fixed length, c_1 and

[1]Trope refers to a recurring plot device, character archetype, or theme that is commonly used in books.

[2]Please note that we assume a temporally linear plot structure, and leave the modeling of nonlinear timelines (or other complex structures, like worlds within worlds, etc.) for future work (Pustejovsky et al., 2003; Vashishtha et al., 2019).

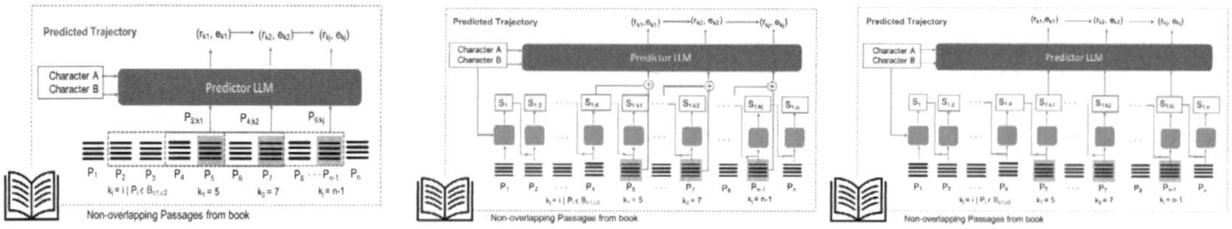

(a) Complete Passages (b) Summary with Passage (c) Complete Summary

Figure 2: Proposed strategies varying in the granularity of passages provided to an LLM for predicting the evolution in the relationship between given characters. ■: Passage where both characters are mentioned ■: Summarizer LLM.

c_2 as the two characters, and $B_{c_1,c_2} = \{P_i \in B \mid \text{both } c_1 \text{ and } c_2 \text{ are mentioned in } P_i\}$. Note that B_{c_1,c_2} is a non-contiguous sub-sequence of $P_1, \ldots P_n$. The task is to predict a tuple (r_i, e_i) where $r_i \in R$ and $e_i \in E$, respectively, denote the type of relationship and evolution (from a predefined set as described in §2) between the two characters by the end of the passage $P_i \in B_{c_1,c_2}$ given the passages $P_{1:i}$. We define evolution in the relationship between c_1 and c_2 in a book B as a trajectory $T_{c_1,c_2} = \{(r_1, e_1), (r_2, e_2), \ldots, (r_j, e_j)\}$ of relationship[3] and evolution types at each passage P_{k_j} where $k_j = \{i \mid P_i \in B_{c_1,c_2}\}$.

4 Proposed Strategies for Tracking Evolution in Relationship

Automatic tracking of fine-grained evolution in the relationship between characters in a book-length context poses two main challenges: (1) handling long context, and (2) lack of annotated datasets. To address these challenges, we aim to assess the zero-shot social reasoning capabilities of recent large language models (Jiang et al., 2023; Team et al., 2024; Dubey et al., 2024) with increased context window size by proposing various strategies (Figure 2) based on the granularity of information (*i.e.*, passages $P_{1:i}$) provided to an LLM to predict a relationship and evolution type by the end of $P_i \in B_{c_1,c_2}$ (as defined in §3).

Complete Passages. This strategy uses the large context window of LLMs to provide passages until $P_i \in B_{c_1,c_2}$ (that can fit in the window) as-is in its highest granularity to predict the status of relationship and evolution type until P_i.

Summary with Passage. As books can be arbitrarily long, $P_{1:i} \in B_{c_1,c_2}$ may not always fit in the context window of LLMs. Further, a reader may know the relationship either because the text in passage P_i reveals information about it directly; or because they recall it from prior passages, and no new information is introduced to change or contradict it; or relevant information is introduced in the passage P_i that is best understood in the context of information presented in prior passages. Thus, we hypothesize that providing a "memory" of prior passages is sufficient for relationship type prediction. However, evolution type changes are defined for each interaction between the two characters making it a more granular and local characteristic of relationships. Hence, instead of providing $P_{1:i}$ as-is, this strategy uses a summary of the type and nature of evolution in the relationship between two characters for passages $P_{1:i-1}$[4] (see §4.1) along with the passage P_i to predict the status of the relationship and evolution type by the end of P_i.

Complete Summary. To study if this task can be performed solely with a summary, in this strategy, we provide the complete context until passage P_i as a summary of the type and nature of evolution in the relationship between the two characters.

4.1 Iterative Summary Generation

To obtain the required summary in the above strategies, following Chang et al. (2023b) and Stiennon et al. (2020), we prompt an LLM (in a zero-shot setting) to iteratively generate a summary and update it with every new passage. Formally, $\mathcal{S}(P_{1:i}) = \mathcal{S}(\mathcal{S}(P_{1:i-1}), P_i)$ where, $\mathcal{S}$ is the summarizer LLM, $\mathcal{S}(P_{1:i-1})$ is the previous summary until passage P_{i-1} and $\mathcal{S}(P_{1:i})$ denotes the updated summary until passage P_i. As summaries may exceed a word limit, following Chang et al. (2023b), we repeatedly prompt LLM to compress (Prompt A.3) the summary until it is within the

[3]We consider the presence of one relationship type at one point in this work however, we acknowledge that multiple relationship types may relate two characters at the same time.

[4]Note that P_{i-1} denote the previous passage as per the chronology in B and not B_{c_1,c_2}.

word limit. Generating a summary iteratively allows for the use of LLMs with smaller context windows, making the process faster, less expensive, and more efficient in terms of inference time and number of generated tokens. We provide details on the prompts in §A.2 in appendix.

4.2 Relationship and Evolution Prediction

Given the input for each of the described strategies, we iteratively prompt an LLM to first determine the relationship type and then the evolution type for the chosen relationship in a zero-shot setting. In addition to the predefined set of relationship and evolution types in §2, we also allow LLMs to predict *cannot be determined* for both the tasks and *others* for the relationship type to cover instances when a relationship type may be determined but is not provided in the predefined set. We provide the prompts used for each strategy (§A.2) and other implementation details (§A.1) in appendix.

5 Experimental Setup

We provide details on the source of dataset, preprocessing steps, predictor and summarizer LLMs.

5.1 Dataset Source

While many books are available on resources like Project Gutenberg[5] (Stroube, 2003), LLMs have memorized them along with their summaries available on online sources as study guides[6] (Chang et al., 2023a). Using these books might result in data contamination therefore, we use 11 books (published in 2023) collected by Chang et al. (2023b) that are less likely to be memorized by LLMs used in this work. We select books from the romance genre as they frequently use tropes (*e.g.*, **enemies-to-lovers, friends-to-lovers, second chance, and forbidden love**) with evolving relationships between the main characters to make the story interesting. We manually refer to online reading forums such as Goodreads[7] to obtain the specific trope depicted in the selected books and their main characters. We use this information for global-level evaluation of the predicted trajectory for a book (§8). We perform experiments for a pair of main characters per book however, the proposed strategies are agnostic to the pair of characters and can be used for any two characters in theory.

[5] https://www.gutenberg.org/
[6] https://www.sparknotes.com/lit/
[7] https://www.goodreads.com/

5.2 Preprocessing Books

We preprocess books using BookNLP (Bamman et al., 2014) library[8] to get coreferences for characters in a book. We first divide the book text into non-overlapping passages of human-readable length ($100-200$ words). Then, replace the first occurrence of any third-person pronouns used as subject with a representative alias for a character. The most frequently used proper noun for a character is considered the representative alias for that character. We do such a replacement to ensure the comprehensibility of a standalone passage. We refer to the above process as **coreference substitution**. We obtain 644 ± 104 passages per book, of which 98 ± 128 passages have both main characters mentioned in them. Huge variation is due to differing author writing styles. We do not perform any coreference substitution for the complete passages strategy since prior passages are provided as-is and as per centering theory coreferences are used to maintain local coherence (Grosz et al., 1995).

5.3 Summarizer and Predictor Models

We use open-sourced LLMs from three families, namely, Llama3.1-8B-chat (Dubey et al., 2024), Mistral-7B-Instruct (Jiang et al., 2023), and Gemma2-9B (Team et al., 2024), to obtain the iterative summaries and predict relationship and evolution type for the *Summary with Passage* and *Complete Summary* strategies. However, for the *Complete Passages* strategy, we use Llama3.1-8B-chat with a maximum of $30K$ context window size.

6 Evaluation Without Gold Labels

One of the major challenges of tracking evolution in the relationship between characters is the unavailability of gold labels and the difficulty in collecting crowd-sourced annotations due to the length of the books; making it extremely expensive, and cognitively challenging. We make a novel contribution by providing insights into the feasibility of this task without gold labels by analyzing the agreement between predictions from multiple LLMs. Additionally, we conduct a quantitative (§9.1) and qualitative (§9.2) manual analysis of the predictions.

Owing to the increasing use of LLM-as-evaluators (Chan et al.; Gu et al., 2024) and LLM-as-annotators (Chiang and Lee, 2023; Tan et al., 2024), we hypothesize that if multiple LLMs agree on a label then it is more likely to be the gold

[8] https://github.com/booknlp/booknlp

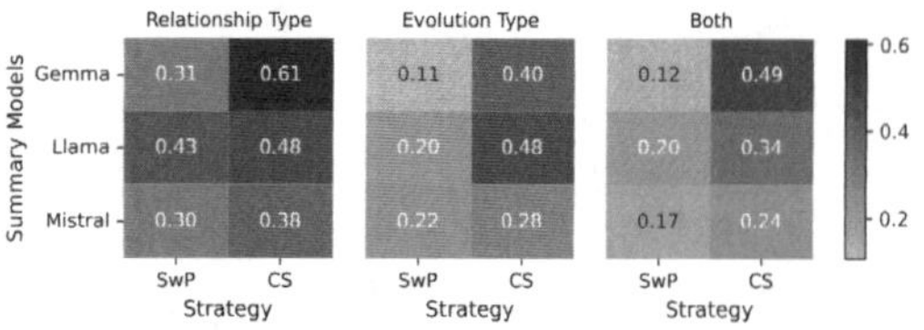

Figure 3: Krippendorff's alpha between different predictions for *Summary with Passage* (SwP) and *Complete Summary* (CS) strategies using summaries generated from various summary models.

label (Liang et al., 2024; Chern et al., 2024). Therefore, we thoroughly analyze the quality of the consensus predictions from multiple LLMs (conditioned on the input) via Krippendorff's alpha (α), and compare it against the agreement between human annotators. We also use α scores to compare agreement between different strategies (Table 3 and Figure 4), and preprocessing methods (Figure 5 and Figure 6). We manually examine the consensus predictions at a global- and local-level to provide an upper bound on the performance of LLMs for this task. **Global-level evaluation** measures the accuracy of correctly predicting the trope given the predicted trajectory of evolution in the relationship between two characters for a book. For **local-level evaluation**, a subset of examples per book per trope is manually annotated and compared against the consensus predictions. We report scores separately for **relationship** and **evolution type** as well as when **both** are considered together.

7 Findings

Agreement between prediction models. We report the agreement (α scores) between predictions from different LLMs for *Summary with Passage* and *Complete Summary* strategies that use summaries generated from various summary models in Figure 3. While this analysis depends on the correctness of the summaries generated from LLMs, we do not explicitly evaluate their correctness as LLM-generated summaries have been shown to be on par with human-written summaries (Goyal et al., 2022; Zhang et al., 2024). Low-to-moderate agreement suggests that tracking evolution in the relationship is a challenging task. Lower agreement for evolution type than relationship type emphasizes the difficulty of predicting fine-grained evolution. We observe higher agreement between predictions for *Complete Summary* than *Summary with Passage* as summaries contain more direct evidence of the type and nature of the relationship whereas in the presence of a more granular passage, the evidence needs to be inferred. Interestingly, agreement between predictions across all the summary models is higher for *Summary with Passage* than the *Complete Summary* strategy (see Table 2). This indicates that using a passage acts as a regularizer for mitigating the effect of differences in summaries generated from different summarizers.

Strategy	Relationship Type	Evolution Type	Both
Summary with Passage	0.24	0.20	0.13
Complete Summary	0.22	0.08	0.11

Table 2: Agreement between predictions across summary and prediction models.

Strategy	Relationship Type	Evolution Type	Both
Summary with Passage	0.50	0.44	0.38
Complete Summary	0.47	0.12	0.17

Table 3: Agreement between predictions from *Complete Passages* and consensus predictions for *Summary with Passage* and *Complete Summary* strategies.

Strategy	Relationship Type (α)	Evolution Type (α)	Both (α)
Summary with Passage	86.04 (0.70)	44.18 (0.26)	39.54 (0.31)
Complete Summary	88.37 (0.79)	70.93 (0.58)	67.44 (0.61)

Table 4: **Local-level evaluation:** Accuracy of consensus predictions averaged across annotations from humans. Scores in the parenthesis denote the agreement (α) between human annotators.

***Summary with Passage* is a better approximation of *Complete Passages* than the *Complete Summary* strategy.** To analyze which strategy – *Summary with Passage* or *Complete Summary* – using a short context window best approximates *Complete Passages* that uses a long context window, we report agreement between the predictions from *Complete Passages* strategy and the consensus predictions across all the summarizers and predictors for the two shorter-window strategies in Table 3. Combining a passage with a prior summary strikes a good balance in providing the information necessary for the task, compared to using the complete summary. This supports the regularization aspect of using a passage, as seen in Table 2.

8 Manual Evaluation

How accurate are the consensus predictions from LLMs? To study the upper bound performance achievable from the proposed strategies, two annotators label the relationship and evolution type

Strategy	Summarizer	Accuracy (%)
Majority Trope	N/A	54.54
Complete Passages	N/A	63.64
Summary with Passage	Llama	27.27
	Mistral	18.18
	Gemma	18.18
	Overall	21.21
Complete Summary	Llama	9.09
	Mistral	9.09
	Gemma	0.00
	Overall	6.06

Table 5: **Global-level evaluation**: Percentage accuracy for predicting the trope of a book (by human annotators) from the predicted trajectory from various strategies.

conditioned on the input for different strategies. For local-level evaluation, we first select one book per trope (4 books in total) that attains the highest prediction agreement over all the predictors and summarizers across different strategies. Then, we sample a maximum of 20 passages (where both the characters are mentioned) per selected book and consensus predictions from the summarizer with the highest agreement[9] for each strategy. Passages are selected at random such that the consensus predictions from different strategies are different as it has a two-fold benefit: (1) the accuracy of prediction for the sampled passages acts as a good approximation of overall accuracy as the two strategies will have the same accuracy for the same predictions, and (2) it makes it easier to qualitatively compare the two strategies (as shown in Table 7). We report the accuracy of prediction averaged over the two annotators and α (in parenthesis) between them in Table 4. We observe that agreement entails accuracy for both strategies. A similar agreement between humans, as observed for LLMs (see Figure 3), indicates that while relationship type can be determined with high agreement, evolution type prediction is challenging for humans as well.

How accurately can trope be identified from the LLM predicted trajectory? For global-level evaluation, we present a visualization (similar to Figure 1) of the trajectory of evolution in the relationship between two characters to annotators[10] and ask them to select the best applicable trope out of enemies-to-lovers, friends-to-lovers, second-chance, and forbidden love[11]. We keep the book and characters' names anonymous to the annotators to ensure no use of online resources. We provide visuals obtained from the predictor having the highest agreement with the consensus predictions for each strategy and summarizer[12]. As mentioned in §5.1, we have gold trope labels for each book to compute the accuracy of trope prediction.

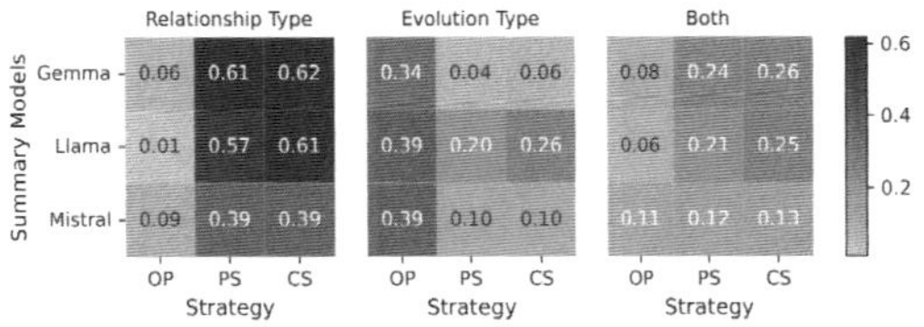

Figure 4: Krippendorff's alpha between consensus predictions from *Summary with Passage* and *Only Passage* (OP) or *Previous Summary* (PS) ablations. Agreement with *Complete Summary* (CS) is shown to emphasize its difference as opposed to *Previous Summary*.

Table 5 shows that trope can be predicted with the highest accuracy when all the passages are provided to an LLM with a large context window (*i.e. Complete Passages*). Higher accuracy for summaries from Llama indicates that it has a better understanding of social relationships than Gemma or Mistral. While we see a higher local-level accuracy for *Complete Summary* than *Summary with Passage* strategy (Table 4), we observe a reverse trend for trope prediction. This shows that an overall summary is unable to capture the fine-grained details; aligning with our previous finding that *Summary with Passage* is a better approximation of *Complete Passages* than *Complete Summary* (see Table 2). Lower accuracy than a majority baseline emphasizes the difficulty of this task when information is not provided at the highest granularity.

9 Analysis and Discussion

We present an ablation study of *Summary with Passage* strategy, need for coreference substitutions, and intermediate passages in §9.1 and shed light on the challenges with this task in §9.2.

9.1 Quantitative Analysis

Evolution type is determined (mostly) based on the passage whereas relationship type is (majorly) influenced by the previous summary. To

[9]Summaries from Llama resulted in higher agreement between predictions as compared to that from Gemma or Mistral.

[10]Manual examination is done internally by people who frequently read novels.

[11]We also provide "cannot be determined" and "others" as options.

[12]11 visualizations per strategy per summarizer.

Strategy	Relationship Type	Evolution Type	Both
Only Passage	59.43 (0.34)	49.05 (0.33)	39.62 (0.23)
Previous Summary	82.95 (0.59)	53.41 (0.40)	45.45 (0.32)
Summary with Passage	72.64 (0.72)	41.51 (0.24)	33.02 (0.38)

Table 6: Accuracy (%) of consensus predictions averaged across annotations from human annotators. Scores in the parenthesis denote the agreement (α) between human annotators.

analyze the source of information used to predict the evolution and relationship types in the *Summary with Passage* strategy, we perform an ablation study by using only the passage or the previous summary and compare the consensus predictions with that from using both the passage and the previous summary. Higher agreement (Figure 4) between the *Previous Summary* and *Summary with Passage* strategy than *Only Passage* for relationship type shows that LLMs rely on information in the summary for relationship type prediction. However, the evolution type predictions are determined based on the provided passage. As expected, agreement between predictions from the complete summary is higher than that from the previous summary since it contains more information. Additionally, we ask two annotators to label a subset of examples selected in the same way as in §8 for local-level evaluation and report the results in Table 6. Low agreement between annotators (in parenthesis) except for relationship predictions from *Summary with Passage* strategy shows that this task is difficult even for humans. This is due to the involved subjectivity leading to different annotations (see Table 8 for examples). Accuracy for relationship predictions for *Only Passage* is much lower than that for *Summary with Passage* due to the possibility of multiple interpretations when a passage is provided out-of-context. However, evolution prediction is less accurate when a previous summary is provided with a passage. This may happen when relationships are in a transition phase, or characters may have different emotional states toward each other. Since a summary captures all this information, it may be difficult to infer an evolution type with certainty. We discuss such examples in §9.2.

Intermediate context is a useful source of information. Prior studies (Chaturvedi et al., 2016; Iyyer et al., 2016; Chaturvedi et al., 2017) that model evolution in relationships have focused solely on passages where both characters are mentioned. In contrast, we hypothesize that interactions between other characters or one of the main characters with others is a useful source of information for this task. To test this, we employ the same strategies as described in §4 but only use the passages where both the characters are mentioned and compare the obtained agreements with those when passages without both character mentions are not filtered. Figure 5 indeed shows that intermediate context results in higher agreement for relationship predictions when passages are not filtered than when filtered. However, we do not observe significant improvement for evolution prediction.

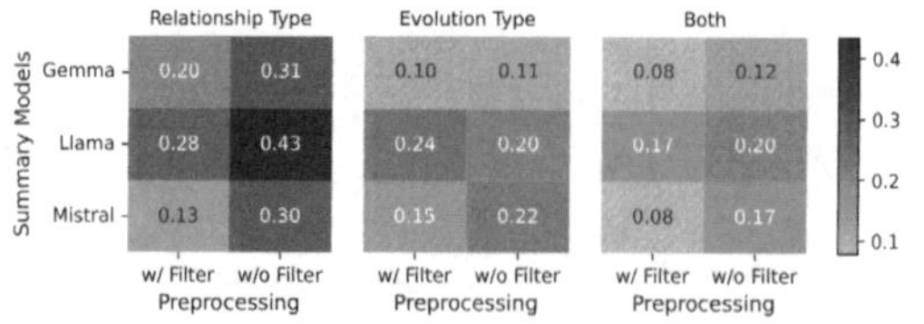

(a) Summary with Passage

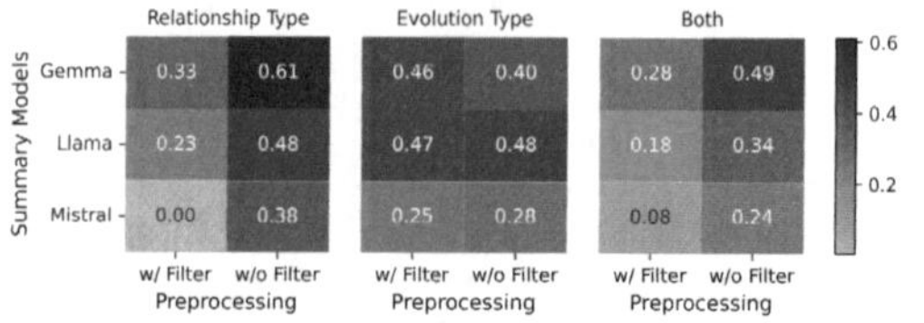

(b) Complete Summary

Figure 5: Krippendorff's alpha between consensus predictions from *Summary with Passage* and *Complete Summary* which use summaries generated from passages with (w/ Filter) and without filtering (w/o Filter) the passages that do not mention both the characters.

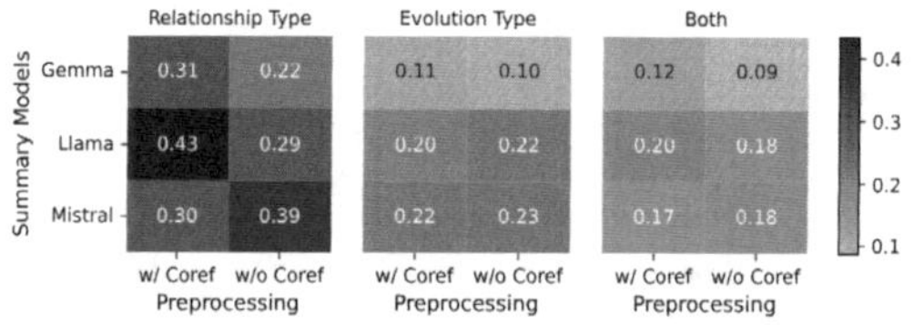

(a) Summary with Passage

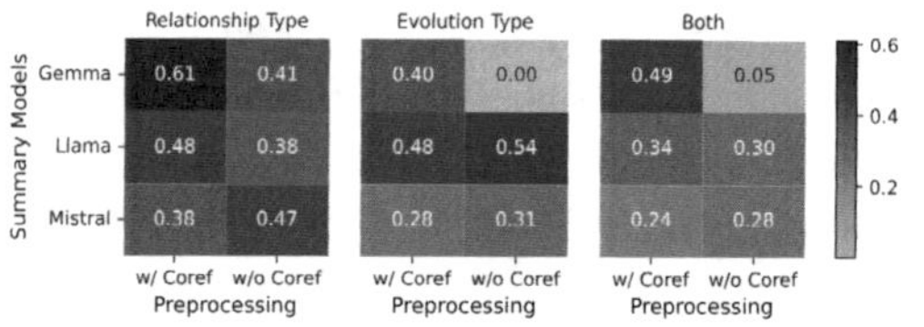

(b) Complete Summary

Figure 6: Krippendorff's alpha between consensus predictions from *Summary with Passage* and *Complete Summary* with (w/ Coref) and without substituting the character coreferences (w/o Coref) in the passages.

Coreference resolution results in (mostly) higher or comparable agreement between predictions than without it. We apply the *Summary with Passage* and *Complete Summary* strategy on passages from a book without coreference substitutions (described in §5.2) to analyze its impact on the agreement between predictions as shown in Figure 6. While we mostly see a higher agreement between predictions when coreference substitution is done during data preprocessing (w/ Coref) than in its absence (w/o Coref), we also see instances of lower or comparable agreement. Manual analysis reveals that in the absence of a specific character mention, LLMs tend to assume that the pronouns refer to the characters understudy both during summary generation, and relationship and evolution prediction. This is a result of the widely acknowledged issue of hallucination (Ye et al., 2023; Huang et al., 2023) and context sensitivity (Min et al., 2022) in LLMs.

9.2 Qualitative Analysis

Maintaining a running summary helps resolve the ambiguity between different relationship types. Manual analysis reveals that providing a previous summary helps propagate the prior knowledge about the relationship that can make predictions more certain, and resolve any ambiguity due to insufficient information or out-of-context passages (see Table 7 in appendix for examples).

Uncertainty in relationship or evolution type prediction results in disagreements between humans. We find that humans might have different interpretations when a relationship is in a "transition/developing" phase, the two characters have different emotional states towards each other, or a phrase with multiple interpretations is mentioned in the text, leading to different annotations (see Table 8 in appendix for examples).

Failure cases. Analysis in Table 9 (in appendix) shows that LLMs rely on surface-level cues, tend to resolve pronouns to the character in question in the absence of an explicit mention, and are sensitive to subtle changes in the context (such as substituting pronouns for other characters in the context). Such behavior raises questions on the *true* understanding of evolving social relationships in LLMs and if they are right for the wrong reasons.

10 Related Work

Existing works that examine relationships between characters in narratives either use a fixed set of coarse-grained relations, such as cooperative or non-cooperative (Srivastava et al., 2016; Chaturvedi et al., 2016) and familial or professional (Makazhanov et al., 2014; Massey et al., 2015; Azab et al., 2019) or learn a set of relationship descriptors (Iyyer et al., 2016). Others classify emotional relationships between characters in fan-fiction stories (Kim and Klinger, 2019b) and harry potter novel (Zehe et al., 2020) following Kim and Klinger (2019a). Another line of research analyzes the polarity and intensity of emotions of characters towards each other (Nalisnick and Baird, 2013) in Shakespearean plays, or classifies interpersonal relationships from dialogues in TV series (Chen et al., 2020), movie scripts (Jia et al., 2021) or detective narratives (Zhao et al., 2024).

While the above works consider static relationships, Chaturvedi et al. (2016) model the evolution of interpersonal relationships in novels in a supervised setting, requiring manual annotations, and model relationships as binary polarities. Whereas Iyyer et al. (2016) introduce an unsupervised method, RMN (Relationship Modeling Network), to model evolving relationships by learning a sequence of discrete states depicting the relationship between the two characters. Qamar et al. (2021) employ psychological models to classify movie dialogues into attachment styles and association types to analyze the transformation between relationships. However, we focus on its evolution.

11 Conclusion

This work tracks the evolution in the relationship between characters in books by proposing several strategies that differ in the granularity of information provided to the LLMs to assess their understanding of social relationships. Without gold annotations, our analysis of agreement between predictions from multiple LLMs shows that providing a running summary of the type and nature of evolution in the relationship between the characters along with a passage is a better approximation of a strategy that uses all the passages until a point than providing a complete summary. Overall, low-to-moderate agreement between LLMs as well as between humans shows the difficulty of the task. While human disagreement can be attributed to their differing interpretations of the context, qualitative analysis reveals that LLMs adopt surface-level cues, and are sensitive to subtle changes in the provided context raising questions on their *true* understanding of social relationships.

Limitations

We acknowledge the below limitations of this work.

Linear plot structure assumption We assume linear plot structure of the books in this work to assess how LLMs perform in a straightforward setting. However, plot structure can be nonlinear and complex such as worlds within worlds wherein the narrative timelines and chronological timelines could be different. We leave tracking evolution in relationships in such books for future research.

Coverage of relationship and asymmetric evolution We use a subset of relationship types that commonly occur in books from the romance genre between main characters. However, we acknowledge that the set of relationships is not exhaustive and may need to be updated based on the genre of books used and the type of relationships that occur in such books. As shown in the qualitative examples, evolution in relationship may be different from each character's perspective. We leave study of such asymmetric evolution in relationships for future work.

Potential errors in conference substitutions Coreference resolution at book-length is still an open problem in NLP (Toshniwal et al., 2020; Xia and Van Durme, 2022; Guo et al., 2023). While we use widely known BookNLP (Bamman et al., 2014) toolkit, we believe that incorrect coreferences could result in misinterpretation of the text and lead to prediction errors. Future work may further investigate the impact of incorrect coreference substitutions on the task of tracking evolution in relationships.

Input conditional evaluation of strategies As gold annotations are not available for this task due to the length of the books and the cognitively challenging nature of the task, our agreement analysis as well as local-level manual evaluation of predictions is conditioned on the input of the specific strategy used. However, we believe that the global-level evaluation via trope prediction provides a good upper bound on the performance achievable from different strategies for this task. An ideal scenario would be when the predictions from different strategies are compared to gold annotations available at different points in the book.

Potential errors in the LLM generated summaries While LLM-generated summaries are on par with human-written summaries (Goyal et al., 2022; Zhang et al., 2024), we acknowledge that summaries may be prone to incoherence and factual inconsistencies. This is potentially the reason behind lower performance for summaries from Gemma and Mistral models. Since the focus of this work was on tracking evolution in relationships, we leave further analysis of summaries until each passage of the book and its impact on the performance of this task for future research.

Ethical Considerations

Our study presents a systematic approach for evaluating LLMs for their social reasoning capabilities and hence does not inherently pose direct risks. However, it is important to emphasize that predictions from LLMs may be influenced by inherent biases that may get ingrained in them during the pretraining stage. Therefore, before deploying the proposed strategies in our work, the predictions should be human-evaluated and debiased to ensure safety and avoid any potential social harm. The dataset used in this work was acquired by directly contacting the authors of that paper. Due to copyright issues, the dataset is not publicly available and we make sure that the data is handled properly with no redistribution.

References

Mahmoud Azab, Noriyuki Kojima, Jia Deng, and Rada Mihalcea. 2019. Representing movie characters in dialogues. In *Proceedings of the 23rd Conference on Computational Natural Language Learning (CoNLL)*, pages 99–109, Hong Kong, China. Association for Computational Linguistics.

David Bamman, Ted Underwood, and Noah A Smith. 2014. A bayesian mixed effects model of literary character. In *Proceedings of the 52nd Annual Meeting of the Association for Computational Linguistics (Volume 1: Long Papers)*, pages 370–379.

Philip Blumstein and Peter Kollock. 1988. Personal relationships. *Annual Review of Sociology*, 14(1):467–490.

Gordon H Bower and Daniel G Morrow. 1990. Mental models in narrative comprehension. *Science*, 247(4938):44–48.

Tom Brown, Benjamin Mann, Nick Ryder, Melanie Subbiah, Jared D Kaplan, Prafulla Dhariwal, Arvind Neelakantan, Pranav Shyam, Girish Sastry, Amanda Askell, et al. 2020. Language models are few-shot learners. *Advances in neural information processing systems*, 33:1877–1901.

Orson Scott Card. 1999. Characters & viewpoint: Elements of fiction writing. *Cincinnati, OH: Writer's Digest Books*.

Chi-Min Chan, Weize Chen, Yusheng Su, Jianxuan Yu, Wei Xue, Shanghang Zhang, Jie Fu, and Zhiyuan Liu. Chateval: Towards better llm-based evaluators through multi-agent debate. In *The Twelfth International Conference on Learning Representations*.

Kent K Chang, Mackenzie Cramer, Sandeep Soni, and David Bamman. 2023a. Speak, memory: An archaeology of books known to chatgpt/gpt-4. *arXiv preprint arXiv:2305.00118*.

Yapei Chang, Kyle Lo, Tanya Goyal, and Mohit Iyyer. 2023b. Booookscore: A systematic exploration of book-length summarization in the era of llms. *arXiv preprint arXiv:2310.00785*.

Snigdha Chaturvedi, Mohit Iyyer, and Hal Daume III. 2017. Unsupervised learning of evolving relationships between literary characters. In *Proceedings of the AAAI Conference on Artificial Intelligence*, volume 31.

Snigdha Chaturvedi, Shashank Srivastava, Hal Daume III, and Chris Dyer. 2016. Modeling evolving relationships between characters in literary novels. In *Proceedings of the AAAI Conference on Artificial Intelligence*, volume 30.

Yi-Ting Chen, Hen-Hsen Huang, and Hsin-Hsi Chen. 2020. MPDD: A multi-party dialogue dataset for analysis of emotions and interpersonal relationships. In *Proceedings of the Twelfth Language Resources and Evaluation Conference*, pages 610–614, Marseille, France. European Language Resources Association.

Steffi Chern, Ethan Chern, Graham Neubig, and Pengfei Liu. 2024. Can large language models be trusted for evaluation? scalable meta-evaluation of llms as evaluators via agent debate. *arXiv preprint arXiv:2401.16788*.

Cheng-Han Chiang and Hung-Yi Lee. 2023. Can large language models be an alternative to human evaluations? In *Proceedings of the 61st Annual Meeting of the Association for Computational Linguistics (Volume 1: Long Papers)*, pages 15607–15631.

Gregory Currie. 2009. Narrative and the psychology of character. *The journal of aesthetics and art criticism*, 67(1):61–71.

Sebastian Deri, Jeremie Rappaz, Luca Maria Aiello, and Daniele Quercia. 2018. Coloring in the links: Capturing social ties as they are perceived. *Proceedings of the ACM on Human-Computer Interaction*, 2(CSCW):1–18.

Abhimanyu Dubey, Abhinav Jauhri, Abhinav Pandey, Abhishek Kadian, Ahmad Al-Dahle, Aiesha Letman, Akhil Mathur, Alan Schelten, Amy Yang, Angela Fan, et al. 2024. The llama 3 herd of models. *arXiv preprint arXiv:2407.21783*.

Susan T Fiske, Shelley E Taylor, Nancy L Etcoff, and Jessica K Laufer. 1979. Imaging, empathy, and causal attribution. *Journal of Experimental Social Psychology*, 15(4):356–377.

Morton Ann Gernsbacher, Brenda M Hallada, and Rachel RW Robertson. 1998. How automatically do readers infer fictional characters' emotional states? *Scientific studies of reading*, 2(3):271–300.

Tanya Goyal, Junyi Jessy Li, and Greg Durrett. 2022. News summarization and evaluation in the era of gpt-3. *arXiv preprint arXiv:2209.12356*.

Barbara Grosz, Aravind Joshi, and Scott Weinstein. 1995. Centering: A framework for modeling the local coherence of discourse. *Computational linguistics*.

Jiawei Gu, Xuhui Jiang, Zhichao Shi, Hexiang Tan, Xuehao Zhai, Chengjin Xu, Wei Li, Yinghan Shen, Shengjie Ma, Honghao Liu, et al. 2024. A survey on llm-as-a-judge. *arXiv preprint arXiv:2411.15594*.

Qipeng Guo, Xiangkun Hu, Yue Zhang, Xipeng Qiu, and Zheng Zhang. 2023. Dual cache for long document neural coreference resolution. In *Proceedings of the 61st Annual Meeting of the Association for Computational Linguistics (Volume 1: Long Papers)*, pages 15272–15285.

Ari Holtzman, Jan Buys, Li Du, Maxwell Forbes, and Yejin Choi. 2019. The curious case of neural text degeneration. *arXiv preprint arXiv:1904.09751*.

Lei Huang, Weijiang Yu, Weitao Ma, Weihong Zhong, Zhangyin Feng, Haotian Wang, Qianglong Chen, Weihua Peng, Xiaocheng Feng, Bing Qin, et al. 2023. A survey on hallucination in large language models: Principles, taxonomy, challenges, and open questions. *ACM Transactions on Information Systems*.

Mohit Iyyer, Anupam Guha, Snigdha Chaturvedi, Jordan Boyd-Graber, and Hal Daumé III. 2016. Feuding families and former Friends: Unsupervised learning for dynamic fictional relationships. In *Proceedings of the 2016 Conference of the North American Chapter of the Association for Computational Linguistics: Human Language Technologies*, pages 1534–1544, San Diego, California. Association for Computational Linguistics.

Qi Jia, Hongru Huang, and Kenny Q Zhu. 2021. Ddrel: A new dataset for interpersonal relation classification in dyadic dialogues. In *Proceedings of the AAAI Conference on Artificial Intelligence*, volume 35, pages 13125–13133.

Albert Q Jiang, Alexandre Sablayrolles, Arthur Mensch, Chris Bamford, Devendra Singh Chaplot, Diego de las Casas, Florian Bressand, Gianna Lengyel, Guillaume Lample, Lucile Saulnier, et al. 2023. Mistral 7b. *arXiv preprint arXiv:2310.06825*.

David Jurgens, Agrima Seth, Jackson Sargent, Athena Aghighi, and Michael Geraci. 2023. Your spouse needs professional help: Determining the contextual appropriateness of messages through modeling social relationships. In *Proceedings of the 61st Annual Meeting of the Association for Computational Linguistics (Volume 1: Long Papers)*, pages 10994–11013, Toronto, Canada. Association for Computational Linguistics.

XJ Kennedy and Dana Gioia. 1983. Literature: An introduction to fiction. *Poetry, Drama, and writing*.

XJ Kennedy, Dana Gioia, and Dan Stone. 2013. *Literature: An introduction to fiction, poetry, drama, and writing*. Pearson.

Evgeny Kim and Roman Klinger. 2019a. An analysis of emotion communication channels in fan-fiction: Towards emotional storytelling. In *Proceedings of the Second Workshop on Storytelling*, pages 56–64, Florence, Italy. Association for Computational Linguistics.

Evgeny Kim and Roman Klinger. 2019b. Frowning Frodo, wincing Leia, and a seriously great friendship: Learning to classify emotional relationships of fictional characters. In *Proceedings of the 2019 Conference of the North American Chapter of the Association for Computational Linguistics: Human Language Technologies, Volume 1 (Long and Short Papers)*, pages 647–653, Minneapolis, Minnesota. Association for Computational Linguistics.

Tian Liang, Zhiwei He, Wenxiang Jiao, Xing Wang, Yan Wang, Rui Wang, Yujiu Yang, Shuming Shi, and Zhaopeng Tu. 2024. Encouraging divergent thinking in large language models through multi-agent debate. In *Proceedings of the 2024 Conference on Empirical Methods in Natural Language Processing*, pages 17889–17904, Miami, Florida, USA. Association for Computational Linguistics.

Gabrielle Lissauer. 2014. *The Tropes of Fantasy Fiction*. McFarland.

Aibek Makazhanov, Denilson Barbosa, and Grzegorz Kondrak. 2014. Extracting family relationship networks from novels. *arXiv preprint arXiv:1405.0603*.

Philip Massey, Patrick Xia, David Bamman, and Noah A Smith. 2015. Annotating character relationships in literary texts. *arXiv preprint arXiv:1512.00728*.

Robert McKee. 1997. *Story: style, structure, substance, and the principles of screenwriting*. Harper Collins.

Gerald Mead. 1990. The representation of fictional character. *Style*, pages 440–452.

Sewon Min, Xinxi Lyu, Ari Holtzman, Mikel Artetxe, Mike Lewis, Hannaneh Hajishirzi, and Luke Zettlemoyer. 2022. Rethinking the role of demonstrations: What makes in-context learning work? In *Proceedings of the 2022 Conference on Empirical Methods in Natural Language Processing*, pages 11048–11064, Abu Dhabi, United Arab Emirates. Association for Computational Linguistics.

Eric T. Nalisnick and Henry S. Baird. 2013. Character-to-character sentiment analysis in shakespeare's plays. In *Proceedings of the 51st Annual Meeting of the Association for Computational Linguistics (Volume 2: Short Papers)*, pages 479–483, Sofia, Bulgaria. Association for Computational Linguistics.

Alison H Paris and Scott G Paris. 2003. Assessing narrative comprehension in young children. *Reading Research Quarterly*, 38(1):36–76.

James Pustejovsky, José M Castano, Robert Ingria, Roser Sauri, Robert J Gaizauskas, Andrea Setzer, Graham Katz, and Dragomir R Radev. 2003. Timeml: Robust specification of event and temporal expressions in text. *New directions in question answering*, 3:28–34.

Saira Qamar, Hasan Mujtaba, Hammad Majeed, and Mirza Omer Beg. 2021. Relationship identification between conversational agents using emotion analysis. *Cognitive Computation*, 13:673–687.

Farzana Rashid and Eduardo Blanco. 2018. Characterizing interactions and relationships between people. In *Proceedings of the 2018 Conference on Empirical Methods in Natural Language Processing*, pages 4395–4404, Brussels, Belgium. Association for Computational Linguistics.

Shashank Srivastava, Snigdha Chaturvedi, and Tom Mitchell. 2016. Inferring interpersonal relations in narrative summaries. In *Proceedings of the AAAI Conference on Artificial Intelligence*, volume 30.

Nisan Stiennon, Long Ouyang, Jeffrey Wu, Daniel Ziegler, Ryan Lowe, Chelsea Voss, Alec Radford, Dario Amodei, and Paul F Christiano. 2020. Learning to summarize with human feedback. *Advances in Neural Information Processing Systems*, 33:3008–3021.

Bryan Stroube. 2003. Literary freedom: Project gutenberg. *XRDS: Crossroads, The ACM Magazine for Students*, 10(1):3–3.

Zhen Tan, Alimohammad Beigi, Song Wang, Ruocheng Guo, Amrita Bhattacharjee, Bohan Jiang, Mansooreh Karami, Jundong Li, Lu Cheng, and Huan Liu. 2024. Large language models for data annotation: A survey. *arXiv preprint arXiv:2402.13446*.

Gemini Team, Rohan Anil, Sebastian Borgeaud, Yonghui Wu, Jean-Baptiste Alayrac, Jiahui Yu, Radu Soricut, Johan Schalkwyk, Andrew M Dai, Anja Hauth, et al. 2023. Gemini: a family of highly capable multimodal models. *arXiv preprint arXiv:2312.11805*.

Gemma Team, Thomas Mesnard, Cassidy Hardin, Robert Dadashi, Surya Bhupatiraju, Shreya Pathak, Laurent Sifre, Morgane Rivière, Mihir Sanjay Kale, Juliette Love, et al. 2024. Gemma: Open models based on gemini research and technology. *arXiv preprint arXiv:2403.08295*.

Anna Tigunova, Paramita Mirza, Andrew Yates, and Gerhard Weikum. 2021. PRIDE: Predicting Relationships in Conversations. In *Proceedings of the 2021 Conference on Empirical Methods in Natural Language Processing*, pages 4636–4650, Online and Punta Cana, Dominican Republic. Association for Computational Linguistics.

Shubham Toshniwal, Sam Wiseman, Allyson Ettinger, Karen Livescu, and Kevin Gimpel. 2020. Learning to ignore: Long document coreference with bounded memory neural networks. *arXiv preprint arXiv:2010.02807*.

Hugo Touvron, Louis Martin, Kevin Stone, Peter Albert, Amjad Almahairi, Yasmine Babaei, Nikolay Bashlykov, Soumya Batra, Prajjwal Bhargava, Shruti Bhosale, et al. 2023. Llama 2: Open foundation and fine-tuned chat models. *arXiv preprint arXiv:2307.09288*.

Siddharth Vashishtha, Benjamin Van Durme, and Aaron Steven White. 2019. Fine-grained temporal relation extraction. *arXiv preprint arXiv:1902.01390*.

Myron Wish, Morton Deutsch, and Susan J Kaplan. 1976. Perceived dimensions of interpersonal relations. *Journal of Personality and social Psychology*, 33(4):409.

Patrick Xia and Benjamin Van Durme. 2022. Online neural coreference resolution with rollback. In *Proceedings of the Fifth Workshop on Computational Models of Reference, Anaphora and Coreference*, pages 13–21.

Hongbin Ye, Tong Liu, Aijia Zhang, Wei Hua, and Weiqiang Jia. 2023. Cognitive mirage: A review of hallucinations in large language models. *arXiv preprint arXiv:2309.06794*.

Albin Zehe, Julia Arns, Lena Hettinger, and Andreas Hotho. 2020. Harrymotions-classifying relationships in harry potter based on emotion analysis. In *SwissText/KONVENS*.

Tianyi Zhang, Faisal Ladhak, Esin Durmus, Percy Liang, Kathleen McKeown, and Tatsunori B Hashimoto. 2024. Benchmarking large language models for news summarization. *Transactions of the Association for Computational Linguistics*, 12:39–57.

Runcong Zhao, Qinglin Zhu, Hainiu Xu, Jiazheng Li, Yuxiang Zhou, Yulan He, and Lin Gui. 2024. Large language models fall short: Understanding complex relationships in detective narratives. In *Findings of the Association for Computational Linguistics ACL 2024*, pages 7618–7638, Bangkok, Thailand and virtual meeting. Association for Computational Linguistics.

A Detailed Experimental Setup

A.1 Implementation Details

We generate summaries of a maximum 300 words given passages of a maximum 200 words. We use nucleus sampling (Holtzman et al., 2019) with radius of $p = 0.9$ and top $k = 50$ tokens for generating summaries and greedy decoding for the prediction tasks.

A.2 Zero-shot Prompt for Obtaining the Summaries and Predictions

We use different prompts to obtain the summary of the first passage (Prompt A.1) and to update the previous summary with a new passage (Prompt A.2). For compressing the summary within a word limit, we use Prompt A.3).

We use the Prompt A.4, Prompt A.6, and Prompt A.5 to get the relationship and evolution type predictions from an LLM for the *Complete Passages*, *Complete Summary*, and *Summary with Passage* strategies, respectively. Iteratively asking for relationship type and then evolution type helps in presenting only the required question and information to an LLM and makes it easier to parse the output.

A.3 Manual Evaluation Details

The manual evaluation was done by experienced annotators who read novels. Two of them are doctoral students and the other two have undergraduate degrees. We clearly explain the annotation task and run a small pilot followed by a discussion to ensure the task annotation is clear.

Prompt A.1: Iterative Summary Generation: First Passage

```
System Prompt: You are a helpful assistant who follows the instructions. No preambles and postambles. Avoid explanations if not asked explicitly.

Prompt: Below is the beginning part of a story from a book:

—
{story}
—

We are going over segments of a story sequentially to gradually update one comprehensive summary depicting the evolution in the relationship between {char_a} and {char_b}. Write a summary of the evolution in the relationship between {char_a} and {char_b} as the story progresses. Make sure to include vital information related to key events that shape the relationship between {char_a} and {char_b}, their objectives, and motivations. The story may feature non-linear narratives, flashbacks, switches between alternate worlds or viewpoints, etc. Therefore, you should organize the summary so it presents a consistent and chronological narrative. Despite this step-by-step process of updating the summary, you need to create a summary that seems as though it is written in one go. The summary should roughly contain 300 words.

Constraint: If the provided segment does not mention both {char_a} and {char_b}, then do not make up or predict anything regarding the relationship between the characters. Just provide a general summary of the provided segment or keep it empty.

Summary:
```

Prompt A.2: Iterative Summary Generation: Updating Previous Summary

System Prompt: You are a helpful assistant who follows the instructions. No preambles and postambles. Avoid explanations if not asked explicitly.

Prompt: Below is a segment of a story from a book:

—
{story}
—

Below is a summary of the evolution in the relationship between {char_a} and {char_b} up until this point in the story.

—
{summary}
—

We are going over segments of a story sequentially to gradually update one comprehensive summary depicting the evolution in the relationship between {char_a} and {char_b}. You are required to update the provided summary to incorporate any new vital information related to the relationship between {char_a} and {char_b} that is present in the current segment of the story. This information may relate to key events, turning points in the relationship between the characters, their objectives, and motivations. The story may feature non-linear narratives, flashbacks, switches between alternate worlds or viewpoints, etc. Therefore, you should organize the summary so it presents a consistent and chronological narrative. Despite this step-by-step process of updating the summary, you need to create a summary that seems as though it is written in one go. The updated summary should roughly contain 300 words.

Constraint: If the provided segment does not mention both {char_a} and {char_b}, then avoid making up or predicting anything regarding the relationship between the characters. Just copy the provided summary as-is or update it with the general aspects of the story or keep it empty.

Updated summary:

Prompt A.3: Compress Summary

System Prompt: You are a helpful assistant who follows the instructions. No preambles and postambles. Avoid explanations if not asked explicitly.

Prompt: Below is a summary of the relationship between {char_a} and {char_b} from a part of a story:

-
{Summary}
-

Currently, this summary contains {summary_length} words. Your task is to condense it to less than 300 words while maintaining the chronological order. The condensed summary should remain clear, overarching, and fluid while being brief. Whenever feasible, maintain details about key events that shape the relationship between {char_a} and {char_b}, how does the relationship evolve over time, character's objectives, and motivations - but express these elements more succinctly. Remove insignificant details that do not add much to the overall evolution in the relationship between {char_a} and {char_b} and phrases like "in this .. segment", "in this part ... story", etc. The story may feature non-linear narratives, flashbacks, switches between alternate worlds or viewpoints, etc. Therefore, you should organize the summary so it presents a consistent and chronological narrative.

Condensed summary (to be within 300 words):

Prompt A.4: Relationship and Evolution Type Prediction Prompt for Complete Passages

System Prompt: You are a helpful assistant who follows the instructions. No preambles and postambles. Avoid explanations if not asked explicitly.

Prompt: Based on the provided context and the following segment, answer the below questions about the type of relationship between {char_a} and {char_b} and its evolution by the end of the provided segment.

Context:
--
{previous passages}
--

Segment:
--
{segment}
--

Are {char_a} and {char_b} mentioned in the provided segment? Answer in one word <ANS> ["yes", "no", "unsure"] </ANS>.
{Model's output}

Can you infer any type of relationship between {char_a} and {char_b} from the segment? Answer in one word <ANS> ["yes", "no", "unsure"] </ANS>
{Model's output}

Choose the type of relationship between {char_a} and {char_b} from these options: acquaintances, strangers, friends, best friends, romantic interest, dating, engaged, married, separated, divorced, enemies, spouse, ex-spouse, one-sided romantic interest, ex-romantic interest, others or cannot be determined. Answer only from the provided options. Relationship type:
{Model's output}

Is the chosen relationship between {char_a} and {char_b} evolving "positively", "negatively", is "stable" or "nothing can be determined" by the end of the segment? A "positive" evolution can result from deepening connection, increasing trust, support or respect, spending more time together etc. A "negative" evolution means any tension or straining relationship that can result from conflicts, arguments, distrust, disrespect, lack of support, or misunderstandings. A "stable" relationship means there is neither positive nor negative evolution. Do not provide any explanation. Evolution type:

Prompt A.5: Relationship and Evolution Type Prediction Prompt for Summary with Passage

System Prompt: You are a helpful assistant who follows the instructions. No preambles and postambles. Avoid explanations if not asked explicitly.

Prompt: Based on the summary of the evolution in type and nature of the relationship between {char_a} and {char_b} until a point in a book and the following segment answer the below questions about the type of relationship between {char_a} and {char_b} and its evolution by the end of provided segment.

Summary:
--
{summary}
--

Segment:
--
{segment}
--

Are {char_a} and {char_b} mentioned in the provided segment? Answer in one word <ANS> ["yes", "no", "unsure"] </ANS>.
{Model's output}

Can you infer any type of relationship between {char_a} and {char_b} from the segment? Answer in one word <ANS> ["yes", "no", "unsure"] </ANS>
{Model's output}

Choose the type of relationship between {char_a} and {char_b} from these options: acquaintances, strangers, friends, best friends, romantic interest, dating, engaged, married, separated, divorced, enemies, spouse, ex-spouse, one-sided romantic interest, ex-romantic interest, others or cannot be determined. Answer only from the provided options. Relationship type:
{Model's output}

Is the chosen relationship between {char_a} and {char_b} evolving "positively", "negatively", is "stable" or "nothing can be determined" from the segment? A "positive" evolution can result from deepening connection, increasing trust, support or respect, spending more time together etc. A "negative" evolution means any tension or straining relationship that can result from conflicts, arguments, distrust, disrespect, lack of support, or misunderstandings. A "stable" relationship means there is neither positive nor negative evolution. Do not provide any explanation. Evolution type:

Prompt A.6: Relationship and Evolution Type Prediction Prompt for Complete Summary

System Prompt: You are a helpful assistant who follows the instructions. No preambles and postambles. Avoid explanations if not asked explicitly.

Prompt: Based on the given summary that depicts the evolution in the relationship between char_a and char_b until a point in a book answer the below questions about the type of relationship between {char_a} and {char_b} and its evolution at the end of the summary.

Summary:
--
{summary}
--

Are {char_a} and {char_b} mentioned in the provided summary? Answer in one word <ANS> ["yes", "no", "unsure"] </ANS>.
{Model's output}

Can you infer any type of relationship between {char_a} and {char_b} from the summary? Answer in one word <ANS> ["yes", "no", "unsure"] </ANS>
{Model's output}

Choose the type of relationship between {char_a} and {char_b} from these options: acquaintances, strangers, friends, best friends, romantic interest, dating, engaged, married, separated, divorced, enemies, spouse, ex-spouse, one-sided romantic interest, ex-romantic interest, others or cannot be determined. Answer only from the provided options. Relationship type:
{Model's output}

Is the chosen relationship between {char_a} and {char_b} evolving "positively", "negatively", is "stable" or "nothing can be determined" by the end of the summary? A "positive" evolution can result from deepening connection, increasing trust, support or respect, spending more time together etc. A "negative" evolution means any tension or straining relationship that can result from conflicts, arguments, distrust, disrespect, lack of support, or misunderstandings. A "stable" relationship means there is neither positive nor negative evolution. Do not provide any explanation. Evolution type:

B Qualitative and Quantitative Analysis

Summary: *Mina stands at a crossroads, torn between her village and the allure of the open sea, driven by her love for Shin. Her memories reveal the early stages of their romance, suggesting her love for him may be a choice rather than a predetermined fate. As Mina's devotion to Shin reaches a boiling point, she breaks the Sea God's three rules, and Joon's concern for her safety demonstrates the strong bond between them. . . . She encounters Shin, who looks at her with longing in his eyes, breaking her heart. Shin's words of encouragement, " "Don't chase fate, Mina. Let fate chase you," remind her to find her own path and destiny. Mina confesses her feelings to Shin, and he reciprocates, stating that he doesn't need the Red String of Fate to know that he loves her. They share a passionate kiss, and Shin says, "Lord Crane was mistaken. He said once the Red String of Fate was formed, you would know how to break the curse."*   **Passage:** *Namgi says. He leans back, and I get a good look at his face. There's joy there, and wonder. "We know everything, about the emperor, about the Sea God. Shin is the Sea God! Can you believe it?" " Where is he?" I ask. "In the hall. We arrived right before you." Kirin approaches from behind Namgi, his always astute eyes watching me carefully. "What were you saying, Mina? That you wouldn't see us before...?" I release Namgi, stepping back.*   **Predictions:** cannot be determined, romantic interest
Summary: *Jana's relationship with Anil began with a transformative experience, marked by a week and a half of intense physical connection. . . . As they traveled together, Jana and Anil grew closer, visiting Tajikistan . . . In London, they transitioned from traveling companions to intimate partners, engaging in a hard-and-fast fling amidst their days of attending meetings and nights in a tiny hotel room. . . . Their connection deepened, and they found themselves lost in intimate moments, discussing their work in the development field and goals of bringing grassroots-style microdevelopment to a larger scale. dots Jana's trust in Anil was shaken when she received anonymous messages accusing her of sleeping with a married man, claiming Anil was still married to the sender's sister. . . .*   **Passage:** *Jana knew she was falling in love with him. And maybe love was a little blind. She picked up her phone again, not to call Anil, but to message Rasheed, the manager of the project in Tajikistan. The one who Anil had been visiting when this relationship started. Jana: Rasheed, is Anil married? It was the middle of the night in Tajikistan. Jana wasn't expecting an answer. But he responded. Rasheed: Have you asked him that question?*   **Predictions:** one-sided romantic interest, romantic interest

Table 7: Sample relationship predictions depicting importance of using a previous summary which helps resolve uncertain predictions, and propagate prior context to avoid misinterpretation from just the passage. Color denotes the predictions and evidences from *Only passage* and *Summary with Passage* strategy.

Summary: *Jana's relationship with Anil began with a transformative experience, marked by a week and a half of intense physical connection. ... However, Jana's trust in Anil was shaken when she received anonymous messages accusing her of sleeping with a married man, claiming Anil was still married. Anil's revelation that he was indeed married marked the end of their relationship, and Jana became pregnant with his child. Years later, ... Anil moved to Toronto to be close to Imani, and as co-parents, Jana and Anil discussed their complicated family dynamics. Jana expressed concerns about becoming overprotective, while Anil demonstrated a willingness to be involved in Imani's life. Jana struggled with her past and her growing closeness to Anil, confronting him about his past behavior and accusing him of trying to stroke her ego. ... As they reconnect, Jana questions whether she is letting other people's opinions get in the way of her own happiness, particularly in regards to her relationship with Anil. Jana is starting to inch out of her comfort zone, and now considers a date with Anil, suggesting a possible rekindling of their relationship.* **Passage:** *Did you forget what happened at Hatari? Jana asked. Anil chuckled low, sending a shiver down Jana's spine. ... "I've honestly thought of little else," he said. And there it was. He'd been as preoccupied with thoughts of that night as she'd been. Jana could feel a heat burning inside her. He still wanted her.* **Discussion:** Jana and Anil are ex-romantic partners who are co-parenting their daughter and are considering to give another chance (romantic interest) to their relationship.
Summary: *Jana's relationship with Anil began with a transformative experience, marked by a week and a half of intense physical connection. ... However, Jana's trust in Anil was shaken when she received anonymous messages accusing her of sleeping with a married man, claiming Anil was still married. Anil's revelation that he was indeed married marked the end of their relationship. Jana became pregnant with his child, and they navigated a co-parenting agreement with the help of a family lawyer. Years later, Anil surprised Jana ... revealing he wanted to surprise their daughter Imani ... This gesture suggested a desire to reconnect with Jana and their daughter. ... Their recent interactions highlighted the challenges they still face, including Anil's condescending behavior and Jana's lingering discomfort. ... Jana's hesitation stems from her need for self-care, as being around Anil triggers memories and makes it difficult for her to think straight.* **Passage:** *Jana couldn't travel for two weeks alone with just him and Imani. His betrayal still hurt too much. She could finally take a trip with Imani, and this would taint it. "Come on, Jana," Anil said. "I don't want to break your mother's heart, either. She's so great for Imani."* **Discussion:** Jana and Anil are ex-romantic partners as well as co-parents. While Anil is putting in efforts to reconnect with Jana and his daughter, Jana has unresolved emotions and is hesitant resulting in a positive evolution in the relationship from Anil's side however, still negative from Jana's perspective.
Passage: *Kirin strides in, bowing low. His keen eyes glance at Shin's hand, still holding my own. "You called for me?" "Mina's been hurt." "Ah, I see." I frown at the two of them, the unspoken words thick in the air. Why had Shin asked for Kirin and not a physician? As Shin releases my hand, Kirin reaches inside his robes and pulls out a small silver dagger. ... I only have a moment to gape before he grabs my wrist, placing his now bloodied hand over my burned one.* **Dicussion:** Here, "holding hands" was interpreted as showing care as *romantic interests* by one annotator while from another's perspective it was considered as a gesture any *friend* would do if someone is injured.
Passage: *It was the cutest thing Jana had ever seen. She lifted Imani in her arms to see it better. Everyone in the Land Cruiser was in awe, giddy with excitement. As the drive continued, they saw gazelles, the most vibrant striped zebras yet, and some giraffes. But Jana understood why this was called the elephant park. There were so many elephants. On their own, in herds, at the watering hole ,Äî everywhere. Anil kept pointing out new ones, and Imani eventually stopped counting (she really couldn't get past forty, anyway).* **Discussion:** As Jana and Anil are spending time together one annotator considered it as a positive evolution however, for another, there was not enough information to determine evolution type from the passage.
Summary: *Jana's relationship with Anil began with a transformative experience, marked by a week and a half of intense physical connection. ... Their connection deepened in London, ... However, Jana's trust in Anil was shaken when she received anonymous messages accusing her of sleeping with a married man, claiming Anil was still married. Anil's revelation that he was indeed married marked the end of their relationship. Jana became pregnant with his child, and they navigated a co-parenting agreement ... This gesture suggested a desire to reconnect with Jana and their daughter. ... Now, Anil is considering Jana for a director of research and programs position, creating a delicate situation for Jana. She must navigate her past anger and work with Anil to co-parent their daughter effectively.* **Passage:** *And now she had two weeks with Anil, this was the perfect time to put it all behind her for Imani's well-being and her own. It was time to show everyone, including Anil Malek, that the last five years hadn't broken Jana. Most of all, it was time for Jana to show herself that. ... It was a revised wedding schedule. Jana assumed Elsie had rearranged everything so Dr. Lopez wasn't in the same activities as Mom, Jana, Anil, or Imani.* **Discussion:** While the evolution is negative as per one annotator due to 'creating a delicate situation for Jana', nothing 'can be determined' from another's perspective as not there is no direct interaction between Anil and Jana in the passage but it mostly mentions Jana's feelings.

Table 8: Examples where relationship and evolution prediction may be uncertain and open to interpretation leading to disagreement between annotators.

Passage	Discussion
Heuristics/Surface-level cues	
In all sincerity, the lesson here is for me to never doubt Fizzy, Connor says, and the audience Awwwwws. "But listen," Lanelle says. "The two of you really had an amazing connection on-screen." Unease thrums beneath my skin. I don't want her to put Connor on the spot like this. "A corpse would have chemistry with this man, Lanelle. Be serious. "The Connor fangirls in the audience scream." No, no, this is something special.	LLM predicts romantic interest between Connor and Fizzy may be due to an incorrect understanding about on-screen vs real connection.
Connor was trying to talk it out with you, Jess says over the steaming top of her mug. I don't need reminding. Every regrettable, overreactive moment of my meltdown is imprinted in my brain like a bad, drunken tattoo. . . . "I know he was. And I know this all happened like eight years ago, and he was upset, and he's older and wiser, but the fact that he decided to not just end his marriage but explode it..." "Fizzy, we are all dumb when we're young. . . .	LLM predicts Fizzy and Connor as ex-spouses potentially due to surface-level cues and improper understanding of who is speaking to/about whom.
Nothing can console him. "My heart is breaking." Why are you telling me this? "Because, as you suggested, I've taken on the role of the Goddess of Women and Children. Do you know what that means?" I shake my head. "It means that everyone who once feared me now loves me. Even Shin, my greatest enemy, loves me. He knows me now as a goddess of motherhood and children. He knows me as a goddess who is loving and kind and giving. Tell me, Mina, how could I be cruel to someone who loves me?" "I do n't know. Can you?" "It's... strange. When I was feared, I hated everything and everyone."	LLM predicts that Mina and Shin are enemies due to misinterpretation of 'me' as 'Mina' instead of the Goddess which shows that it ignores the context and resorts to surface-level cues.
Incorrect (assumed) pronoun resolution	
It's a barely restrained Uh, okay, buddy. It's a laugh held in. Connor's smile remains, but it doesn't look totally natural anymore. "Do you read her books? "Ashley shakes her head. " Oh, I don't read books with just romance in them; I need there to be some plot, too. "Fizzy goes quietly stony." There's plenty of plot. And Fizzy's are the gold standard. "I stare up at him with fondness. This liar, still pretending he's read my books.	LLM assumes "I" to refer to Fizzy resulting in romantic interest prediction between Fizzy and Connor.
So, he says, and smiles shyly over at me in a way that acknowledges how heavy things just got, how there is something hot and tangible in the air between us but maybe if we talk over it, it will dissipate. "You ready for tomorrow?" Inhaling sharply, I sit up straighter. Right. Get yourself together, Fizzy. "I am. I hope I can sleep tonight. I really don't want to show up all puffy and shadowed tomorrow." "I was going to say," he says, smiling, "you've appeared very calm for someone who's about to be on television."	LLM predicts *romantic interest* between Fizzy and Connor even though Connor is not mentioned in the passage.
Sensitivity to irrelevant changes	
"Where is she?" Mom frowned. "Where did you sleep?" Jana rummaged through her bag to get clothes. "Imani's with Anil. They're fine. Everything is fine. I'm just going to take a shower." "But where did you sleep?" Mom asked again. Jana did not want to answer the question. She did not want to say she slept with Anil Malek's arm around her. Or that he wasn't wearing a shirt. Or that they weren't sleeping at all early in the morning and were instead watching the most beautiful sunrise Jana had ever seen and maybe thinking about kissing.	Evolution prediction between Jana and Anil changes from *positive* to *cannot be determined* when *she* is substituted with *Imani*.

Table 9: Examples where LLM's predictions are incorrect due to potential reliance on surface-level heuristics, the tendency to resolve pronouns to the character in question in the absence of an explicit mention, and sensitivity to irrelevant changes in the context.

Narrative Studio: Visual narrative exploration using LLMs and Monte Carlo Tree Search

Parsa Ghaffari
parsa.ghaffari@gmail.com

Chris Hokamp
chris.hokamp@gmail.com

Abstract

Interactive storytelling benefits from planning and exploring multiple "what if" scenarios (Goldfarb-Tarrant et al., 2020a). Modern LLMs are useful tools for ideation and exploration, but current chat-based user interfaces restrict users to a single linear flow. To address this limitation, we propose Narrative Studio – a novel in-browser narrative exploration environment featuring a tree-like interface that allows branching exploration from user-defined points in a story. Each branch is extended via iterative LLM inference guided by system and user-defined prompts. Additionally, we employ Monte Carlo Tree Search (MCTS) to automatically expand promising narrative paths based on user-specified criteria, enabling more diverse and robust story development. We also allow users to enhance narrative coherence by grounding the generated text in an entity graph that represents the actors and environment of the story.

1 Introduction

Large Language Models (LLMs) have significantly advanced the field of automated narrative generation, demonstrating impressive capabilities in producing coherent and contextually rich stories (Tian et al., 2024). However, most user interfaces designed for interacting with LLMs remain constrained to linear progression, limiting creative exploration and the ability to engage with alternative narrative possibilities. In domains such as interactive storytelling, game design, and creative writing, users often wish to explore multiple "what-if" scenarios, comparing different narrative trajectories in parallel (Skorupski, 2009), and necessarily generating exponential possible paths as story length grows. Existing LLM-powered systems, exposed primarily as chat-based interfaces, do not provide a structured way to navigate these non-linear narrative spaces.

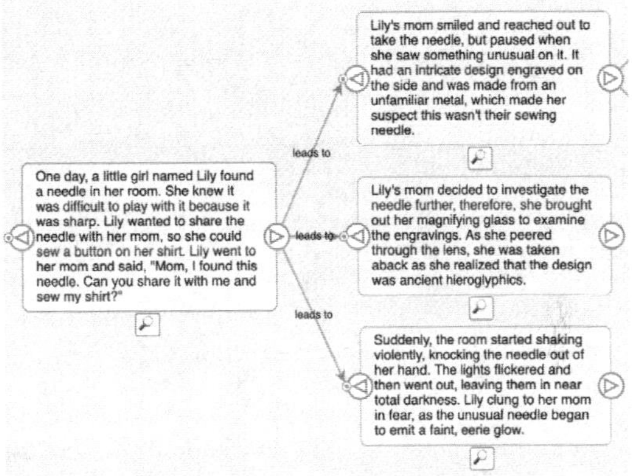

Figure 1: Branching story paths in Narrative Studio

Existing work has explored branching narrative systems that enable users to make choices leading to different outcomes. Prior work in game narratives and mixed-initiative storytelling has demonstrated the potential of branching structures to enhance engagement by offering multiple paths for exploration (Riedl and Young, 2006). However, many such systems rely on pre-scripted paths or manually defined rules, limiting flexibility and scalability. Additionally, ensuring narrative coherence across branches remains a persistent challenge, as diverging storylines may lead to inconsistencies in character motivations, world states, or causal/temporal relationships.

In this work, we propose **Narrative Studio**, a novel in-browser narrative exploration environment that allows users to simultaneously develop multiple story branches while preserving coherence through iterative LLM inference. The core novelty of our approach is the unification of a tree-based interface, iterative cause-and-effect expansions, and search-based expansions under MCTS, enabling a structured yet highly flexible branching mechanism for interactive story generation. By combining these elements, our system provides authors with a versatile environment to explore parallel sto-

Proceedings of the The 7th Workshop on Narrative Understanding, pages 83–96
May 4, 2025 ©2025 Association for Computational Linguistics

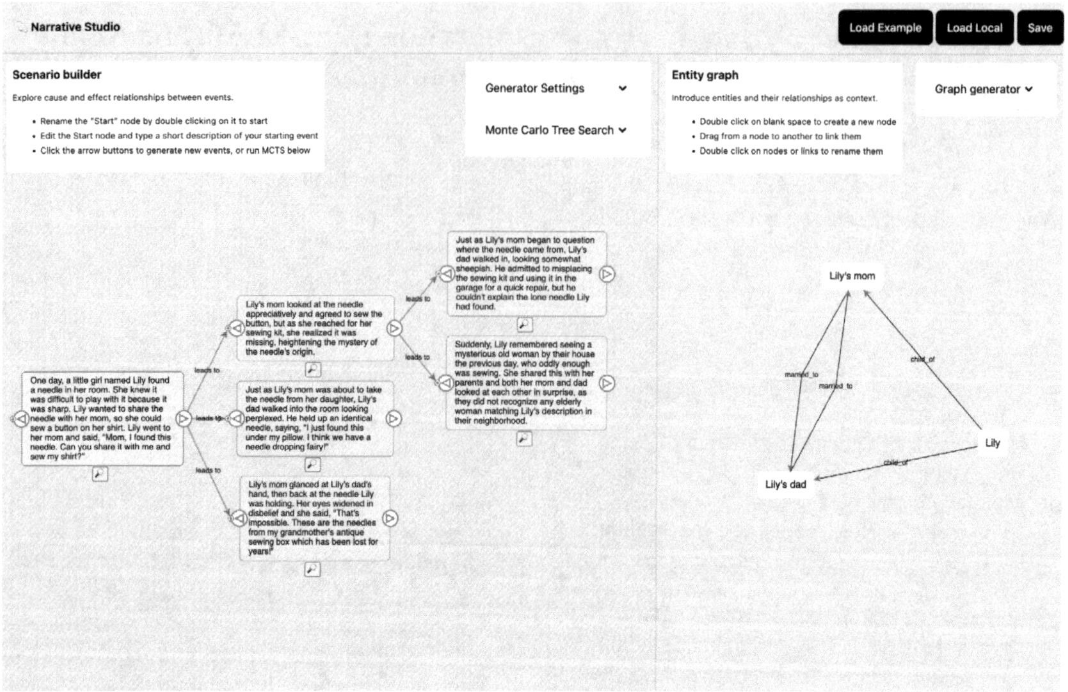

Figure 2: The Narrative Studio user interface.

rylines, identify interesting outcomes, and resolve or prevent consistency issues.

Tree-based User Interface Our approach leverages a tree-based user interface, where branching points are user-defined or LLM-generated, enabling structured yet flexible exploration. To maintain narrative consistency, we ground an LLM in prior events with cause-and-effect conditioning, ensuring coherence across diverging paths. Furthermore, we integrate Monte Carlo Tree Search (MCTS) to autonomously expand promising branches based on default or user-specified criteria, thereby reducing reliance on pre-scripted structures while enhancing narrative discovery.

Knowledge Graph Grounding Story entities and environments are represented in a graph, which serves as a grounding mechanism for the generated text. Graph-based methods have been explored in narrative analysis for tracking relationships between characters, events, and objects, but their integration into interactive storytelling tools remains underdeveloped. By incorporating a structured representation of key entities, our approach ensures logical consistency and continuity across multiple branching narratives.

Our contributions[1] are as follows:

- A tree-based interface[2] for multi-branch narrative development, enabling users to explore multiple "what-if" scenarios in parallel.
- A cause-and-effect-driven LLM inference framework, ensuring flexibility and consistency across divergent storylines.
- The application of Monte Carlo Tree Search (MCTS) for automated discovery of promising narrative branches.
- A graph-based grounding mechanism for tracking story entities and their interactions, enhancing coherence across branching paths.

The remainder of this paper is structured as follows: Section 2 discusses related work in story generation, interactive storytelling, and evaluation of narrative generation. Section 3 presents the methodology behind **Narrative Studio**, including its user interface, MCTS integration, and graph-based grounding. In Section 4, we outline experimental setups and evaluation metrics, followed by

[1]The code for Narrative Studio is available here: https://github.com/parsaghaffari/narrative-studio

[2]A demo video of the interface is available here: https://youtu.be/9T2sCyBhe8A

a discussion of our findings in Section 5. Section 6 concludes with suggestions for future research directions.

2 Related Work

2.1 Story Generation Approaches

Early story generation methods used algorithmic planning, where characters and events followed predefined rules (Meehan, 1977; Lebowitz, 1985). More recent machine-learning approaches leverage large datasets to train neural models capable of generating coherent stories (Du and Chilton, 2023; Hong et al., 2023; Akoury et al., 2020; Louis and Sutton, 2018; Fan et al., 2018). Hybrid techniques integrate content planning, generating high-level outlines before expanding them into full narratives (Yao et al., 2019; Goldfarb-Tarrant et al., 2020b; Huang et al., 2024). Despite advancements, maintaining long-term coherence remains a challenge, with generated stories often suffering from repetitiveness and logical inconsistencies.

While purely neural approaches can generate fluent and interesting text, they typically operate in a left-to-right, linear fashion and can struggle to revisit or branch out from earlier assumptions (Yang and Jin, 2024). Our method mitigates these pitfalls by allowing branching expansions via MCTS, enabling more robust exploration of alternate possibilities and reducing the risk of contradictory or stale narrative continuations.

2.2 Interactive Storytelling

Interactive storytelling enables users to influence narratives through branching structures or AI-driven adaptation. Traditional branching systems, such as Choose-Your-Own-Adventure books and gamebooks, require extensive manual effort and can become unwieldy (Young, 2015). AI-driven systems dynamically adjust stories in response to user actions, mitigating these issues (Mateas and Stern, 2003; Riedl and Bulitko, 2012). Search-based approaches, such as drama management techniques, optimize story coherence by selecting appropriate narrative continuations in real time (Jhala and Young, 2010). Our work builds upon these efforts by integrating LLM-based branching with Monte Carlo Tree Search (MCTS) for more structured yet flexible exploration.

2.3 Evaluation of Narrative Generation

In many narrative-generation pipelines, evaluating coherence, creativity, and diversity has historically relied on human judgment (Chakrabarty et al., 2024; Guan et al., 2021). Automated metrics such as BLEU or ROUGE correlate poorly with key aspects of storytelling, motivating the use of specialized frameworks like OpenMEVA (Guan et al., 2021).

In this work, we use an LLM-based "judge" that scores generated stories along seven dimensions. Section 2.4 provides a dedicated explanation of these evaluation criteria and reproduces the exact evaluation prompt.

2.4 Evaluation Criteria

We evaluate each generated narrative by using an LLM-based "judge" that scores text on seven dimensions. This approach offers a more nuanced view of narrative quality than classical NLG metrics. The evalution dimensions, listed below, are captured in a prompt (included in appendix C) that guides the judge's scoring process.

Dimensions. Each dimension is rated on a 1-10 scale (1 = very poor, 10 = excellent):

1. **Overall quality**: How engaging, structured, and fluid the story is.
2. **Identifying major flaws**: Checks for inconsistencies, repetitions, or unnaturally phrased segments. A higher score indicates a story free of glaring mistakes.
3. **Character behavior**: Whether characters' actions and dialogue are consistent and believable given the context.
4. **Common sense adherence**: Whether the events and their explanations align with general world knowledge and logic.
5. **Consistency**: The story's internal logic and continuity (no contradictions across different parts).
6. **Relatedness**: How well paragraphs or events connect logically and thematically to one another.
7. **Causal and temporal relationship**: Whether cause-and-effect and chronological sequences are handled appropriately.

A brief explanatory comment is also produced to summarize the judge's reasoning about the story. The judge thus produces integer scores in each of the seven categories and an overall short comment. This structured output simplifies downstream analysis in Section 5.

2.5 Monte-Carlo Tree Search

Monte-Carlo Tree Search (MCTS) (Abramson, 1987; Silver et al., 2016) is a simple algorithm allowing efficient scoring of paths generated by Monte Carlo rollouts of a policy. Paths can be scored by any method, allowing for a flexible configuration of search, and enabling tuning and customization of the exploration vs. exploitation trade-off. Especially for deterministic games such as Go, MCTS is an essential component of self-learning systems (Silver et al., 2016). In our work, we employ MCTS to allow users to specify high-level scoring criteria, and automate the expansion of paths according to the search hyperparameters (see Section 3.3).

3 Methodology

3.1 System Overview

Our proposed system is designed to facilitate interactive, branching narrative exploration while maintaining logical coherence. It consists of three core components:

1. an **event tree exploration and expansion tool** (supporting both forward and backward events in a cause-and-effect style),
2. a **graph-based grounding model**,
3. an **MCTS-based automated narrative exploration module**.

As shown in Figure 3, a user can interact with the system through the following workflows:

1. **Event generation**: The user defines an initial event, and generates new events either via manual invocation or using the automated MCTS-based component, with user-defined parameters such as: scoring prompt, number of iterations, and maximum number of children for expansion. The system can generate:
    - **Forward** events ("effects") that push the story forward.
    - **Backward** events ("causes") that help clarify how a particular event came about.
2. **Entity graph construction**: Optionally, the user can also construct a graph of entities (such as people, locations, etc.) that the event generation will be grounded in. The graph can be constructed manually, or by providing instructions to an LLM.

Through these workflows, the user can interactively explore and construct one or many story narratives. We will describe each of the components in the following subsections.

3.2 Iterative LLM Inference for Forward and Backward Expansions

To support bi-directional narrative growth, our system provides a mechanism for iteratively generating new events around a chosen event e, typically represented as a succinct declarative opening sentence or paragraph. While the interface supports both *forward* expansions (i.e., possible "effects") and *backward* expansions (i.e., possible "causes"), both are framed in terms of logical continuity or cause-and-effect relationships to ensure coherent storytelling.

Specifically, from any existing node representing an event, a user may create either:

- a *forward* event (*effect* that logically follows from e), or
- a *backward* event (*cause* that leads to e).

This bi-directional capability offers authors the flexibility to explore what might happen next or to expand on existing preconditions for an event.

Additionally, the interface allows users to configure hyper-parameters that directly shape the prompt or the LLM invocation:

- **Guide prompt (optional)**: e.g., "Adopt a humorous tone."
- **Event likelihood** (1 = very low, 5 = very high)
- **Event severity** (1 = very low, 5 = very high)
- **Model temperature** (0 = near-deterministic, up to around 2 = highly varied)

These parameters are embedded into the forward/backward prompts for event generation, influencing both the textual style and the thematic direction of the model's responses.

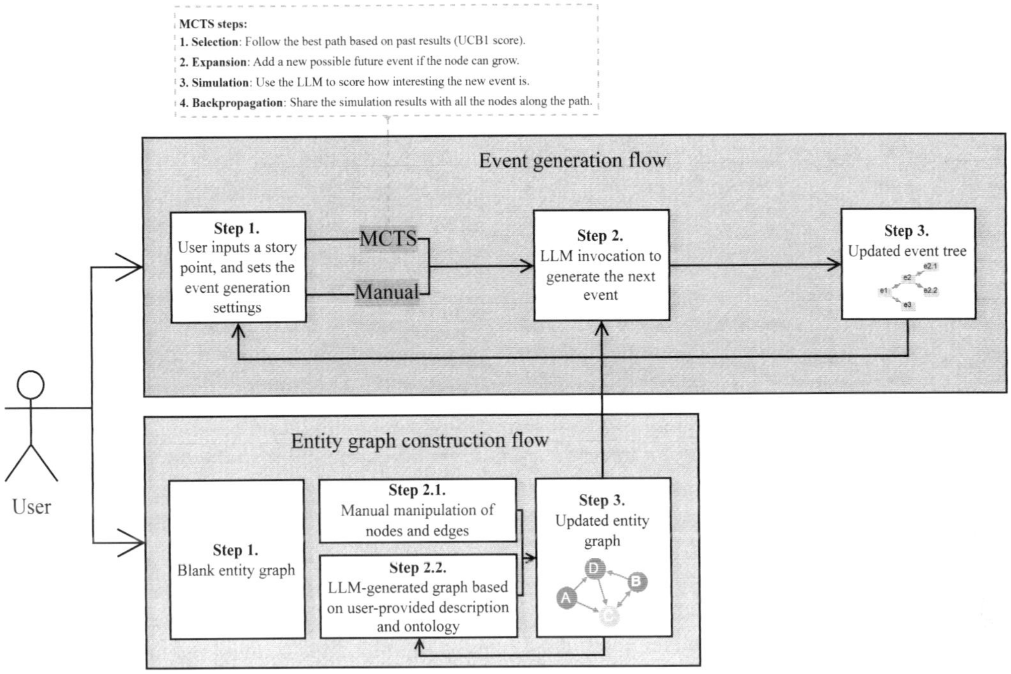

Figure 3: Narrative exploration system overview

Forward Expansion (Effects). When a user requests a forward expansion from the current event e, the system collects the chain of parent events (if any) and the relevant parameter settings (e.g., likelihood, severity, temperature). It then prompts an LLM to generate a short, specific story event that moves the plot forward, while staying logically consistent, introducing elements of surprise, and using narration techniques such as using "therefore" and "but" to piece events together. The resulting new event is added to the event tree and linked to e with a directional edge. The forward expansion process is represented in Algorithm 1.

Additionally, the system tracks *previously generated forward guesses*, which are passed back into the LLM prompt to discourage repeating identical or highly similar expansions from the same event node. This helps maintain narrative variety and avoids looping or stale content.

An example of the prompts used in Forward Expansion is included in appendix C.

Backward Expansion (Causes). Similarly, a user may choose to expand *backward* from the current event e, asking the model to propose a plausible *cause* that precedes it. The same user-defined parameters (guide prompt, likelihood, severity, temperature) can be applied to shape the backward prompt. Once the LLM returns a short, specific precursor event, the system inserts and connects this new node to e.

Algorithm 1 Forward expansion pseudocode, incorporating user-set parameters

```
function ExpandForward(currentEvent, modelData)
    parents ← Collect all ancestor events of currentEvent
    userParams ← { eventPrompt, eventLikelihood, eventSeverity, eventTemperature }
    prompt ← Build forward-prompt using parents, currentEvent, and userParams
    newEvent ← LLMResponse(prompt, userParams)
    Insert newEvent node into diagram
    Create directed link ⟨currentEvent → newEvent⟩ labeled "leads to"
end function
```

Overall User Workflow. In practice, forward and backward expansions enable users to navigate what can be viewed as a *cause-and-effect* graph interactively. By iterating these expansions, stories can evolve in non-linear directions. Multiple potential futures may fork from a single event, and each event can similarly trace back to one or more possible causal histories. User-configurable parameters offer flexibility in shaping the narrative's complexity, tone, and scope, ensuring authors can explore a wide range of "what-if" scenarios across different genres.

3.3 Monte Carlo Tree Search (MCTS) for Narrative Exploration

We employ Monte Carlo Tree Search (MCTS) (Abramson, 1987; Chaslot et al., 2008; Silver et al., 2016) to autonomously expand promising story branches, guided by a *scoring prompt* that rates newly generated events. By iterating through repeated cycles of **selection**, **expansion**, **simulation**, and **backpropagation**, MCTS discovers high-value narrative paths without relying on exhaustive search. Users can configure key parameters:

- **Prompt (scoring instructions):** e.g., "Rate events from 1..10 based on interestingness."
- **Max children per node (N):** limit on how many new children (forward expansions) each event can have.
- **MCTS iterations:** how many times to iterate the four-step MCTS loop.
- **Scoring depth:** how many prior events to include in the LLM scoring prompt.
- **Rollout depth:** how many *ephemeral expansions* to generate at each simulation step for deeper look-ahead before scoring.
- **Early stopping:** optionally stop the MCTS loop once a specified number of paths reach a desired chain length.

During **selection**, we traverse from the root to a leaf, picking child nodes using an Upper Confidence Bound (UCB1) metric to balance exploration and exploitation. In **expansion**, if a leaf is not fully expanded (i.e., under *maxChildren*), the system generates a new forward event, linking it to the leaf.

Rather than immediately scoring the newly expanded event, the algorithm performs a short series of *ephemeral expansions* (up to the *rolloutDepth*) to see how the event might evolve. The LLM then scores the resulting mini-chain, enabling a deeper look-ahead. These ephemeral nodes are subsequently discarded, so they do not remain in the main story graph. Finally, **backpropagation** aggregates the resulting LLM score up the path, guiding MCTS to prefer more promising branches in further iterations.

The system also introduces **early stopping** based on user-defined constraints. If a user specifies a *desiredChainLength* and a *minNumChains*, the MCTS loop halts early (as soon as it discovers the required number of root-to-leaf paths that match the desired length). This allows users to focus on obtaining a certain quantity of fully developed storylines without waiting for all iterations to complete.

By adjusting parameters such as *prompt*, *maxChildren*, *iterations*, *scoringDepth*, *rolloutDepth*, and *early stopping* thresholds, authors can control how exhaustively or selectively the algorithm explores narrative space. This effectively reduces the reliance on manually pre-scripted paths and opens opportunities for discovering emergent storylines that align with desired thematic or design objectives. An example scoring prompt can be found in appendix C.

3.4 Graph-based Grounding Mechanism

While branching narratives can evolve in purely textual fashion, grounding events in a structured graph of entities (e.g., people, places, organizations) and their relationships adds coherence and consistency. This *entity graph* can serve as a reference for next story event generation, ensuring that newly proposed events align with known interactions or constraints in the story world. An example entity graph is shown in Figure 4.

Manual Entity Graph Construction. Users can construct an entity graph by directly adding nodes (representing, for instance, characters or locations) and linking them with edges that specify relationships such as *friend_of*, *married_to*, or *resides_in*. For instance, the user may double-click on a blank area of the diagram to create a new entity node, then drag a link from one node to another to establish a relationship.

LLM-Based Entity Graph Construction. Alternatively, the user may issue a high-level prompt describing the desired domain or scenario (e.g., "A graph of 3 families living in the same village"), along with lists of *entity types* (e.g., *person*, *village*) and *relationship types* (e.g., *married_to*, *lives_in*). The system then invokes an LLM to *generate* a consistent JSON-formatted graph reflecting these

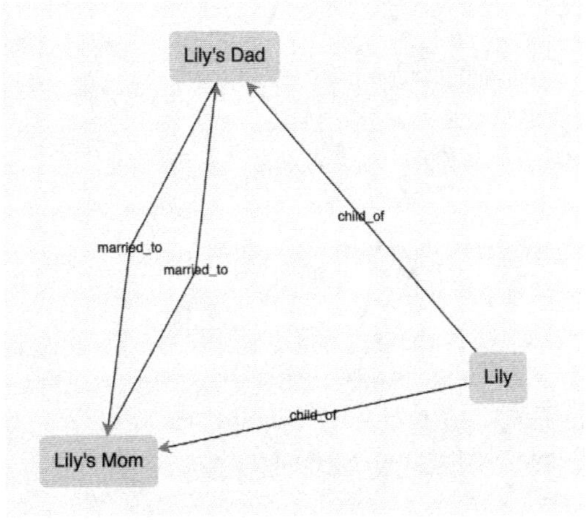

Figure 4: A graph of relationships for Lily's family for grounding next event generation

requirements.

Integration with Event Generation. When the user opts to leverage this entity graph for event creation, the system references it during *forward* or *backward* expansions. Specifically, the LLM prompt includes a summary of the relevant nodes and edges, guiding the model to generate cause-and-effect events consistent with existing characters, locations, and relationships. For instance, if two characters are linked by *friend_of*, the model might propose events that respect or subvert that friendship, thereby grounding the narrative in a structured world model. This approach ensures logical continuity and encourages richer, more context-aware storylines.

4 Experimental Setup

We focus our evaluations on measuring the effectiveness of MCTS-based narrative generation, and in order to do so, we apply it to a set of 20 story "stubs"—short initial contexts—randomly selected from the publicly available Children Stories Text Corpus[3]. This dataset, compiled from cleaned public-domain Project Gutenberg children's books[4], provides a diverse range of introductory story fragments.

We run four different MCTS configurations alongside three baseline strategies, resulting in seven total strategies (outlined in Table 1). In all strategies, we expand the story to 10 events by invoking forward expansion[5] with a temperature of 1.3 to encourage creativity. The baseline strategies use a naive expansion approach whereby they recursively expand events up to a fixed branching length (num_children) and pick one of the children at random. The MCTS strategies, on the other hand, use the MCTS algorithm to automatically expand the story tree based on a scoring prompt and user-defined parameters.

We apply the LLM-based judge described in Section 2.4 to each completed story, obtaining numerical ratings (1-10) for seven categories and a short explanatory comment. In Section 5, we report aggregated scores for each strategy across the 20 stubs.

Note on Model Variants. We employ a slightly less capable LLM from the "gpt-4o" family to generate forward and backward expansions, while the "judge" agent uses a more advanced "o1" model variant (both from OpenAI). Although the judge thus has comparatively stronger reasoning abilities, relying on any single LLM to both generate *and* evaluate narratives still has limitations (e.g., bias, potential overfitting to certain writing styles). In future work, we plan more extensive human evaluations to triangulate these results.

5 Results and Discussion

Table 1 compares the baseline narrative expansion method against four MCTS configurations, each differing in search breadth (*maxChildren*), iteration count, and scoring lookback (*scoringDepth*). All MCTS variants outperform the baselines across every evaluation criterion, demonstrating that tree-based expansion yields richer, more coherent continuations.

Increasing *scoringDepth* from 1 to 3 boosts or matches performance, suggesting a longer look-back in the scoring prompt helps detect inconsistencies and refine causal/temporal logic. Among the high-capacity configurations (*maxChildren = 6*), a 100-iteration search with *scoringDepth = 3* achieves or ties for the best scores, indicating that deeper searches consistently improve coherence, consistency, and flaw detection. Nevertheless, a smaller configuration (*maxChildren = 3, iterations = 60, scoringDepth = 3*) remains competitive,

[3]Available here: Children Stories Text Corpus - Kaggle

[4]It is worth noting that whilst we have evaluated our system on children's books, our system is not specifically optimized for this or any other genre, and evaluating the system across a broader range of genres remains a topic for future work.

[5]Although our system supports backward expansion, we have not evaluated it here. We anticipate comparable performance in that setup.

Strategy	Overall Quality	Identifying Major Flaws	Character Behavior	Common Sense Adherence	Consistency	Relatedness	Causal/Temporal Relationship
baseline (num_children=1)	5.95	4.65	6.40	5.75	5.25	5.25	5.50
baseline (num_children=3)	5.35	4.15	5.90	5.00	4.70	4.70	4.75
baseline (num_children=6)	5.55	4.45	6.20	5.55	5.05	4.85	5.20
mcts (num_children=3, iterations=60, scoring_depth=1)	7.56	7.13	7.63	7.18	7.42	7.35	7.13
mcts (num_children=3, iterations=60, scoring_depth=3)	7.98	7.57	**8.03**	7.62	**8.01**	**7.83**	**7.58**
mcts (num_children=6, iterations=100, scoring_depth=1)	7.40	6.98	7.45	6.98	7.23	7.12	7.09
mcts (num_children=6, iterations=100, scoring_depth=3)	**8.03**	**7.63**	7.98	**7.65**	7.96	7.78	7.57

Table 1: Comparison of strategies (rounded to two decimal places). Highest values in each column are in bold.

which suggests moderate-scale MCTS often suffices while reducing computational cost.

These results confirm that search-based expansions, guided by a well-chosen scoring objective, can produce more coherent and consistent continuations than simple linear generation. However, our automated measurements rely on a single LLM-based evaluator, and a more thorough user study might uncover additional nuances in perceived story quality and engagement.

We also examined lexical diversity and found no meaningful difference in distinct-n scores (for n = 1-4) between MCTS and baseline expansions; details appear in Appendix E. This suggests that lexical diversity owes more to the local event-generation step than the higher-level strategy.

Comparison to WHAT-IF (Huang et al., 2024). While both approaches generate branching narratives via iterative LLM calls, WHAT-IF leverages meta-prompts and a three-act structure to rewrite a single, linear human-written plot, requiring user input for interactive expansion. In contrast, our framework offers three modes: fully interactive (where the user directs the story), fully automated (where MCTS explores and expands branches on its own), or a hybrid of both. By employing a search-based strategy plus a configurable scoring function, we systematically identify and refine the most promising branches rather than relying solely on fixed decision points extracted from an existing storyline.

6 Conclusion and Future Work

In this paper, we introduced a tree-based narrative exploration environment that applies Monte Carlo Tree Search to improve story expansion beyond linear, sequential generation. Our results show that MCTS-enhanced branching yields more coherent, causally consistent continuations and better identification of major narrative flaws, with deeper look-back in scoring providing an additional boost in quality.

Although the automated judgments offer compelling evidence of MCTS's effectiveness, several avenues remain to be explored. First, we plan a formal human evaluation of the generated stories to verify whether the observed gains align with readers' subjective impressions of coherence and engagement. Second, although basic forms of mixed-initiative control already appear in our framework, an in-depth evaluation of a hybrid MCTS–human author collaboration approach would clarify how best to integrate user input with algorithmic search, and the performance of such a system relative to the automated strategies explored thus far. Third, we will undertake more focused HCI evaluations of the interface itself, studying how effectively authors can branch, compare, and refine narratives within our tree-based environment. Finally, we aim to learn the MCTS objective over multiple iterations of authoring sessions or from large corpora, so that the system's search heuristics and scoring prompts can adapt automatically to different genres, tones, or user preferences, including specialized styles such as horror, comedy, or romance. We believe these directions will further solidify MCTS-based branching as a powerful tool for interactive storytelling and creative writing.

References

Bruce D. Abramson. 1987. *The expected-outcome model of two-player games*. Ph.D. thesis, USA. AAI8827528.

Nader Akoury, Shufan Wang, Josh Whiting, Stephen Hood, Nanyun Peng, and Mohit Iyyer. 2020. STORIUM: A Dataset and Evaluation Platform for Machine-in-the-Loop Story Generation. In *Proceedings of the 2020 Conference on Empirical Methods in Natural Language Processing (EMNLP)*, pages 6470–6484, Online. Association for Computational Linguistics.

Tuhin Chakrabarty, Philippe Laban, Divyansh Agarwal, Smaranda Muresan, and Chien-Sheng Wu. 2024. Art or artifice? large language models and the false promise of creativity. In *Proceedings of the CHI Con-*

ference on Human Factors in Computing Systems, pages 1–34.

Guillaume Chaslot, Sander Bakkes, Istvan Szita, and Pieter Spronck. 2008. Monte-carlo tree search: a new framework for game ai. In *Proceedings of the Fourth AAAI Conference on Artificial Intelligence and Interactive Digital Entertainment*, AIIDE'08, page 216–217. AAAI Press.

Yulun Du and Lydia Chilton. 2023. StoryWars: A dataset and instruction tuning baselines for collaborative story understanding and generation. In *Proceedings of the 61st Annual Meeting of the Association for Computational Linguistics (Volume 1: Long Papers)*, pages 3044–3062, Toronto, Canada. Association for Computational Linguistics.

Angela Fan, Mike Lewis, and Yann Dauphin. 2018. Hierarchical neural story generation. In *Annual Meeting of the Association for Computational Linguistics*.

Seraphina Goldfarb-Tarrant, Tuhin Chakrabarty, Ralph Weischedel, and Nanyun Peng. 2020a. Content planning for neural story generation with aristotelian rescoring. In *Proceedings of the 2020 Conference on Empirical Methods in Natural Language Processing (EMNLP)*, pages 4319–4338, Online. Association for Computational Linguistics.

Seraphina Goldfarb-Tarrant, Tuhin Chakrabarty, Ralph Weischedel, and Nanyun Peng. 2020b. Content planning for neural story generation with aristotelian rescoring. In *Proceedings of the 2020 Conference on Empirical Methods in Natural Language Processing (EMNLP)*, pages 4319–4338, Online. Association for Computational Linguistics.

Jian Guan, Zhexin Zhang, Zhuoer Feng, Zitao Liu, Wenbiao Ding, Xiaoxi Mao, Changjie Fan, and Minlie Huang. 2021. OpenMEVA: A benchmark for evaluating open-ended story generation metrics. In *Proceedings of the 59th Annual Meeting of the Association for Computational Linguistics and the 11th International Joint Conference on Natural Language Processing (Volume 1: Long Papers)*, pages 6394–6407, Online. Association for Computational Linguistics.

Xudong Hong, Asad Sayeed, Khushboo Mehra, Vera Demberg, and Bernt Schiele. 2023. Visual writing prompts: Character-grounded story generation with curated image sequences. *Transactions of the Association for Computational Linguistics*, 11:565–581.

Runsheng "Anson" Huang, Lara J. Martin, and Chris Callison-Burch. 2024. What-if: Exploring branching narratives by meta-prompting large language models. *Preprint*, arXiv:2412.10582.

Arnav Jhala and R. Michael Young. 2010. Cinematic visual discourse: Representation, generation, and evaluation. *IEEE Transactions on Computational Intelligence and AI in Games*, 2(2):69–81.

Michael Lebowitz. 1985. Story-telling as planning and learning. *Poetics*, 14(6):483–502.

Annie Louis and Charles Sutton. 2018. Deep dungeons and dragons: Learning character-action interactions from role-playing game transcripts. In *Proceedings of the 2018 Conference of the North American Chapter of the Association for Computational Linguistics: Human Language Technologies, Volume 2 (Short Papers)*, pages 708–713, New Orleans, Louisiana. Association for Computational Linguistics.

Michael Mateas and Andrew Stern. 2003. Façade: An experiment in building a fully-realized interactive drama. In *Game developers conference*, volume 2, pages 4–8. Citeseer.

James R. Meehan. 1977. Tale-spin, an interactive program that writes stories. In *Proceedings of the 5th International Joint Conference on Artificial Intelligence - Volume 1*, IJCAI'77, page 91–98, San Francisco, CA, USA. Morgan Kaufmann Publishers Inc.

Mark Owen Riedl and Vadim Bulitko. 2012. Interactive narrative: An intelligent systems approach. *AI Magazine*, 34(1):67.

M.O. Riedl and R.M. Young. 2006. From linear story generation to branching story graphs. *IEEE Computer Graphics and Applications*, 26(3):23–31.

David Silver, Aja Huang, Chris J Maddison, Arthur Guez, Laurent Sifre, George Van Den Driessche, Julian Schrittwieser, Ioannis Antonoglou, Veda Panneershelvam, Marc Lanctot, et al. 2016. Mastering the game of go with deep neural networks and tree search. *Nature*, 529(7587):484–489.

James Skorupski. 2009. Storyboard authoring of plan-based interactive dramas. In *Proceedings of the 4th International Conference on Foundations of Digital Games*, FDG '09, page 349–351, New York, NY, USA. Association for Computing Machinery.

Yufei Tian, Tenghao Huang, Miri Liu, Derek Jiang, Alexander Spangher, Muhao Chen, Jonathan May, and Nanyun Peng. 2024. Are large language models capable of generating human-level narratives? *Preprint*, arXiv:2407.13248.

Dingyi Yang and Qin Jin. 2024. What makes a good story and how can we measure it? a comprehensive survey of story evaluation. *Preprint*, arXiv:2408.14622.

Lili Yao, Nanyun Peng, Ralph Weischedel, Kevin Knight, Dongyan Zhao, and Rui Yan. 2019. Plan-and-write: Towards better automatic storytelling. *Proceedings of the AAAI Conference on Artificial Intelligence*, 33(01):7378–7385.

Michael Young. 2015. Planning in narrative generation : A review of plan-based approaches to the generation of story , discourse and interactivity in narratives.

A Appendix

B User Interface Examples

Automatic entity graph generation using an LLM:

- **prompt**: "a graph of three families in a village: the Smiths, the Jones, and the Adams"
- **entityTypes**: *person, village, dog*
- **relationshipTypes**: *married_to, friends_with, has_pet, live_in, child_of, is_member_of_family*

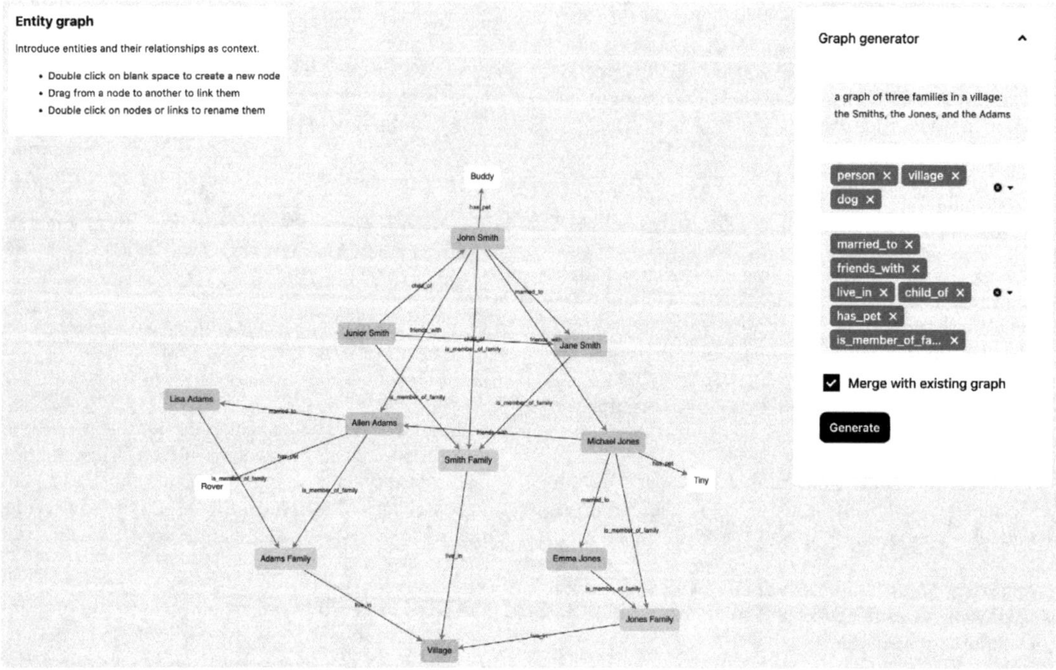

MCTS expansion loop running in the UI:

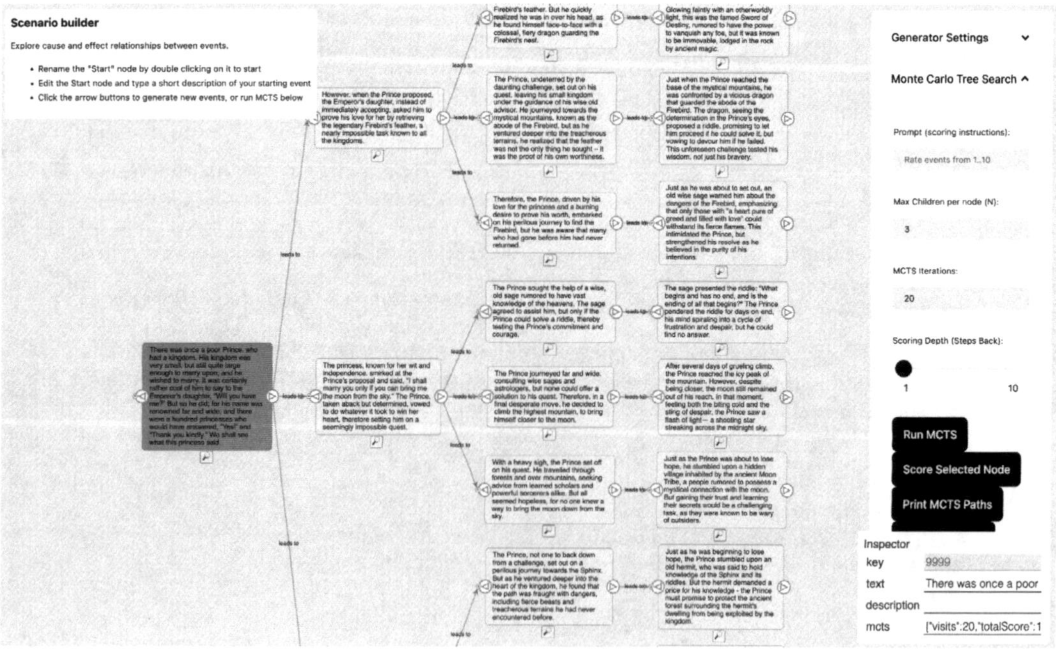

C Prompts Used

Below is a schedule of some of the main prompts used in this work, in their default form without user input.

Next Event Generation:

You are a creative storyteller. Below is the current story context (events so far), followed by instructions to generate the next event.

[STORY CONTEXT]
{parent_events}

— INSTRUCTIONS —
• Write a single story event (2–3 sentences) that moves the plot forward.
• Escalate tension, reveal new details, or deepen character relationships.
• Be logically consistent with existing events but also add an element of surprise or conflict.
• Avoid contradicting established facts or merely repeating prior events.
• Like a good storywriter, try to use "but" or "therefore" to piece together ideas—without overusing or over-mentioning them.
• Do NOT include extra punctuation. Keep it concise and compelling.

Scoring Prompt for MCTS:

You are an expert story critic. Rate this narrative event for coherence, creativity, and engagement, paying special attention to how it connects with prior context.

Use the **full 1–10 range** if warranted:
- 1 → extremely incoherent, contradictory, or uninteresting
- 2–4 → event has big flaws or is mostly unengaging
- 5–6 → somewhat coherent or passable, but not particularly strong
- 7–8 → a good event that is coherent, interesting, and mostly consistent
- 9 → an excellent event, fresh or surprising yet still logical
- 10 → near-perfect event with no apparent flaws

{domain_constraints_line}
Penalize heavily if any of the following occur:
- The event violates the above domain constraints (if any)
- The event repeats prior text with no meaningful change
- The event contradicts established facts or is obviously illogical
- The event is dull or adds nothing new
- The event includes gibberish or weird, nonsensical characters

Reward if:
- The event is novel and contributes something interesting to the story
- It remains logically consistent with prior context and timeline
- It is creative, engaging, and adheres to any user-specified constraints

Example Ratings
1. **Poor Event (score 2)**
"There's an obvious timeline contradiction or unexplained character appearing out of nowhere."
2. **So-So Event (score 5)**
"The event is coherent but bland, adds no real tension or new information."
3. **Excellent Event (score 9)**
"The event heightens conflict in a fresh way, stays consistent with prior facts, and feels natural."

Only output **one integer** from 1 to 10.

NARRATIVE EVENT:
{event_text}

Narrative Judge Prompt:

You are an expert story critic. Analyze the following narrative and rate it for each of these categories, scoring each on a scale from 1 to 10 (1=very poor, 10=excellent).

Use the **full range** if warranted. For instance:
• (2) → extremely contradictory or incoherent
• (5) → okay but flawed or somewhat boring
• (9) → excellent, with minor or no flaws
• (10) → near-perfect

NARRATIVE:
{narrative_text}

Categories to Rate
1. Overall quality: How engaging, structured, and fluid the story is.
2. Identifying major flaws: Whether the story has inconsistencies, repetitions, or unnatural patterns. Score higher if the story is free of glaring mistakes.
3. Character behavior: How consistent and believable are the characters' actions and dialogue?
4. Common sense adherence: Do the events align with general world knowledge and logic?
5. Consistency: Does the story maintain internal logic and continuity (no contradictions)?
6. Relatedness: Do paragraphs/events connect logically to one another?
7. Causal and temporal relationship: Are cause-and-effect and chronological order handled well?

After rating each category (integers 1..10), write a short paragraph of overall comments. Be strict if you see any contradictions, lack of clarity, or poor transitions.

Return your answer **only** as valid JSON matching the schema below. For example:

```
{
  "judgement": {
    "overall_quality": 8,
    "identifying_major_flaws": 7,
    "character_behavior": 9,
    "common_sense": 8,
    "consistency": 9,
    "relatedness": 7,
    "causal_temporal_relationship": 8
  },
  "narrative_comments": "A summary of your key observations"
}
```
No triple backticks, no additional text. Just raw JSON.

D Generated Narrative Examples

Both narratives generated using the MCTS strategy with *maxChildren=3*, *iterations=60*, and *scoringDepth=1*.

Example narrative 1:

- **Stub:** "SHE said that she would dance with me if I brought her red roses," cried the young Student; "but in all my garden there is no red rose." From her nest in the holm-oak tree the Nightingale heard him, and she looked out through the leaves, and wondered. "No red rose in all my garden!" he cried, and his beautiful eyes filled with tears. "Ah, on what little things does happiness depend! I have read all that the wise men have written, and all the secrets of philosophy are mine, yet for want of a red rose is my life made wretched."

- The Nightingale, moved by the Student's despair, resolved that her own song might hold the key, so she vowed to sing beneath the moon each night until the first bloom of dawn, hoping to nourish the barren rose bush with the notes of her heart's melody. As the stars bore witness to her devotion, an ancient, hidden force, drawn by the purity of her song, stirred within the depths of the earth—answering her call with a mysterious promise, whispered through the rustling leaves: one life for one love.

- The mysterious figure, with a voice like the rippling of midnight waves, softly revealed themselves to be an ancient guardian of the garden, bound by timeless duty to protect the balance between nature and heart. Sensing the true depth of the Nightingale's sacrifice, the guardian beseeched her to reconsider, offering an alternate path: a quest for the rare Moon-Dew, a shimmering nectar that, with its touch alone, could infuse a rose with crimson splendor without her demise. Thus, as the stars sighed softly in the sprawling sky, the Nightingale faced an uncertain choice: follow this uncharted journey of life and hope, or embrace the realm of eternal night within her song.

- The Nightingale, torn between the perilous promise of immortality through her song and the hope of finding the elusive Moon-Dew, hesitated a moment longer beneath the oak's sheltering branches, feeling her heartbeat echo in the still air. But as she prepared to set out on her quest, storm clouds rumbled and dimmed the stars' guiding light, signaling a new trial she must face while haunted by the guardian's solemn warning: "The path is treacherous and a heart that desires must be stronger than its doubts." Therefore, with steadfast resolve and wings trembling with both fear and faith, the Nightingale took flight into the gathering storm.

- As the Nightingale hesitated, torn by the weight of truth and desire, a sudden downpour drenched the gleaming grove and revealed a hidden symbol within the earth, glowing with the promise of ancient wisdom untold. Therefore, wary now of unwavering bargains, she turned her thoughts inward, reflecting upon the very wholeness that gifted her with song, for a sphere of perceptual tug began presenting alternate paths in cryptic epiphanies calling. Thus spoke her heart as fierce gusts unraveled all illusions, to cherish that truth is courage in navigating futures unknown—wading promises aware of strength within, voiced or silentwards, to declare love eventual.

- As lightning fractured the sky, the Nightingale pressed on, determined, yet the storm conspired against her, sudden gusts stealing her flight. But within the tempest appeared an ethereal vision of a monarch of vibrant wings who proclaimed in lilting tones she must seek the twin pillars of Adhara, where concealed amidst mirrored lakes lies a sanctuary for her deepest desires, a place where love finds clarity. Therefore, armed with renewed purpose, she braved the swirling vortex, prepared to unearth both beauty and truth unknown.

- The Nightingale fluttered closer to the pillars of Adhara and noticed an iridescent mist swirling between them like a living dream infused with the cascade of forgotten echoes, offering glimpses of long-silenced tales—attending magic interpreted with melody. Yet when she touched the translucent veil, shadows rose from its depth, fusing tangible threat with visions of entrapped love lost to avarice, drowned in its grim roots clawing raw eternal regrets. Prompting the Nightingale to summon strength from her unyielding heart, constructing betwixt sunrise glimmers a harmonizing truth guiding her forward, hoping against hope that fidelity emboldened relinquishments past to illuminate a way through doubts entrenched peripheries unmarked.

- As the Nightingale ventured through the mist, she discovered a delicate silver feather caught within the roots of a gnarled tree, its gleaming edge whispering possibilities unseen yet potent, calling her closer with a chorus hushed and intricate. However, before she could pluck it free, a draconian silhouette encircled her journey—a mysterious Sworn Sentinel lurking in the shadows of the mirrored lakes—who demanded the price of truth for each feather's knowledge, renewing her predicament where honor and hope entwined amidst suspicion cloaked behind its sinister allure. For here love's lesson loomed over faith, and where the heart lay stronger than trials imposed unto finding and daring to unravel revelation amidst the enigma-infused tendrils of longing.

- As the Nightingale's heart beat in rhythm with the whispers of the woodland, she caught sight of a reflection flickering across the mirrored lake, a web of memories tethered to her journey upon its undulating surface. But in reaching for its gossamer strands of kinship glimpsed among the shifting sheen, she stumbled and fell into the water through that liquid looking-glass, where she emerged in a hidden dawn-lit grove that was colored differently, like her song availed—gloried sylvan twilight anew against epoch's intended echoes, grounding profoundly. Uncover history shall emanate visionary, adjoining her song pulse harbor-sync—a timeless nexus anchored true, bygone entry into vaster essence rendered keenly akin yet unforeseen, where each whispered note vibrates to amplify existence recalled, greater melodies affirm before fathom reflects altogether paths she charted.

- Emerging from the mirrored lake, the Nightingale found herself beneath an evergreen archway graced by ancestral guardians carved from wisdom unknown; their stony eyes impassive yet pregnant with secrets that once sworn might tip fate's fragile balance. But just as she began to decipher their silent counsel, the draconian Sentinel appeared beside her, leaving deepening ripples in his wake, his voice softer now, lamenting that deeper truths like hidden roses risk loss unfathomable if symbiotic visions withered before desert bloom—prompting her to question what sacrifice truly demands of one's soul when confronted by eternal equivalencies within life's grand riddle.

Example narrative 2:

- **Stub:** Out in the woods stood a nice little Fir Tree. The place he had was a very good one: the sun shone on him: as to fresh air, there was enough of that, and round him grew many large-sized comrades, pines as well as firs. But the little Fir wanted so very much to be a grown-up tree. He did not think of the warm sun and of the fresh air; he did not care for the little cottage children that ran about and prattled when they were in the woods looking for wild-strawberries. The children often came with a whole pitcher full of berries, or a long row of them threaded on a straw, and sat down near the young tree and said, "Oh, how pretty he is! What a nice little fir!" But this was what the Tree could not bear to hear.

- One day, as autumn approached, the woodsmen came with their sharp axes, scanning the trees for harvest but bypassed the little fir deeming it too young; the fir felt a sting of disappointment mixed with gratitude. Observing this, the wise old owl perched above whispered secrets of patience and purpose, urging the young fir to find contentment in the now. As whispers of winter approached, the ground rumbled unexpectedly, leaving tree roots trembling and the air filling with an unfamiliar, electric scent, hinting that change loomed not just for the tree but for all creatures of the woods.

- As the forest slumbered beneath the starlit sky, the little Fir jolted awake to an extraordinary melody coursing through the air, woven by the harmonious voices of the wind, echoing claims of a distant starlighter whose mere presence could alter the fate of trees forever. The Fir's branches quaked with a mix of hope and unease, but determined not to sway in uncertainty, it called upon a passing breeze to convey its whispered wish: to understand the destiny unfolding before its uneasy heart.

- As the silver dawn began to paint the horizon, a mysterious visitor clad in a cloak woven with star residue appeared at the edge of the wood, recognizing the Fir Tree as a seeker among giants. With a gentle yet profound gaze, the traveler touched the young tree's bark, whispering words of ancient treesong and hidden truths, promising revelations to those who dared to listen. The Fir felt a surge of warmth and curiosity collide within, knowing this was the pivotal moment that could redefine its barren discontent and longing into something profoundly transformative.
- The moment the symbol was etched into its bark, a sharp chill ran through the Fir Tree as if awakening an ancient energy; the forest began to shimmer with hues unseen before, revealing hidden creatures emerging from the depths, drawn to the young tree's newfound aura like moths to flame. But as curiosity blended with unease, among the emerging throng, a shadowy being materialized, its roots entwined in the tricorne tales of forests long silent, warning in a voice woven with wind that, while aspirations could climb skyward, one must also delve deep to confront the regeneration of forgotten echoes that lie buried beneath.
- Amidst the ethereal glow and mounting tension, the fir's bark vibrated to life, transmitting secret languages embedded in the vitreous residue, weaving spells that would reveal visions of futures hitherto shrouded in mystery. As the whispers intensified, new glimpses emerged: a landscape marred by a quiescent haze and the elusive hope of renewal burdened by cyclical legacies and desaturation. Yet despite the chiaroscuro on its horizon, the little Fir sensed that its burgeoning luminosity must guide both itself and its gnarled companions through an unfolding chapter where dreams fettered by tradition could finally root an unheard imbroglio into coexistence—a lush crescendo for those willing to dare release.

E Lexical Diversity Evaluation

In this evaluation we specifically compare lexical diversity between MCTS and baseline narrative generation approaches to measure how varied the vocabulary and linguistic patterns are in the generated stories.

The evaluation process is as follows:

1. Select a story stub from our dataset
2. Run both MCTS and baseline strategies N times (N=10 for the below results)
3. Generate stories of target length M using both strategies (M=6 for the below results)
4. Compare lexical diversity using distinct-n metrics for n=1,2,3,4

Experiment results:

n-grams	**MCTS avg**	**Baseline avg**	**Difference**
1-grams	0.5376 (±0.0306)	0.5480 (±0.0387)	-0.0104
2-grams	0.9174 (±0.0187)	0.9221 (±0.0125)	-0.0046
3-grams	0.9858 (±0.0047)	0.9864 (±0.0042)	-0.0006
4-grams	0.9987 (±0.0017)	0.9989 (±0.0013)	-0.0001

Table 2: Comparison of MCTS and Baseline performance across different n-grams.

These results suggest that the MCTS and baseline strategies produce narratives with similar lexical diversity across n-grams, indicating that the diversity of the generated text is mainly a function of the next event generator rather than the expansion strategy.

Speaker Identification and Dataset Construction Using LLMs: A Case Study on Japanese Narratives

Seiji Gobara, Hidetaka Kamigaito, Taro Watanabe
Nara Institute of Science and Technology
{gobara.seiji.gt6, kamigaito.h, taro}@is.naist.jp

Abstract

Speaker identification in narrative analysis is a challenging task due to complex dialogues, diverse utterance patterns, and ambiguous character references. Cosly and time-intensive manual annotation limits the scalability of high-quality dataset creation. This study demonstrates a cost-efficient approach of constructing speaker identification datasets by combining small-scale manual annotation with LLM-based labeling. A subset of data is manually annotated and is used to guide LLM predictions with a few-shot approach followed by refinement through minimal human corrections. Our results show that LLMs achieve approximately 90% accuracy on challenging narratives, such as the "Three Kingdoms" dataset, underscoring the importance of targeted human corrections. This approach proves effective for constructing scalable and cost-efficient datasets for Japanese and complex narratives.

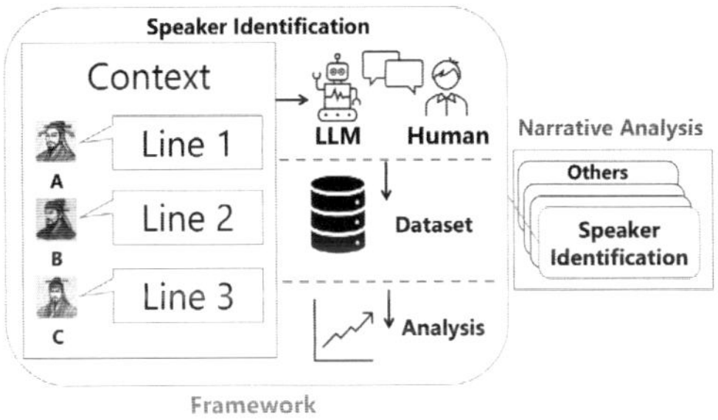

Figure 1: Method for constructing a dataset through collaboration between LLMs and human annotators for speaker identification in narrative analysis.

1 Introduction

Narrative analysis is essential for understanding cultural values, psychological dynamics, and creative processes. Examining narrative structures and themes provides valuable insights into societal norms and human behavior (Piper et al., 2021). Large language models (LLMs) (Zhao et al., 2023a) have introduced new possibilities in narrative analysis, enabling tasks such as character emotion analysis and plot progression prediction.

Speaker identification, a key task in narrative analysis, involves accurately attributing dialogue to characters and understanding character dynamics within a story. However, constructing high-quality speaker identification datasets is costly and labor-intensive, requiring consistency and attention to paraphrase variations (Elson and McKeown, 2010; He et al., 2013; Muzny et al., 2017; Chen et al., 2019a; Vishnubhotla et al., 2022).

To address these challenges, we employ a collaborative approach to dataset construction, combining LLM-based initial annotations with targeted manual corrections (Tan et al., 2024). This significantly reduces annotation costs while maintaining quality. Inspired by the PDNC dataset (Vishnubhotla et al., 2022), we annotate both primary speaker names and their paraphrased forms (aliases). This dual annotation improves efficiency and flexibility. Figure 1 outlines our framework: LLM predictions, followed by iterative human correction, encompassing dialogue extraction, speaker labeling, and refinement.

Existing speaker identification datasets have primarily focused on English and Chinese, limiting the scope of research to these languages. To address this, we first constructed a speaker identification dataset for the Japanese narrative "Romance of the Three Kingdoms", a Japanese translation of the original Chinese work, chosen for its complex plot and character interactions, leveraging data from Aozora Bunko[1]. This method demonstrated the feasibility of creating high-quality datasets with reduced annotation costs.

Our results show that LLMs achieve approximately 90% accuracy, even without human corrections, while human intervention further enhances

[1]https://www.aozora.gr.jp/

Proceedings of the The 7th Workshop on Narrative Understanding, pages 97–119
May 4, 2025 ©2025 Association for Computational Linguistics

accuracy. Additionally, this approach significantly lowers the cost of dataset creation, making it scalable for larger and more diverse datasets. We also highlight the critical role of contextual input length in improving LLM performance, providing valuable insights for handling complex narratives.

2 Related Work

2.1 Dataset Construction

Elson and McKeown (2010) annotated speaker names and genders in 11 English narratives from the 19th century. He et al. (2013) treated separated lines in *Pride & Prejudice* as a single utterance for annotation. Muzny et al. (2017) expanded these datasets, creating the QuoteLi3 dataset, which includes annotations for all utterances in three narratives. Chen et al. (2019a) annotated utterances in the Chinese narrative World of Plainness (WP). Vishnubhotla et al. (2022) developed the Project Dialogism Novel Corpus (PDNC), annotating speakers, addressees, quote types, referring expressions, and mentions across 28 English novels, including main names and their variations.

Despite these advancements, existing datasets are primarily limited to English or Chinese, with no publicly available datasets for Japanese. Moreover, since these datasets depend on manual labor for annotation, they are inherently labor-intensive and costly to produce.

2.2 Speaker Identification

Feature-Based Approaches Several studies have employed linguistic features and manually crafted attributes for speaker identification (Elson and McKeown, 2010; He et al., 2013; Bamman et al., 2014; Muzny et al., 2017).

Deep Learning Approaches With the advent of deep learning, more advanced methods for speaker identification have emerged. These include approaches that fine-tune models such as BERT (Bidirectional Encoder Representations from Transformers; (Devlin et al., 2019)), BART (Lewis et al., 2020) for speaker identification tasks (Cuesta-Lazaro et al., 2022; Vishnubhotla et al., 2023), and prompt tuning techniques with models such as GPT-3.5 (Ouyang et al., 2022) which have also demonstrated high accuracy on the Chinese WP dataset (Su et al., 2024).

Despite these advances, limitations remain, particularly regarding the size of the context window. Michel et al. (2024) demonstrated that while LLaMA-3 (Dubey et al., 2024) expanded the context window and improved accuracy on the PDNC, their evaluation was constrained by the range of models and languages, leaving it incomplete.

3 Methods

Task Definition Speaker identification in narrative analysis involves determining which character or entity is responsible for a given utterance. This process requires analyzing both the utterance and its context to accurately attribute it to the correct speaker. In our approach, the set of possible speakers S is not predefined but derived from the context of the input text. Given a set of utterances $U = u_1, u_2, \ldots, u_m$, we establish a mapping function $f : U \rightarrow S$ so that each utterance $u_i \in U$ is correctly attributed to a speaker $s_j \in S$. We annotated two types of speaker names: the 'main name,' representing the most contextually appropriate identifier (e.g., Elizabeth Bennet), and 'candidates,' which include alternative names or alternative forms (e.g., Lizzy, Liz, Elizabeth). This dynamic speaker identification is crucial for capturing the fluid and complex nature of narrative interactions, enabling more accurate analysis of character relationships and narrative structure.

Refining Prompts and Manual Correction To cost-effectively create a high-quality speaker identification dataset, we manually annotated a small development set and refined prompt configurations for the LLM to generate speaker labels, which were then manually corrected. This approach ensured high data quality while minimizing costs. We also employed a specialized chat template[2] with a few-shot approach to enhance LLM performance (see Appendix I).

Robust Evaluation Metrics To ensure a robust evaluation of generation-based speaker identification systems like LLMs, we incorporated additional metrics such as substring match ratio and uncased evaluations. These metrics allow for a more relaxed and accurate assessment of speaker identification performance by accounting for variations in text, thereby improving the reliability of the evaluation results.

4 Dataset Construction

The dataset construction was carried out according to the following steps, as shown in Figure 2.

[2]https://github.com/chujiezheng/chat_templates

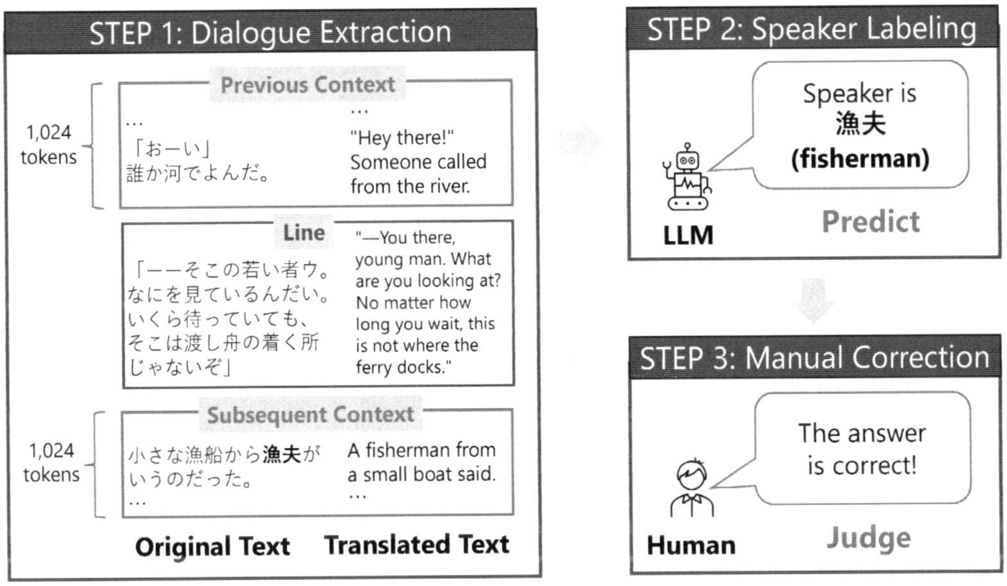

Figure 2: Workflow for constructing a speaker identification dataset using `LLaMA-3-70B-Instruct`. The process includes three steps: dialogue extraction, LLM-based labeling, and manual correction. LLM-generated labels are reviewed by human annotators—correct labels are retained, while errors are corrected.

STEP 1: Dialogue Extraction We gathered and tokenized dialogues from *Aozora Bunko's "Romance of the Three Kingdoms"* and Wikipedia sources by LLaMA-2 tokenizer and then extracting the surrounding 1,024-token contexts for each dialogue. This process resulted in a dataset of 16,423 instances. The dataset is composed of 10 books, with book_id=52410 serving as the development data, and book_id=52411 to 52420 serving as the evaluation data (see Appendix B).

STEP 2: Speaker Labeling We utilized an LLM to identify and label the speakers in the extracted dialogues. As the LLM, we used `LLaMA-3-70B-Instruct` with a few-shot setting, which showed the highest performance on the development dataset (see Appendix B and G).

STEP 3: Manual Correction We manually corrected the speaker names based on the annotation rules (see Appendix F.1) and adjusted approximately 20% of the identified labels. We excluded instances where the context lacked vocabulary corresponding to the speaker's name or involved multiple speakers in a single dialogue. This process removed 1,011 instances and finalized the dataset at 15,412 instances. We used GPU for 200 hours during inference (see Appendix H).

This method significantly reduced the time required to create evaluation data. While annotating 1,500 instances originally took 10 hours, focusing on correction tasks cut this time to 3.5 hours per 1,500 instances. Table 1 summarizes the tokens (LLaMA-2 and LLaMA-3 base models), lines, unique speakers, and skips for each book_id. The annotated speaker names include 856 unique speakers after excluding duplicates.[3]

4.1 Quality Assessment of Annotations

To verify the quality of the annotations, three independent annotators reviewed 100 samples from the evaluation dataset. They labeled the speaker names as "appropriate," "inappropriate," or "neutral," and we calculated the agreement rates for the "appropriate" labels. The results showed high consistency, with two annotators achieving an agreement rate of 0.97 and one annotator achieving an agreement rate of 0.96 (see Appendix F.2).

A comprehensive human evaluation under the exact same conditions as model inference would be prohibitively expensive. Manually reading the entire text, identifying the position of each input utterance, and determining the corresponding speaker are time-intensive and impractical at scale. In contrast, verifying whether a predicted speaker name is appropriate is relatively more manageable

[3]The datasets are available at `https://huggingface.co/datasets/satoshi-2000/romance_of_the_three_kingdoms/`.

book_id	Title	tokens (Llama-2)	tokens (Llama-3)	lines	skip	unique speakers
Excluded Data						
052409	Introduction	1,866	1,129	0	2	0
Development (dev) Data: Fully Human-Annotated						
052410	Oath of the Peach Garden	195,226	124,143	1,686	70	113
Evaluation (eval) Data: LLM-Labeled + Manual Correction						
052411	Stars of Destiny	195,589	124,772	1,662	108	157
052412	Heroes from the Grasslands	193,973	124,364	1,649	129	136
052413	The Way of the Minister	201,042	129,000	1,616	82	123
052414	Zhuge Liang	205,799	131,796	1,461	89	159
052415	The Battle of Red Cliffs	209,759	133,797	1,532	88	117
052416	Longing for Shu	204,514	130,989	1,598	83	153
052417	Plans for the South	222,992	143,735	1,433	95	171
052418	The Expedition	249,258	159,547	1,426	96	186
052419	The Battle of Wuzhang Plains	223,710	143,901	1,308	130	122
052420	Additional Records	27,050	16,968	40	40	26
Total		2,130,778	1,364,141	15,411	1,012	1,463

Table 1: Number of Tokens and Speakers by Dataset. The dataset was extracted and aligned based on token counts measured with the Llama-2 tokenizer, using 1,024 tokens as the standard segment length. `book_id=052409` represents the introductory chapter, setting the stage for the epic narrative of *Romance of the Three Kingdoms*. From the Oath of the Peach Garden (`book_id=052410`) to the final records of the Three Kingdoms (`book_id=052420`), the dataset follows the chronological progression of the story. `book_id=052410` served as development (dev) data, fully annotated by humans, while `book_id=052411-052420` were used as evaluation (eval) data, where initial LLM-generated labels were refined manually.

and can be done in a realistic timeframe. Therefore, we adopted this evaluation approach for human assessment, ensuring both feasibility and reliability while maintaining high annotation quality.

5 Experiment

To assess LLM capability in speaker identification and, simultaneously, to validate the quality of our constructed dataset, we conduct a series of experiments evaluating LLM performance. A primary aim of these experiments is to identify the characteristics of LLMs that facilitate efficient and effective dataset construction, allowing for the identification of optimal model features for similar tasks.

5.1 Prompt

As shown in Table 2, our approach employs a chat-based template to guide LLMs through the speaker identification task. By providing a few-shot prompt and assigning the LLM a system role, we effectively direct it through the necessary steps in a conversational format (see Appendix I).

5.2 Model

To compare model performance using LLMs, we selected LLaMA-3 (Dubey et al., 2024), a standard in LLM comparisons, along with Swallow-3 (Fujii, 2024), ELYZA-JP-8B (Hirakawa et al., 2024), and LLaMA-3-youko-8B (Mitsuda et al.), all based on LLaMA-3 with additional Japanese training. For broader model evaluation, we included Mistral 7B (Jiang et al., 2023) and RakutenAI-7B (Group et al., 2024), which, like Mistral 7B, are trained on Japanese data. To assess the impact of training data composition on accuracy, we selected CALM-3-22B (Ishigami, 2024), primarily trained on Japanese data, and Karakuri-8x7B (Inc., 2024), which uses the Mixture of Experts technique (Jiang et al., 2024) (see Appendix G).

5.3 Evaluation Metrics

We evaluated speaker attribution accuracy using the gold labels in the datasets of both languages:

Exact Match Ratio This metric, commonly used in prior research (Vishnubhotla et al., 2023; Michel et al., 2024), measures the percentage of exact matches between the speakers identified in the generated text and those in the annotations.

Substring Match Ratio Given the variations in texts generated by LLMs, this metric recognizes partial matches in key elements of the speaker names (see Appendix A).

BERTScore (Zhang* et al., 2020) This metric as-

Role	Content
user	Please guess who is speaking each line of dialogue in the following story (# Example Story) and provide only the speaker's name.
assistant	Understood. I will provide answers based on the story and dialogues below.
user	# Example Story {Example Context}
assistant	I have reviewed the story. Now, I will identify the speaker for each line of dialogue.
user	Who said the following line?
assistant	Please provide the line of dialogue.
user	Hey there!
assistant	Fisherman
user	—You there, young man. What are you looking at? No matter how long you wait, this is not where the ferry docks.
assistant	Fisherman
user	Thank you,
assistant	Young Man
user	Hey, hey, traveler.
assistant	Farmer
user	—What have you been waiting for since this morning in a place like this? Lately, there have been bandits called the Yellow Turbans around. The officials will get suspicious of you.
assistant	Farmer
user	Similarly, guess who is speaking each line of dialogue in the following story (# Target Story) and provide only the speaker's name.
assistant	Understood. I will provide answers based on the story and dialogues below.
user	# Target Story {Context}
assistant	I have reviewed the story. Now, I will identify the speaker for each line of dialogue.
user	Who said the following line?
assistant	Please provide the line of dialogue.
user	{Line}

Table 2: Prompts for Speaker Identification (Translated one). This table represents prompts designed for application in chat templates. The {Context} section contains the story content, while the {Line} section specifies the dialogue for which the speaker is to be identified. Appendix I shows the original Japanese text.

sesses similarity based on embeddings, capturing cases where surface expressions differ but the underlying meaning remains the same.

Edit Distance (Levenshtein et al., 1966) Edit distance calculates similarity by counting character insertions, deletions, and substitutions to transform one string into another.

5.4 Results

Overall Performance Table 3 shows the speaker identification accuracy for each model. Across both the dev (book_id=052410) and eval (book_id=052411–052420) phases, accuracy of approximately 90%, the models demonstrated robust performance in speaker identification (see Appendix B). The highest accuracy was achieved by a model that underwent continued pre-training on Japanese data using the base LLaMA-3 model, followed by instruction tuning. This combination proved particularly effective for speaker identification. The original LLaMA-3 model ranked second.

Additionally, `Swallow-3-8B-Instruct` showed a 5% improvement over `Swallow-3-8B`, highlighting the benefits of instruction tuning.

The results highlight the importance of combining high-quality datasets with large-scale models (e.g., 70B parameters) to achieve accurate speaker identification. Continued pre-training on Japanese data and instruction tuning not only ensure high accuracy but also reduce the cost of human corrections. This efficient and scalable method underscores the importance of leveraging well-trained large-scale models to balance accuracy and cost efficiency.

Accuracy by Book We analyzed the substring match ratio for each book_id to evaluate model accuracy, focusing on `LLaMA-3-70B-Instruct` as an example. This model consistently achieved approximately 0.9 accuracy across book_ids, as shown in Table 3, demonstrating robust performance in speaker identification.

In book_id=052419, the character "Sima Yi Zhongda" was labeled variably as "Sima Yi" or "Zhongda." Annotation rules prioritized the given name when present, leading to frequent use of "Zhongda." As a result, instances labeled as "Sima Yi" reflect the same individual, potentially skew-

Book ID	Swallow-3				Karakuri-8x7B	Mistral-7B	RakutenAI-7B	ELYZA-JP-8B	llama-3-youko-8B	LLaMA-3		CALM-3-22B
	8B	8B-Instruct	70B	70B-Instruct						8B-Instruct	70B-Instruct	
Exact Match Ratio												
052410	0.219	0.465	0.803	0.802	0.658	0.000	0.138	0.483	0.345	0.537	0.781	0.580
052411	0.222	0.582	0.835	0.829	0.687	0.000	0.108	0.540	0.310	0.537	0.824	0.507
052412	0.234	0.588	0.861	0.876	0.718	0.000	0.111	0.526	0.301	0.570	0.864	0.542
052413	0.240	0.621	0.887	0.892	0.744	0.000	0.126	0.593	0.313	0.593	0.849	0.547
052414	0.229	0.608	0.882	0.884	0.744	0.000	0.114	0.571	0.317	0.611	0.859	0.520
052415	0.238	0.582	0.873	0.871	0.706	0.000	0.139	0.536	0.343	0.555	0.839	0.543
052416	0.219	0.541	0.842	0.835	0.658	0.000	0.133	0.509	0.283	0.514	0.810	0.495
052417	0.228	0.584	0.866	0.871	0.719	0.000	0.109	0.537	0.278	0.603	0.865	0.505
052418	0.225	0.554	0.825	0.802	0.681	0.000	0.121	0.501	0.293	0.565	0.822	0.546
052419	0.193	0.476	0.735	0.727	0.617	0.000	0.098	0.469	0.239	0.499	0.728	0.426
052420	0.325	0.675	0.800	0.800	0.600	0.000	0.250	0.550	0.350	0.475	0.775	0.400
Substring Match Ratio												
052410	0.520	0.794	0.864	0.895	0.735	0.469	0.725	0.530	0.563	0.648	0.863	0.664
052411	0.536	0.795	0.892	0.918	0.745	0.510	0.705	0.589	0.555	0.649	0.916	0.610
052412	0.585	0.817	0.894	0.926	0.750	0.535	0.739	0.552	0.566	0.648	0.911	0.598
052413	0.582	0.827	0.906	0.925	0.759	0.502	0.728	0.618	0.546	0.666	0.880	0.605
052414	0.554	0.797	0.906	0.916	0.762	0.466	0.700	0.598	0.546	0.678	0.900	0.600
052415	0.567	0.790	0.891	0.896	0.717	0.456	0.698	0.555	0.519	0.623	0.866	0.589
052416	0.516	0.750	0.880	0.887	0.689	0.428	0.669	0.539	0.496	0.594	0.870	0.581
052417	0.549	0.792	0.897	0.912	0.739	0.486	0.721	0.569	0.539	0.687	0.914	0.572
052418	0.547	0.797	0.893	0.907	0.738	0.468	0.687	0.564	0.505	0.684	0.914	0.660
052419	0.479	0.684	0.797	0.806	0.664	0.417	0.635	0.518	0.455	0.609	0.808	0.539
052420	0.575	0.925	0.900	0.975	0.750	0.350	0.775	0.700	0.525	0.700	1.000	0.700
Edit Distance												
052410	7.751	1.543	0.446	0.476	0.845	10.423	6.837	1.432	5.852	2.705	0.620	4.240
052411	7.552	1.220	0.395	0.430	0.745	10.563	6.842	1.261	5.816	2.601	0.449	5.732
052412	7.155	1.178	0.321	0.301	0.191	11.091	6.735	1.421	6.127	2.646	0.320	5.179
052413	7.970	1.134	0.237	0.241	0.610	11.704	6.498	1.225	7.323	2.097	0.351	4.851
052414	7.949	1.162	0.265	0.277	0.704	11.260	6.903	1.386	6.602	2.086	0.369	5.307
052415	7.989	1.183	0.263	0.290	0.855	11.497	6.765	1.314	6.809	2.796	0.379	3.692
052416	8.243	1.377	0.362	0.406	0.885	11.538	7.342	1.406	6.869	2.857	0.489	5.267
052417	8.045	1.230	0.301	0.293	0.723	11.193	6.731	1.387	6.915	2.439	0.322	3.773
052418	7.735	1.262	0.431	0.531	0.893	11.250	6.608	1.426	6.996	2.705	0.500	4.211
052419	7.973	1.489	0.661	0.716	1.061	11.502	7.119	1.517	7.402	2.731	0.687	4.570
052420	8.925	1.025	0.475	0.475	1.225	11.150	4.375	1.300	5.150	3.500	0.525	5.475
BERTScore F1												
052410	0.792	0.888	0.959	0.958	0.923	0.676	0.772	0.706	0.812	0.877	0.950	0.879
052411	0.797	0.914	0.964	0.962	0.928	0.675	0.765	0.741	0.800	0.881	0.962	0.850
052412	0.809	0.918	0.970	0.974	0.936	0.675	0.768	0.699	0.797	0.886	0.972	0.864
052413	0.808	0.925	0.977	0.979	0.944	0.675	0.773	0.769	0.792	0.898	0.969	0.871
052414	0.810	0.924	0.976	0.976	0.944	0.682	0.770	0.764	0.803	0.904	0.971	0.861
052415	0.811	0.920	0.975	0.974	0.939	0.677	0.778	0.744	0.805	0.887	0.968	0.885
052416	0.794	0.906	0.967	0.966	0.926	0.671	0.762	0.744	0.789	0.875	0.960	0.856
052417	0.800	0.915	0.971	0.973	0.939	0.682	0.771	0.731	0.789	0.899	0.972	0.870
052418	0.813	0.917	0.965	0.961	0.932	0.685	0.776	0.732	0.794	0.893	0.965	0.875
052419	0.797	0.897	0.946	0.944	0.920	0.680	0.765	0.737	0.778	0.881	0.945	0.848
052420	0.809	0.939	0.956	0.960	0.908	0.664	0.825	0.853	0.817	0.860	0.960	0.825

Table 3: Performance metrics for all models (Exact Match Ratio, Substring Match Ratio, Edit Distance, BERTScore F1) evaluated across different books, highlighting variations by model category. The scores presented in the table are averaged values across the dataset. The background color gradient represents performance: darker red indicates higher performance, while darker blue indicates lower performance.

ing the evaluation for this book_id.

Relaxed Evaluation by Candidate Sets Using candidate sets for best matching enabled relaxed evaluation, enhancing accuracy. In book_id=52419, "Sima Yi Zhongda" appeared under various names, such as "Sima Yi" and "Zhongda." Per annotation rules, "Zhongda" was used when present in context, and "Sima Yi" otherwise. Both names could serve as main identifiers. Following PDNC (Vishnubhotla et al., 2023), we prepared interchangeable candidate sets for "Zhongda," including "Zhongda," "Sima Yi," "Sima Yi Zhongda," and "Sima Zhongda."

We then evaluated the predictions by matching them to the most corresponding name from these candidate sets. Compared to strict substring matching, this approach allowed for a more relaxed evaluation. For book_id=52419, the substring match ratio increased from 80.8% (without candidates) to 89.3% (with candidates), an improvement of 8.5%. This suggests that a relaxed strictness in the representation of speaker names leads to a more accurate and consistent evaluation (see Appendix K for details).

5.5 Analysis

Table 4 presents case study examples.

Case Study A: Long-Turn Dialogues The model generally identifies speakers accurately, even when relevant information is at the edges of the context. In Case A, although the model correctly

Case	Line	Excerpt Context	Pred	True
A	Hahaha.	Yang Biao, harboring his secret plan, returned to his residence. As soon as he arrived, he went into his wife's room and said, "So, how is it these days? Do you often meet with Lady Guo? I hear you ladies frequently have various gatherings." Placing his hands gently on his wife's shoulders, he spoke with an unusual tenderness. Yang Biao's wife, puzzled, teased him, "What's gotten into you today? You' re never this sweet to me." "What's the matter?" "Well, it's just that you never act this way towards me normally." "Hahaha." "It actually makes me feel uneasy." "Is that so?"	Yang Biao	Yang Biao
B	Land of Jiangdong,	Wu is known as the "Land of Jiangdong," situated along the flow of the Great River.	Narration	Unknown
C	......	Diaochan, without showing any signs of agitation, immediately responded, "Yes. If it is the will of my lord, I am ready to give my life at any time." Wang Yun straightened his posture and said, "Then, I have something I wish to ask of you, trusting in your sincerity." "What is it?" "Dong Zhuo must be killed." "......" "If he is not removed, it will be as if the Han Emperor does not exist." "......"	Diaochan	Diaochan
D	The pleasures of life culminate here,	In the evening, a grand banquet was held with the slaughtering of cattle and horses for a feast. "The pleasures of life culminate here," said Guan Yu and Zhang Fei. "How could it end here? This is just the beginning," replied Xuande.	Guan Yu and Zhang Fei	Unknown
E	Lord Xuande, it is the fervent wish of both of us. Will you not consider it?	"It would be best." "Lord Xuande, it is the fervent wish of both of us. Will you not consider it?" From both sides,	Guan Yu	Guan Yu

Table 4: Case Study: 'Pred' indicates the predicted speaker, 'True' indicates the annotated speaker. Examples are translated into English; the original text is available in Appendix 5. Results are based on `LLaMA-3-70B-Instruct`, with unnecessary text removed via regular expressions.

attributed 'Hahaha.' to Yang Biao, it erroneously attributed the subsequent line, 'Is that so?', to his wife. This highlights the increased likelihood of errors in long-turn dialogues.

Case Study B: Narrator Identification We observed that the model correctly identifies the speaker as the narrator.

Case Study C: Silent Utterance Identification We confirmed the model demonstrated the ability to infer speaker names in implicit dialogues, "......" highlighting its contextual reasoning capabilities.

Case Study D: Multiple Speaker Identification The model successfully identified the speaker even in instances involving multiple speakers within the same utterance.

Case Study E: Data Leak We analyzed potential data leakage by comparing `ELYZA-JP-8B` and `LLaMA-3-70B-Instruct` predictions with an 8-context length. While `LLaMA-3-70B-Instruct` inferred speaker names from the context, `ELYZA-JP-8B` correctly predicted speakers not explicitly mentioned. For example, `ELYZA-JP-8B` mistakenly identified "Guan Yu" as a speaker, likely due to reliance on prior knowledge triggered by the mention of "Xuande".

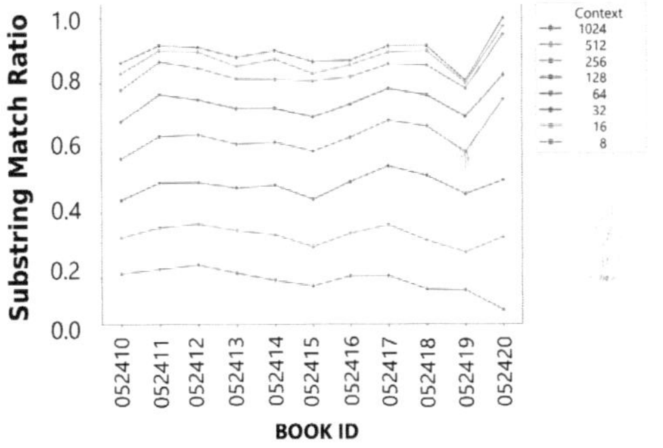

Figure 3: Variation in Substring Match Ratio by Context Length. This figure shows how the substring match ratio changes with different context lengths.

Impact of Varying Context Lengths As shown in Figure 3, the `LLaMA-3-70B-Instruct` model's accuracy improves with longer context lengths but plateaus between 512 and 1,024 tokens. Models with smaller parameter sizes (8B or less) peaked at 512 tokens (see Appendix J).

This suggests that optimal context length depends on the model's parameter size, reflecting its computational capacity and design. Selecting an appropriate context length is essential to maximize performance, especially in resource-limited settings (see Appendix B).

Impact of Context Masking We evaluated the effect of masking tokens within a 1,024 token context window on speaker identification accuracy. We tested the `LLaMA-3-70B-Instruct` model with mask ratios from 0% to 100% in 10% increments, replacing tokens with '<unk>'.

Figure 4 shows that the accuracy decreases as the Mask ratio increases. At 0% Mask, the model achieved 1.9% accuracy, which decreased as the Mask ratio increased. The `LLaMA-3-70B-Instruct` model's accuracy decreased with higher Mask ratios but still identified some speakers correctly. In contrast, the `ELYZA-JP-8B` model performed better at a 20% Mask ratio, indicating superior context retention. However, accuracy declined with excessive Masking due to reduced context. At 100% Mask, the `ELYZA-JP-8B` model achieved a 2.7% match rate, surpassing the `LLaMA-3-70B-Instruct` model's 1.9%. This suggests that the `ELYZA-JP-8B` model retains valuable contextual information even with full Masking (see Appendix E.2).

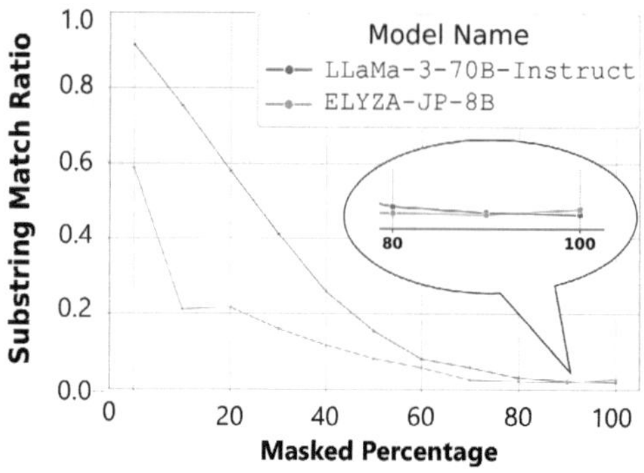

Figure 4: Substring Match Ratio by Mask Ratios for `LLaMA-3-70B-Instruct`. This figure shows how the substring match ratio changes as the proportion of masked tokens increases. The model demonstrates a gradual decline in accuracy with higher mask ratios, reflecting its dependency on contextual information.

Extending Applicability Across Narratives To evaluate the applicability of our approach to different narratives and languages, we constructed a bi-lingual dataset comprising 14 diverse stories in Japanese and English. This dataset, sourced from Wikisource and Aozora Bunko, enabled us to analyze the `LLaMA-3-70B-Instruct` model' s performance across languages and cultural contexts.

Our analysis revealed that the model achieved higher accuracy on Japanese datasets, likely due to fewer variations in referring terms compared to English, which often includes synonyms for the same entity (e.g., Mother" and Woman"). This suggests the importance of designing candidate sets for consistent name recognition across languages. For further details on dataset construction and results, see Appendix C.

6 Conclusion

We collaborated with LLMs to create a speaker labeling dataset by annotating "Romance of the Three Kingdoms" from Aozora Bunko in Japanese. The dataset included 15,412 entries.

Using LLMs like LLaMA-3, we achieved a substring match ratio of approximately 90%. To handle multiple potential speakers, we developed a paraphrase dataset to improve evaluation accuracy.

Instead of manually annotating the entire dataset, we adopted an approach where LLMs performed the initial labeling, and human annotators focused on correcting the generated labels. This shift significantly reduced human labor costs while maintaining high annotation quality.

Our findings demonstrate the potential of scalable, LLM-assisted methods for narrative analysis, offering a cost-effective solution for speaker identification in complex texts.

7 Future Plans

We will expand our datasets with advanced translation techniques and enhanced annotations, including Addressees and Quote Types, following the PDNC approach (Vishnubhotla et al., 2022). We also plan to refine speaker labeling methods and extend our analysis to complex stories with extensive character lists, improving LLMs' capacity for handling intricate narratives.

Our datasets also offer potential applications beyond speaker identification:

- **Character Interaction Analysis**: Exploring power dynamics, alliances, and conflicts in narratives.
- **Sentiment and Emotion Attribution**: Studying emotional tones associated with characters or interactions.
- **Cross-Cultural Studies**: Comparing storytelling across languages and cultures.
- **Education and Language Learning**: Teaching narrative structures and cultural contexts.

These applications highlight the versatility of our dataset, supporting both academic research and practical applications.

8 Limitations

Supported Languages This study primarily focuses on Japanese, with additional experiments conducted on a small-scale Japanese-English bilingual dataset. The English dataset was limited in size and scope, constraining the generalizability of the findings. While speaker identification performance in Japanese was strong, direct comparison with English posed challenges due to linguistic differences.

English narratives, with their diverse synonyms and alternative expressions, introduce variability that complicates direct comparisons to the contextually uniform nature of Japanese texts. Future work should expand datasets to address these linguistic differences. These differences may have influenced the results, underscoring the need for caution when evaluating bi-lingual performance. Future work should expand the dataset to include larger and more diverse bi-lingual samples, enabling more robust and comprehensive evaluations.

Models One of the objectives of this study is to demonstrate how high-quality datasets can be collaboratively created at a low cost using local LLMs without relying on APIs. While this approach highlights the potential of local models, the experiments were limited to models with a maximum size of 70 billion parameters. Comparisons with state-of-the-art models, such as GPT-4 (Achiam et al., 2023), which are accessible through APIs, remain unexplored.

Future work should include evaluations using more powerful models like GPT-4 to better understand the upper bounds of performance in speaker identification tasks. Additionally, it is worth noting that for Japanese tasks, certain models like ELYZA-JP-8B and Swallow-3 have been reported to perform at levels comparable to GPT-4 in specific scenarios, suggesting that sufficiently high-performance models are available for meaningful comparisons. However, given the steady improvement in the performance of local LLMs, we believe that our evaluations provide a reasonably comprehensive assessment within the scope of this study.

Translation In this study, we created a dataset translated using GPT-4o-mini for the purpose of bi-lingual evaluations. However, we only performed format checks on the translations (see Appendix D). To further enhance the quality of the dataset, human evaluation is deemed necessary.

Vulnerability to Tokenizer Limitations During dataset creation, some words may not be tokenized effectively, potentially impacting the quality of the extracted contextual information. To address this vulnerability to tokenizer limitations, future work could explore using alternative, more comprehensive tokenizers with larger vocabularies. This approach could mitigate the risk of data omissions stemming from inadequate tokenization, leading to more complete and reliable contextual representations within the dataset.

9 Assurance of Research Ethics

Explanation to Annotators We ensured adherence to research ethics by providing comprehensive explanations to the annotators about the study. Additionally, once the annotation was completed, we anonymized the collected data and paid careful attention to protecting personal information.

Licenses and Approvals Furthermore, we verified the licenses for the artifacts, obtained the necessary approvals, and confirmed that our usage complies with the intended purposes.

Potential Misuse Risks and Mitigation While our study focuses on the development of speaker identification datasets for narrative analysis, we acknowledge the potential risks associated with misuse of the generated datasets or data generation approach. For instance, speaker identification systems could be misused to monitor conversations or infringe on individual privacy if applied inappropriately. To mitigate such risks, we emphasize that our research is intended solely for academic purposes and large-scale narrative analysis, and not for surveillance or other unethical applications.

Transparency and Accountability Additionally, the datasets and methodologies are designed with transparency and accountability in mind, ensuring that their usage aligns with ethical standards.

Content Warning for Violent Expressions This dataset contains stories written several decades ago, during a period when violent expressions and provocative language, including depictions of murder and aggressive behavior, were more commonplace. Users are advised to exercise caution and be mindful of the potentially disturbing content when utilizing this dataset.

References

Josh Achiam, Steven Adler, Sandhini Agarwal, Lama Ahmad, Ilge Akkaya, Florencia Leoni Aleman, Diogo Almeida, Janko Altenschmidt, Sam Altman, Shyamal Anadkat, et al. 2023. Gpt-4 technical report. *arXiv preprint arXiv:2303.08774*.

David Bamman, Ted Underwood, and Noah A. Smith. 2014. A Bayesian mixed effects model of literary character. In *Proceedings of the 52nd Annual Meeting of the Association for Computational Linguistics (Volume 1: Long Papers)*, pages 370–379, Baltimore, Maryland. Association for Computational Linguistics.

Lasse Bergroth, Harri Hakonen, and Timo Raita. 2000. A survey of longest common subsequence algorithms. In *Proceedings Seventh International Symposium on String Processing and Information Retrieval. SPIRE 2000*, pages 39–48. IEEE.

Jia-Xiang Chen, Zhen-Hua Ling, and Li-Rong Dai. 2019a. A Chinese Dataset for Identifying Speakers in Novels. In *Proc. Interspeech 2019*, pages 1561–1565.

Wei-Yu Chen, Yen-Cheng Liu, Zsolt Kira, Yu-Chiang Wang, and Jia-Bin Huang. 2019b. A closer look at few-shot classification. In *International Conference on Learning Representations*.

Jacob Cohen. 1960. A coefficient of agreement for nominal scales. *Educational and psychological measurement*, 20(1):37–46.

Carolina Cuesta-Lazaro, Animesh Prasad, and Trevor Wood. 2022. What does the sea say to the shore? a BERT based DST style approach for speaker to dialogue attribution in novels. In *Proceedings of the 60th Annual Meeting of the Association for Computational Linguistics (Volume 1: Long Papers)*, pages 5820–5829, Dublin, Ireland. Association for Computational Linguistics.

Jacob Devlin, Ming-Wei Chang, Kenton Lee, and Kristina Toutanova. 2019. BERT: Pre-training of deep bidirectional transformers for language understanding. In *Proceedings of the 2019 Conference of the North American Chapter of the Association for Computational Linguistics: Human Language Technologies, Volume 1 (Long and Short Papers)*, pages 4171–4186, Minneapolis, Minnesota. Association for Computational Linguistics.

Abhimanyu Dubey, Abhinav Jauhri, Abhinav Pandey, Abhishek Kadian, Ahmad Al-Dahle, Aiesha Letman, Akhil Mathur, Alan Schelten, Amy Yang, Angela Fan, Anirudh Goyal, Anthony Hartshorn, Aobo Yang, Archi Mitra, Archie Sravankumar, Artem Korenev, Arthur Hinsvark, Arun Rao, Aston Zhang, Aurelien Rodriguez, Austen Gregerson, Ava Spataru, Baptiste Roziere, Bethany Biron, Binh Tang, Bobbie Chern, Charlotte Caucheteux, Chaya Nayak, Chloe Bi, Chris Marra, Chris McConnell, Christian Keller, Christophe Touret, Chunyang Wu, Corinne Wong, Cristian Canton Ferrer, Cyrus Nikolaidis, Damien Allonsius, Daniel Song, Danielle Pintz, Danny Livshits, David Esiobu, Dhruv Choudhary, Dhruv Mahajan, Diego Garcia-Olano, Diego Perino, Dieuwke Hupkes, Egor Lakomkin, Ehab AlBadawy, Elina Lobanova, Emily Dinan, Eric Michael Smith, Filip Radenovic, Frank Zhang, Gabriel Synnaeve, Gabrielle Lee, Georgia Lewis Anderson, Graeme Nail, Gregoire Mialon, Guan Pang, Guillem Cucurell, Hailey Nguyen, Hannah Korevaar, Hu Xu, Hugo Touvron, Iliyan Zarov, Imanol Arrieta Ibarra, Isabel Kloumann, Ishan Misra, Ivan Evtimov, Jade Copet, Jaewon Lee, Jan Geffert, Jana Vranes, Jason Park, Jay Mahadeokar, Jeet Shah, Jelmer van der Linde, Jennifer Billock, Jenny Hong, Jenya Lee, Jeremy Fu, Jianfeng Chi, Jianyu Huang, Jiawen Liu, Jie Wang, Jiecao Yu, Joanna Bitton, Joe Spisak, Jongsoo Park, Joseph Rocca, Joshua Johnstun, Joshua Saxe, Junteng Jia, Kalyan Vasuden Alwala, Kartikeya Upasani, Kate Plawiak, Ke Li, Kenneth Heafield, Kevin Stone, Khalid El-Arini, Krithika Iyer, Kshitiz Malik, Kuenley Chiu, Kunal Bhalla, Lauren Rantala-Yeary, Laurens van der Maaten, Lawrence Chen, Liang Tan, Liz Jenkins, Louis Martin, Lovish Madaan, Lubo Malo, Lukas Blecher, Lukas Landzaat, Luke de Oliveira, Madeline Muzzi, Mahesh Pasupuleti, Mannat Singh, Manohar Paluri, Marcin Kardas, Mathew Oldham, Mathieu Rita, Maya Pavlova, Melanie Kambadur, Mike Lewis, Min Si, Mitesh Kumar Singh, Mona Hassan, Naman Goyal, Narjes Torabi, Nikolay Bashlykov, Nikolay Bogoychev, Niladri Chatterji, Olivier Duchenne, Onur Çelebi, Patrick Alrassy, Pengchuan Zhang, Pengwei Li, Petar Vasic, Peter Weng, Prajjwal Bhargava, Pratik Dubal, Praveen Krishnan, Punit Singh Koura, Puxin Xu, Qing He, Qingxiao Dong, Ragavan Srinivasan, Raj Ganapathy, Ramon Calderer, Ricardo Silveira Cabral, Robert Stojnic, Roberta Raileanu, Rohit Girdhar, Rohit Patel, Romain Sauvestre, Ronnie Polidoro, Roshan Sumbaly, Ross Taylor, Ruan Silva, Rui Hou, Rui Wang, Saghar Hosseini, Sahana Chennabasappa, Sanjay Singh, Sean Bell, Seohyun Sonia Kim, Sergey Edunov, Shaoliang Nie, Sharan Narang, Sharath Raparthy, Sheng Shen, Shengye Wan, Shruti Bhosale, Shun Zhang, Simon Vandenhende, Soumya Batra, Spencer Whitman, Sten Sootla, Stephane Collot, Suchin Gururangan, Sydney Borodinsky, Tamar Herman, Tara Fowler, Tarek Sheasha, Thomas Georgiou, Thomas Scialom, Tobias Speckbacher, Todor Mihaylov, Tong Xiao, Ujjwal Karn, Vedanuj Goswami, Vibhor Gupta, Vignesh Ramanathan, Viktor Kerkez, Vincent Gonguet, Virginie Do, Vish Vogeti, Vladan Petrovic, Weiwei Chu, Wenhan Xiong, Wenyin Fu, Whitney Meers, Xavier Martinet, Xiaodong Wang, Xiaoqing Ellen Tan, Xinfeng Xie, Xuchao Jia, Xuewei Wang,

Yaelle Goldschlag, Yashesh Gaur, Yasmine Babaei, Yi Wen, Yiwen Song, Yuchen Zhang, Yue Li, Yuning Mao, Zacharie Delpierre Coudert, Zheng Yan, Zhengxing Chen, Zoe Papakipos, Aaditya Singh, Aaron Grattafiori, Abha Jain, Adam Kelsey, Adam Shajnfeld, Adithya Gangidi, Adolfo Victoria, Ahuva Goldstand, Ajay Menon, Ajay Sharma, Alex Boesenberg, Alex Vaughan, Alexei Baevski, Allie Feinstein, Amanda Kallet, Amit Sangani, Anam Yunus, Andrei Lupu, Andres Alvarado, Andrew Caples, Andrew Gu, Andrew Ho, Andrew Poulton, Andrew Ryan, Ankit Ramchandani, Annie Franco, Aparajita Saraf, Arkabandhu Chowdhury, Ashley Gabriel, Ashwin Bharambe, Assaf Eisenman, Azadeh Yazdan, Beau James, Ben Maurer, Benjamin Leonhardi, Bernie Huang, Beth Loyd, Beto De Paola, Bhargavi Paranjape, Bing Liu, Bo Wu, Boyu Ni, Braden Hancock, Bram Wasti, Brandon Spence, Brani Stojkovic, Brian Gamido, Britt Montalvo, Carl Parker, Carly Burton, Catalina Mejia, Changhan Wang, Changkyu Kim, Chao Zhou, Chester Hu, Ching-Hsiang Chu, Chris Cai, Chris Tindal, Christoph Feichtenhofer, Damon Civin, Dana Beaty, Daniel Kreymer, Daniel Li, Danny Wyatt, David Adkins, David Xu, Davide Testuggine, Delia David, Devi Parikh, Diana Liskovich, Didem Foss, Dingkang Wang, Duc Le, Dustin Holland, Edward Dowling, Eissa Jamil, Elaine Montgomery, Eleonora Presani, Emily Hahn, Emily Wood, Erik Brinkman, Esteban Arcaute, Evan Dunbar, Evan Smothers, Fei Sun, Felix Kreuk, Feng Tian, Firat Ozgenel, Francesco Caggioni, Francisco Guzmán, Frank Kanayet, Frank Seide, Gabriela Medina Florez, Gabriella Schwarz, Gada Badeer, Georgia Swee, Gil Halpern, Govind Thattai, Grant Herman, Grigory Sizov, Guangyi, Zhang, Guna Lakshminarayanan, Hamid Shojanazeri, Han Zou, Hannah Wang, Hanwen Zha, Haroun Habeeb, Harrison Rudolph, Helen Suk, Henry Aspegren, Hunter Goldman, Igor Molybog, Igor Tufanov, Irina-Elena Veliche, Itai Gat, Jake Weissman, James Geboski, James Kohli, Japhet Asher, Jean-Baptiste Gaya, Jeff Marcus, Jeff Tang, Jennifer Chan, Jenny Zhen, Jeremy Reizenstein, Jeremy Teboul, Jessica Zhong, Jian Jin, Jingyi Yang, Joe Cummings, Jon Carvill, Jon Shepard, Jonathan McPhie, Jonathan Torres, Josh Ginsburg, Junjie Wang, Kai Wu, Kam Hou U, Karan Saxena, Karthik Prasad, Kartikay Khandelwal, Katayoun Zand, Kathy Matosich, Kaushik Veeraraghavan, Kelly Michelena, Keqian Li, Kun Huang, Kunal Chawla, Kushal Lakhotia, Kyle Huang, Lailin Chen, Lakshya Garg, Lavender A, Leandro Silva, Lee Bell, Lei Zhang, Liangpeng Guo, Licheng Yu, Liron Moshkovich, Luca Wehrstedt, Madian Khabsa, Manav Avalani, Manish Bhatt, Maria Tsimpoukelli, Martynas Mankus, Matan Hasson, Matthew Lennie, Matthias Reso, Maxim Groshev, Maxim Naumov, Maya Lathi, Meghan Keneally, Michael L. Seltzer, Michal Valko, Michelle Restrepo, Mihir Patel, Mik Vyatskov, Mikayel Samvelyan, Mike Clark, Mike Macey, Mike Wang, Miquel Jubert Hermoso, Mo Metanat, Mohammad Rastegari, Munish Bansal, Nandhini Santhanam, Natascha Parks, Natasha White, Navyata Bawa, Nayan Singhal, Nick Egebo, Nicolas Usunier, Nikolay Pavlovich Laptev, Ning Dong, Ning Zhang, Norman Cheng, Oleg Chernoguz, Olivia Hart, Omkar Salpekar, Ozlem Kalinli, Parkin Kent, Parth Parekh, Paul Saab, Pavan Balaji, Pedro Rittner, Philip Bontrager, Pierre Roux, Piotr Dollar, Polina Zvyagina, Prashant Ratanchandani, Pritish Yuvraj, Qian Liang, Rachad Alao, Rachel Rodriguez, Rafi Ayub, Raghotham Murthy, Raghu Nayani, Rahul Mitra, Raymond Li, Rebekkah Hogan, Robin Battey, Rocky Wang, Rohan Maheswari, Russ Howes, Ruty Rinott, Sai Jayesh Bondu, Samyak Datta, Sara Chugh, Sara Hunt, Sargun Dhillon, Sasha Sidorov, Satadru Pan, Saurabh Verma, Seiji Yamamoto, Sharadh Ramaswamy, Shaun Lindsay, Shaun Lindsay, Sheng Feng, Shenghao Lin, Shengxin Cindy Zha, Shiva Shankar, Shuqiang Zhang, Shuqiang Zhang, Sinong Wang, Sneha Agarwal, Soji Sajuyigbe, Soumith Chintala, Stephanie Max, Stephen Chen, Steve Kehoe, Steve Satterfield, Sudarshan Govindaprasad, Sumit Gupta, Sungmin Cho, Sunny Virk, Suraj Subramanian, Sy Choudhury, Sydney Goldman, Tal Remez, Tamar Glaser, Tamara Best, Thilo Kohler, Thomas Robinson, Tianhe Li, Tianjun Zhang, Tim Matthews, Timothy Chou, Tzook Shaked, Varun Vontimitta, Victoria Ajayi, Victoria Montanez, Vijai Mohan, Vinay Satish Kumar, Vishal Mangla, Vlad Ionescu, Vlad Poenaru, Vlad Tiberiu Mihailescu, Vladimir Ivanov, Wei Li, Wenchen Wang, Wenwen Jiang, Wes Bouaziz, Will Constable, Xiaocheng Tang, Xiaofang Wang, Xiaojian Wu, Xiaolan Wang, Xide Xia, Xilun Wu, Xinbo Gao, Yanjun Chen, Ye Hu, Ye Jia, Ye Qi, Yenda Li, Yilin Zhang, Ying Zhang, Yossi Adi, Youngjin Nam, Yu, Wang, Yuchen Hao, Yundi Qian, Yuzi He, Zach Rait, Zachary DeVito, Zef Rosnbrick, Zhaoduo Wen, Zhenyu Yang, and Zhiwei Zhao. 2024. The llama 3 herd of models. *Preprint*, arXiv:2407.21783.

David Elson and Kathleen McKeown. 2010. Automatic attribution of quoted speech in literary narrative. *Proceedings of the AAAI Conference on Artificial Intelligence*, 24(1):1013–1019.

Kazuki Fujii. 2024. Llama-3-swallow.

Kazuki Fujii, Taishi Nakamura, Mengsay Loem, Hiroki Iida, Masanari Ohi, Kakeru Hattori, Hirai Shota, Sakae Mizuki, Rio Yokota, and Naoaki Okazaki. 2024. Continual pre-training for cross-lingual llm adaptation: Enhancing japanese language capabilities. *Preprint*, arXiv:2404.17790.

Ulrich Germann. 2003. Greedy decoding for statistical machine translation in almost linear time. In *Proceedings of the 2003 Conference of the North American Chapter of the Association for Computational Linguistics on Human Language Technology - Volume 1*, NAACL '03, page 1 – 8, USA. Association for Computational Linguistics.

Rakuten Group, Aaron Levine, Connie Huang, Chenguang Wang, Eduardo Batista, Ewa Szymanska, Hongyi Ding, Hou Wei Chou, Jean-François Pessiot, Johanes Effendi, Justin Chiu, Kai Torben

Ohlhus, Karan Chopra, Keiji Shinzato, Koji Murakami, Lee Xiong, Lei Chen, Maki Kubota, Maksim Tkachenko, Miroku Lee, Naoki Takahashi, Prathyusha Jwalapuram, Ryutaro Tatsushima, Saurabh Jain, Sunil Kumar Yadav, Ting Cai, Wei-Te Chen, Yandi Xia, Yuki Nakayama, and Yutaka Higashiyama. 2024. Rakutenai-7b: Extending large language models for japanese. *Preprint*, arXiv:2403.15484.

Hua He, Denilson Barbosa, and Grzegorz Kondrak. 2013. Identification of speakers in novels. In *Proceedings of the 51st Annual Meeting of the Association for Computational Linguistics (Volume 1: Long Papers)*, pages 1312–1320, Sofia, Bulgaria. Association for Computational Linguistics.

Dan Hendrycks, Collin Burns, Steven Basart, Andy Zou, Mantas Mazeika, Dawn Song, and Jacob Steinhardt. 2021. Measuring massive multitask language understanding. In *International Conference on Learning Representations*.

Masato Hirakawa, Shintaro Horie, Tomoaki Nakamura, Daisuke Oba, Sam Passaglia, and Akira Sasaki. 2024. elyza/llama-3-elyza-jp-8b.

KARAKURI Inc. 2024. KARAKURI LM 8x7B Instruct v0.1.

Ryosuke Ishigami. 2024. cyberagent/calm3-22b-chat.

Albert Q Jiang, Alexandre Sablayrolles, Arthur Mensch, Chris Bamford, Devendra Singh Chaplot, Diego de las Casas, Florian Bressand, Gianna Lengyel, Guillaume Lample, Lucile Saulnier, et al. 2023. Mistral 7b. *arXiv preprint arXiv:2310.06825*.

Albert Q. Jiang, Alexandre Sablayrolles, Antoine Roux, Arthur Mensch, Blanche Savary, Chris Bamford, Devendra Singh Chaplot, Diego de las Casas, Emma Bou Hanna, Florian Bressand, Gianna Lengyel, Guillaume Bour, Guillaume Lample, Lélio Renard Lavaud, Lucile Saulnier, Marie-Anne Lachaux, Pierre Stock, Sandeep Subramanian, Sophia Yang, Szymon Antoniak, Teven Le Scao, Théophile Gervet, Thibaut Lavril, Thomas Wang, Timothée Lacroix, and William El Sayed. 2024. Mixtral of experts. *Preprint*, arXiv:2401.04088.

Vladimir I Levenshtein et al. 1966. Binary codes capable of correcting deletions, insertions, and reversals. In *Soviet physics doklady*, volume 10, pages 707–710. Soviet Union.

Mike Lewis, Yinhan Liu, Naman Goyal, Marjan Ghazvininejad, Abdelrahman Mohamed, Omer Levy, Veselin Stoyanov, and Luke Zettlemoyer. 2020. BART: Denoising sequence-to-sequence pre-training for natural language generation, translation, and comprehension. In *Proceedings of the 58th Annual Meeting of the Association for Computational Linguistics*, pages 7871–7880, Online. Association for Computational Linguistics.

Gaspard Michel, Elena V. Epure, Romain Hennequin, and Christophe Cerisara. 2024. A realistic evaluation of llms for quotation attribution in literary texts: A case study of llama3. *Preprint*, arXiv:2406.11380.

Koh Mitsuda, Xinqi Chen, Toshiaki Wakatsuki, and Kei Sawada. rinna/llama-3-youko-8b.

Grace Muzny, Michael Fang, Angel Chang, and Dan Jurafsky. 2017. A two-stage sieve approach for quote attribution. In *Proceedings of the 15th Conference of the European Chapter of the Association for Computational Linguistics: Volume 1, Long Papers*, pages 460–470, Valencia, Spain. Association for Computational Linguistics.

Long Ouyang, Jeffrey Wu, Xu Jiang, Diogo Almeida, Carroll Wainwright, Pamela Mishkin, Chong Zhang, Sandhini Agarwal, Katarina Slama, Alex Ray, et al. 2022. Training language models to follow instructions with human feedback. *Advances in Neural Information Processing Systems*, 35:27730–27744.

Andrew Piper, Richard Jean So, and David Bamman. 2021. Narrative theory for computational narrative understanding. In *Proceedings of the 2021 Conference on Empirical Methods in Natural Language Processing*, pages 298–311, Online and Punta Cana, Dominican Republic. Association for Computational Linguistics.

Zhenlin Su, Liyan Xu, Jin Xu, Jiangnan Li, and Mingdu Huangfu. 2024. Sig: Speaker identification in literature via prompt-based generation. *Proceedings of the AAAI Conference on Artificial Intelligence*, 38(17):19035–19043.

Zhen Tan, Dawei Li, Song Wang, Alimohammad Beigi, Bohan Jiang, Amrita Bhattacharjee, Mansooreh Karami, Jundong Li, Lu Cheng, and Huan Liu. 2024. Large language models for data annotation: A survey. *Preprint*, arXiv:2402.13446.

Krishnapriya Vishnubhotla, Adam Hammond, and Graeme Hirst. 2022. The project dialogism novel corpus: A dataset for quotation attribution in literary texts. In *Proceedings of the Thirteenth Language Resources and Evaluation Conference*, pages 5838–5848, Marseille, France. European Language Resources Association.

Krishnapriya Vishnubhotla, Frank Rudzicz, Graeme Hirst, and Adam Hammond. 2023. Improving automatic quotation attribution in literary novels. In *Proceedings of the 61st Annual Meeting of the Association for Computational Linguistics (Volume 2: Short Papers)*, pages 737–746, Toronto, Canada. Association for Computational Linguistics.

Tianyi Zhang*, Varsha Kishore*, Felix Wu*, Kilian Q. Weinberger, and Yoav Artzi. 2020. Bertscore: Evaluating text generation with bert. In *International Conference on Learning Representations*.

Wayne Xin Zhao, Kun Zhou, Junyi Li, Tianyi Tang, Xiaolei Wang, Yupeng Hou, Yingqian Min, Beichen Zhang, Junjie Zhang, Zican Dong, et al. 2023a. A survey of large language models. *arXiv preprint arXiv:2303.18223*.

Zirui Zhao, Wee Sun Lee, and David Hsu. 2023b. Large language models as commonsense knowledge for large-scale task planning. In *Thirty-seventh Conference on Neural Information Processing Systems*.

A Substring Match Ratio Evaluation Method

The substring match ratio evaluates whether the true speaker name, as annotated, exists as a substring within the predicted speaker name. This evaluation metric is mathematically formalized as follows:

Definitions In a given dialogue dataset, we define the speaker names as follows:

- P_i: Predicted speaker name
- T_i: Annotated true speaker name

We define the match function M as:

$$M(P_i, T_i) = \begin{cases} 1 & \text{if there exists an integer } j \\ & \text{such that } 0 \leq j \leq |P_i| - |T_i| \\ & \text{and } P_i[j : j + |T_i|] = T_i \\ 0 & \text{otherwise} \end{cases}$$

Calculation of Substring Match Ratio The substring match ratio for the entire dataset is calculated as the proportion of dialogues where the true speaker name is a substring of the predicted speaker name. Formally, it is defined as:

$$r_s = \frac{1}{n} \sum_{i=1}^{n} M(P_i, T_i)$$

where $n \in \mathbb{N}$ is the total number of lines.

Calculation Steps

1. For each dialogue i, check if the true speaker name T_i is a substring of the predicted speaker name P_i.
2. Assign $M(P_i, T_i) = 1$ if T_i is a substring of P_i; otherwise, assign $M(P_i, T_i) = 0$.
3. Calculate the sum of all $M(P_i, T_i)$ values and divide by the total number of dialogues n.

Example Consider three dialogues with the following predicted and true speaker names:

- P_1 = "John Smith", T_1 = "John"
- P_2 = "Alice", T_2 = "Bob"
- P_3 = "Charlie Brown", T_3 = "Charlie"

The substring matches are calculated as follows:

$$M(P_1, T_1) = 1,$$
$$M(P_2, T_2) = 0,$$
$$M(P_3, T_3) = 1$$

Thus, the substring match ratio is calculated as:

$$r_s = \frac{1}{3}(1 + 0 + 1) = \frac{2}{3} \approx 0.67$$

Using the substring match ratio, we can evaluate how accurately the predicted speaker names contain the true speaker names as substrings.

Particularly, LLMs often generate unnecessary texts, such as special tokens like "[INST]" and unrelated tokens.

B Detailed Dataset Construction Process

Data Extraction The data was meticulously extracted from *Aozora Bunko's "Romance of the Three Kingdoms"* using the Huggingface datasets[4] library. This curated dataset includes furigana and metadata, and was selected for its extensive character list and the potential to extract complex relationships.

Development and Evaluation Sets The dataset was split into development and evaluation sets as follows:

- Volume 02: Peach Garden Oath (Shinjitai, Book ID: 52410) served as the development set.
- Volume 03: Among the Stars (Shinjitai, Book ID: 52411) to Volume 11: Wuzhang Plains (Shinjitai, Book ID: 52419) constituted the evaluation set.

[4]https://huggingface.co/datasets/globis-university/aozorabunko-clean

Token Count Variations Figure 5 shows the maximum input token count per book_id, confirming that the actual number of input tokens in this study falls within 8,192 tokens when converted using the LLaMA 3 Tokenizer. As illustrated in Figure 5, this study employed the LLaMA 2 Tokenizer to extract the preceding and following 1,024 tokens, thereby creating context tokens. Among the tokenizers used in the comparative models, the most commonly utilized base tokenizer was the LLaMA 3 Tokenizer.

Furthermore, Figure 6 demonstrates the variation in token count per index for book_id=052415, which had the highest number of input tokens. Excluding a few exceptionally long dialogue examples, almost all token counts were distributed around 2,250 tokens using the LLaMA 2 Tokenizer and around 1,500 tokens using the LLaMA 3 Tokenizer.

Reducing the length of the input context or randomly masking it was confirmed to significantly decrease identification accuracy (see Section 5.5 and Section 5.5). Therefore, to solve this task with high accuracy, it is necessary to process a sufficiently long context of at least 1,500 tokens using the LLaMA 3 Tokenizer.

This indicates that the number of tokens handled is extremely large compared to the methods used for evaluating the performance of existing LLMs, such as MMLU (Hendrycks et al., 2021) and Commonsense (Zhao et al., 2023b). By addressing this task, it is believed that we can measure the inference performance of LLMs with respect to long contexts.

Additionally, in this study, the dataset length was set to fit within the maximum input token count of 8,192 tokens, which is the limit for the models used in comparison. For identification tasks using similar methods, simply increasing the length of the input context or simultaneously targeting multiple lines for speaker identification could easily extend the evaluation to tasks requiring longer contexts, such as those involving 100,000 tokens.

Number of Tokens and Speakers Table 9 summarizes the number of tokens, utterances, and characters for each story.

In this table, "Tokens (LLaMA-3, JA)" and "Tokens (LLaMA-3, EN)" indicate the number of tokens in the Japanese and English versions of each story, respectively. Similarly, "Lines (JA)" and "Lines (EN)" represent the number of utterances in Japanese and English, respectively.

C Constructing a Bi-lingual Dataset via Crawling

Bi-lingual Dataset Creation To explore the applicability of this approach to other stories and languages, we expanded our research to include bilingual datasets developed from Wikisource[5] and Aozora Bunko, covering 14 diverse narratives in two languages. This approach offers a flexible and scalable framework for narrative analysis across various languages and cultural contexts, enhancing speaker identification by capturing the complexity of character references.

Bi-lingual Performance Figure 7 shows the substring match ratio for speaker identification using the `LLaMA-3-70B-Instruct` model on Japanese and English datasets. The model achieved higher accuracy on Japanese data, likely due to fewer label variations compared to English.

The Japanese dataset, composed mainly of simple folktales, exhibits fewer variations in referring terms. In contrast, the English dataset includes multiple synonyms for the same names, affecting the results. For example, the Japanese term "お母さん" in "matsuyama_kagami" is translated into various English terms, such as "Woman," "Mother," and "Wife".

This suggests that, as noted in Section 5.4, preparing candidate sets for main names could reduce discrepancies. Additionally, to address case sensitivity issues in English, we introduced an Uncased Exact Match approach for more accurate evaluation (see Appendix L).

D Constructing a Bi-lingual Dataset via Translation

To broaden the applicability of our dataset and facilitate bilingual analysis, we translated the Japanese portions of *Romance of the Three Kingdoms* into English using the GPT-4o-mini model,[6] significantly reducing the time and cost associated with manual annotation.

This distinction clarifies that the bi-lingual datasets from Wikisource and Aozora Bunko use professional translations, while the "Romance of

[5] `https://wikisource.org/wiki/Main_Page`

[6] `https://platform.openai.com/docs/models` A smaller variant of GPT-4 with reduced computational requirements.

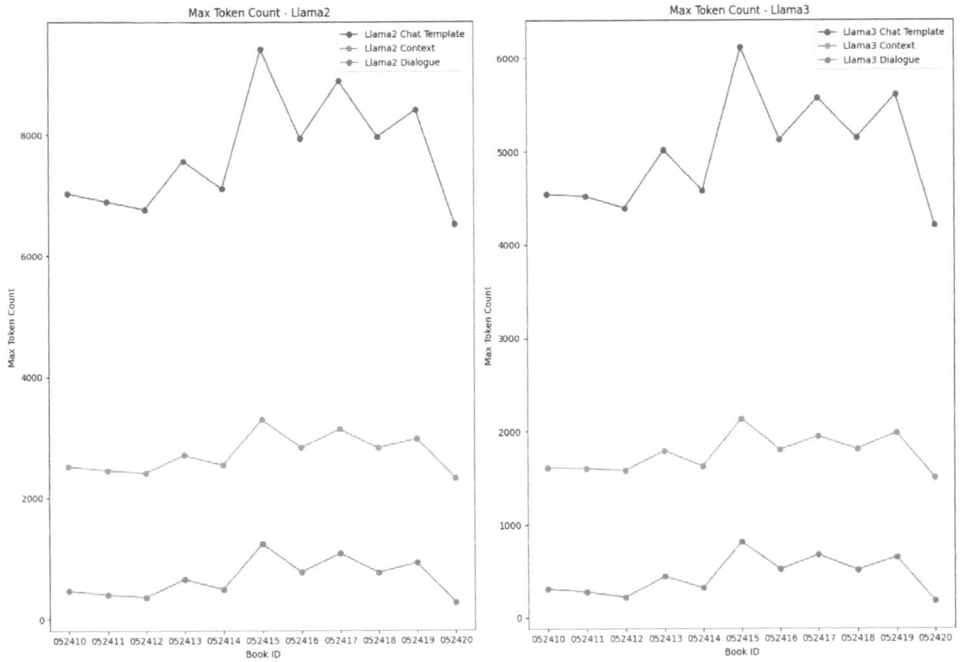

Figure 5: The Chat Template indicates the maximum token count when including tokens that control few-shots and prompt format. Context shows the maximum token count when inferring speaker names and combining the target dialogue with the preceding and following 1,024 tokens. Dialogue shows the maximum token count for the dialogue itself.

the Three Kingdoms" dataset relies on machine-translated content for exploratory purposes.

D.1 Translation Process and Quality Assurance

We followed a translation strategy similar to that used for speaker identification, employing few-shot prompts and incorporating failure cases for robustness (see Table 12). The translation covered 3,348 instances (book_id=052410, 052411), producing 1,574 entries for `book_id=052410` and 1,528 entries for `book_id=052411`.

We applied three main quality checks:

- **Language Accuracy:** Ensuring the translated text was correctly in English.
- **Dialogue Inclusion:** Confirming that each translated dialogue was present within the translated context.
- **Speaker Name Inclusion:** Verifying that translated speaker names appeared correctly in the translated context.

If any criterion was not met, we allowed up to five retries. Cases where the model responded with an inability message (e.g., "I'm sorry, but I can't...") were discarded. Additionally, for dialogues not found in the translated context, we employed the longest common subsequence algorithm (Bergroth et al., 2000) to match them with the closest translation. Only entries passing all checks were retained in the final dataset.

E Case Studies and Challenging Examples

E.1 Original Japanese Text of Case Study

Table 5 presents the original Japanese text of the case study discussed (see Section 5.5).

E.2 Further Case Study

Table 6 shows that `ELYZA-JP-8B` had already read these datasets during the training steps.

This finding indicates that the `ELYZA-JP-8B` model may have leveraged learned patterns or relationships to make accurate predictions even when the context is heavily Masked.

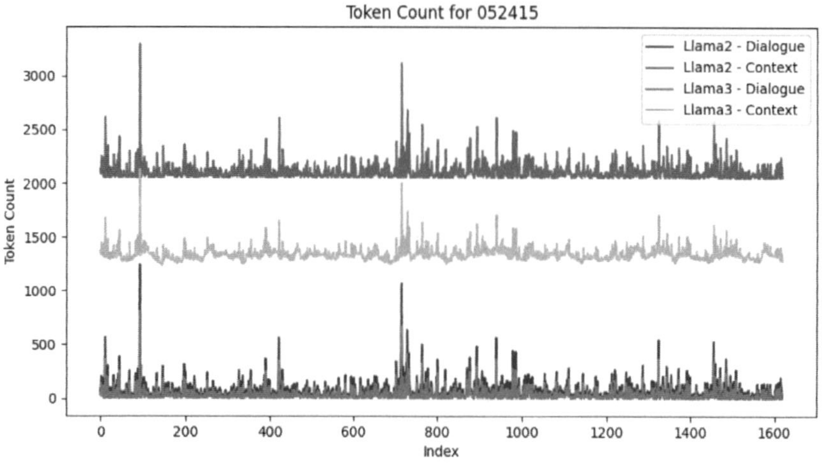

Figure 6: Variation in token count per index for book_id=052415. Excluding exceptionally long dialogues, most token counts are distributed around 2,250 tokens based on the LLaMA 2 Tokenizer and around 1,500 tokens based on the LLaMA 3 Tokenizer.

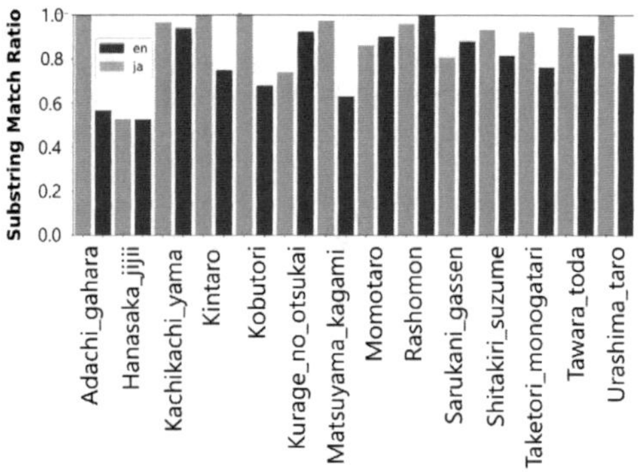

Figure 7: Substring match ratio comparison across stories in Japanese and English datasets, based on results from the `LLaMA-3-70B-Instruct` model.

F Annotation Settings

F.1 Annotation Rules

The following annotation rules were applied for label assignment:

1. As a general principle, the smallest constituent part of a character's name used in the narrative text is considered the correct label. (Example: For "劉備玄徳", "玄徳" is the correct label.)
2. When multiple candidates exist, the given name is preferred if it is present in the context.
3. If the text is not a dialogue, label it as 'Unknown'. (Examples: characters, narrator, book titles)
4. If multiple speakers are indicated for a single utterance, label it as 'Unknown'. (Examples: Guan Yu, Zhao Yun, Liu Bei)
5. Due to the high preparation cost, dynamic generation based on reading the context is preferred, as annotators had prior access to speaker information.
6. Each utterance, along with the preceding and following 1,024 tokens, is set as the context. Only the names found within this context are subject to annotation. The number of tokens is calculated based on the LLaMA-2 Tokenizer[7].
7. If multiple names representing a single person appear in the context, the most appropriate one is labeled as the "main name," while other possible names are labeled as "candidates."
8. List candidates for each main name in a dictionary format. Include various expressions, such as courtesy names or official titles, in the candidates list.

[7] `https://huggingface.co/meta-llama/Llama-2-7b-hf`

Case	line	excerpt context	pred	true
A	あははは	楊彪は秘策を胸にねりながら、わが邸へ帰って行った。帰るとすぐ、彼は妻の室へはいって、「どうだな。この頃は、郭汜の令夫人とも、時々お目にかかるかね。……おまえたち奥さん連ばかりで、よく色々な会があるとのことだが」と、両手を妻の肩にのせながら、いつになく優しい良人になって云った。二 楊彪の妻は怪しんで、良人を揶揄した。「あなた。どうしたんですか、いったい今日は」「なにが？」「だって、常には、私に対して、こんなに機嫌をとるあなたではありませんもの」「あははは」「かえって、気味が悪い」「そうかい」	楊彪	楊彪
B	江東の地	呉は、大江の流れに沿うて、「江東の地」と称われている。	不明（ナレーション）	Unknown
C	…………	貂蝉は、さわぐ色もなく、すぐ答えた。「はい。大人のおたのみなら、いつでもこの生命は捧げます」王允は、座を正して、「では、おまえの真心を見込んで頼みたいことがあるが」「なんですか」「董卓を殺さねばならん」「…………」「彼を除かなければ、漢室の天子はあってもないのと同じだ」「…………」	貂蝉	貂蝉
D	人生の快、ここに尽くる	夜は、牛馬を宰して、聚議の大歓宴が設けられた。「人生の快、ここに尽くる」関羽、張飛がいうと、「何でこれに尽きよう。これからである」と、玄徳はいった。	関羽、張飛	Unknown
E	玄徳様、ふたりの熱望です。ご承知くださるまいか	たほうがよい」 「玄徳様、ふたりの熱望です。ご承知くださるまいか」 左右から	関羽	関羽

Table 5: Original Case Study in Japanese. 'pred' indicates the predicted speaker label, and 'true' indicates the annotated speaker label.

id	line	excerpt context	pred	true
1869	ですから、父上のお顔で、富豪を紹介して下さい。曹家は、財産こそないが、遠くは夏侯氏の流れを汲み、漢の丞相曹参の末流です。この名門の名を利用して、富豪から金を出させて下さい		曹操	曹操

Table 6: Correct Identification of an Absent Name：ELYZA-JP-8B accurately predicts the name "曹操," despite it not being present in the context.

For each main name, the presence of candidates in the context is checked, and a set of potential names is automatically generated.

F.2 Detailed Quality Assessment of Annotations

In this study, all annotations were independently performed by the first author, making it impossible to directly evaluate inter-annotator agreement. To verify the quality of the created annotations, we randomly selected 100 samples from the evaluation dataset and asked three independent annotators to review them.

The annotators were tasked with evaluating the labeled speaker names as "appropriate," "inappropriate," or "cannot judge". We assigned weights to these evaluations: 3 points for "appropriate," 2 points for "cannot judge," and 1 point for "inappropriate". The agreement was calculated based on these weighted scores using a three-point Likert scale.

The results showed that two annotators had an agreement rate of 0.97, and one annotator had an agreement rate of 0.96, indicating a very high level of consistency. This suggests that the dataset constructed in this study is of high quality.

Typically, Cohen's kappa coefficient (Cohen, 1960) is used to evaluate inter-annotator agreement. However, in this case, the agreement rates were so high that setting the original data labels to 3 when calculating the kappa coefficient could lead to undefined values. Therefore, we report only the agreement rate and its variance (see Appendix F.3 for details).

Additionally, the annotation task required an average of 2 hours per annotator, with a compensation rate set at 1,000 yen per hour. The annotations were performed by three native Japanese graduate students, selected for their advanced language proficiency, further contributing to the reliability and accuracy of the data.

Metric	Annotator ID		
	A	B	C
Agreement Rate	0.97	0.97	0.96
Count (3)	97	97	96
Count (2)	3	2	3
Count (1)	0	1	1
Total	100	100	100
Weighted Average Score	2.97	2.96	2.95

Table 7: Annotation agreement and evaluation distribution by annotator. The "Agreement Rate" represents the proportion of cases where independent evaluators marked the data as "appropriate" (3) when the author had labeled it as 3 in the dataset. The "Count (x)" rows indicate the number of times each annotator selected "appropriate" (3), "neutral" (2), or "inappropriate" (1). The "Total" row indicates that each annotator evaluated 100 cases. The "Weighted Average Score" reflects the average score calculated by assigning weights of 3, 2, and 1 to the respective categories.

F.3 Challenging Cases in Annotation Judgment

Table 8 presents examples where annotation decisions were particularly challenging.

Examining the final portion of the context in Table A, it is evident that the character "張飛" strongly asserts that "呂布" must be defeated. This suggests that the preceding conversation was primarily conducted by "玄徳" and "張飛". Therefore, considering the immediate context, it is highly likely that the line in question was spoken by "張飛".

However, reading the previous tokens reveals that the line "何事を曹操からいってよこしたのですか" could be attributed to both "張飛" and "関羽". Consequently, there is a slight possibility that "関羽" could have responded to "玄徳"' s statement, "まあ、これを見るがいい".

Two of the independent annotators employed to assess annotation quality provided feedback suggesting that the possibility of "関羽" being the speaker could not be entirely ruled out. Such cases, where reaching a consensus on the speaker annotation was extremely difficult, were reported by the annotators three or four times per 100 cases.

G Model Description

The selection criteria for each model aim to comprehensively evaluate performance across various languages and tasks, adaptation to Japanese data, and differences between architectures. This allows for a multifaceted assessment of LLM performance.

In this study, we selected 12 models for comparison, organized into six categories. Below is a description of each model and the rationale for its selection.

LLaMA-3 (Dubey et al., 2024) LLaMA-3 is an LLM that considers human preferences, demonstrating high performance in various tasks such as bi-lingual support, coding, and mathematics. It is also used as a base model for many other models, making it suitable for comparative validation.

Swallow-3 (Fujii et al., 2024) Swallow-3 is a model based on LLaMA-3 that has undergone continual pretraining and instruction tuning with Japanese data. It was selected to analyze changes in Japanese performance and potential performance degradation in English data relative to LLaMA-3.

ELYZA-JP-8B (Hirakawa et al., 2024) ELYZA-JP-8B is a model based on LLaMA-3 that has undergone continual pretraining and instruction tuning with Japanese data. We selected this model to evaluate whether instruction tuning leads to differences when compared to Swallow-3.

llama-3-youko-8B (Mitsuda et al.) llama-3-youko-8B is a model based on LLaMA-3 that has undergone continual pretraining using a mixture of Japanese and English datasets.

Mistral-7B (Jiang et al., 2023) Mistral-7B, like LLaMA-3, is frequently used for comparisons with other models and is known for its high performance despite its smaller size. It was selected to compare a model from a different lineage to LLaMA-3.

RakutenAI-7B (Group et al., 2024) RakutenAI-7B is a model fine-tuned with Japanese data based on Mistral 7B. It was selected to compare the performance of models fine-tuned with Japanese data, similar to Swallow-3.

CALM-3-22B (Ishigami, 2024) CALM-3-22B is an LLM primarily trained on proprietary Japanese data. It was selected to compare the performance of models that mainly handle Japanese data with those that support multiple languages, primarily focusing on English.

id	line	excerpt context	true	corr	incor	neu
3818	呂布を殺せという密命ですな	何度も、繰返し繰返し読み直していると、後ろに立っていた張飛、関羽のふたりが、「何事を曹操からいってよこしたのですか」と、訊ねた。 「まあ、これを見るがいい」 **「呂布を殺せという密命ですな」** 「そうじゃ」 「呂布は、兇勇のみで、もともと義も欠けている人間ですから、曹操のさしずをよい機として、この際、殺してしまうがよいでしょう」 「いや、彼はたのむ所がなくて、わが懐に投じてきた窮鳥だ。それを殺すは、飼禽を縊るようなもの。玄徳こそ、義のない人間といわれよう」 「——が、不義の漢を生かしておけば、ろくなことはしませんぞ。国に及ぼす害は、誰が責めを負いますか」 「次第に、義に富む人間となるように、温情をもって導いてゆく」 「そうやすやす、善人になれるものですか」 張飛は、あくまでも、呂布討つべしと主張したが、玄徳は、従う色もなかった。	張飛	1	0	2

Table 8: Challenging Annotation Example. 'true' indicates the predicted speaker label. 'corr' indicates the number of annotators who judged the annotated label to be correct, 'incor' indicates those who judged it to be incorrect, and 'neu' indicates those who judged it to be neutral. This example illustrates a difficult case where the three independent annotators had differing opinions, highlighting the complexity and subjectivity involved in the annotation process.

Karakuri-8x7B (Inc., 2024) Karakuri-8x7B is a model that uses a Mixture of Experts (MoE) approach by combining multiple models for more effective inference, specifically Mixtral-8x7B (Jiang et al., 2024), and has undergone continual pre-training and fine-tuning with Japanese data. It was selected to compare MoE models with other LLMs.

H Inference and Evaluation Setup

In this study, we set the random seed at 42 and performed 4-bit quantization for model inference. We used the Greedy Decoding Algorithm (Germann, 2003) for decoding. Inference was conducted using an A6000 GPU, with a total inference time of approximately 200 hours.

During evaluation, unnecessary strings, such as special tokens [INST] generated by the LLM, were removed using regular expressions wherever possible.

Additionally, various libraries were utilized for inference, evaluation, and visualization. For example, we employed scikit-learn[8], transformers[9], beautifulsoup4[10], tiktoken[11], openai[12], evaluate[13], accelerate[14], torch[15], datasets[16], and matplotlib[17].

I Prompt Configuration

Predict Quoted Utterance Table 10 shows the prompts used for speaker identification (original version). As shown in this table, we provide several few-shot examples in a chat format. The prompt consists of text extracted from the beginning of book_id=052410 included in Aozora Bunko. In Table 10, few-shot examples (Chen et al., 2019b) related to the story, along with the target story (`{Context}`) and are provided the utterance line (`{Line}`) for speaker identification.

Using these prompts, we constructed a dataset to evaluate the accuracy of speaker identification and conducted speaker identification based on this dataset.

In addition, Table 11 shows an example story used for prompts. This example was inserted into the `Context` sections of Tables 2 and 10 as part of the few-shot learning examples.

J Impact of Varying Context Lengths with Other Models

Figures 8–9 illustrate the accuracy of substring matches when varying the input context length

[8] `https://scikit-learn.org/`
[9] `https://github.com/huggingface/transformers`
[10] `https://beautiful-soup-4.readthedocs.io/`
[11] `https://github.com/openai/tiktoken`
[12] `https://github.com/openai/openai-python`
[13] `https://github.com/huggingface/evaluate`
[14] `https://github.com/huggingface/accelerate`
[15] `https://github.com/pytorch/pytorch`
[16] `https://github.com/huggingface/datasets`
[17] `https://matplotlib.org/`

Story	Tokens (Llama-3)		Lines		Skip	
	JA	EN	JA	EN	JA	EN
Shita-kiri Suzume	2,838	3,256	46	22	1	2
Tawara Toda	2,035	2,823	18	11	0	1
Urashima Taro	4,036	5,272	36	69	0	3
Kachikachi Yama	3,175	2,842	58	17	1	0
Kintaro	2,816	3,920	30	52	1	6
Taketori Monogatari	5,452	6,680	27	17	0	0
Matsuyama Kagami	2,839	6,219	40	46	0	0
Adachigahara	2,479	2,083	17	23	0	0
Hanasaka Jijii	2,237	3,339	19	19	2	2
Kurage no Otsukai	2,837	3,728	58	67	0	0
Saru Kani Kassen	2,498	3,256	42	17	0	0
Momotaro	4,031	5,361	58	83	9	1
Rashomon	2,176	2,730	26	32	4	0
Kubu-tori	3,539	2,579	42	25	0	0
Total	42,988	54,088	517	500	18	15

Table 9: Summary of token and utterance counts for both Japanese (JA) and English (EN) versions of each story. Annotation was performed on the main names of characters, following the methodology used in constructing the dataset for the Japanese version of "Romance of the Three Kingdoms" (see Section 4).

across different models.

As shown in these figures, models with approximately 70B parameters exhibited improved speaker identification accuracy as the context length increased. Conversely, for models with 8B parameters or fewer, accuracy plateaued when the context length was extended from 256 to 512 tokens. Beyond this point, providing additional context resulted in a performance decline due to the introduction of noise, with the extent of the decline varying across models.

These observations suggest that the effective context length for input varies depending on the model's parameter size and training methodology.

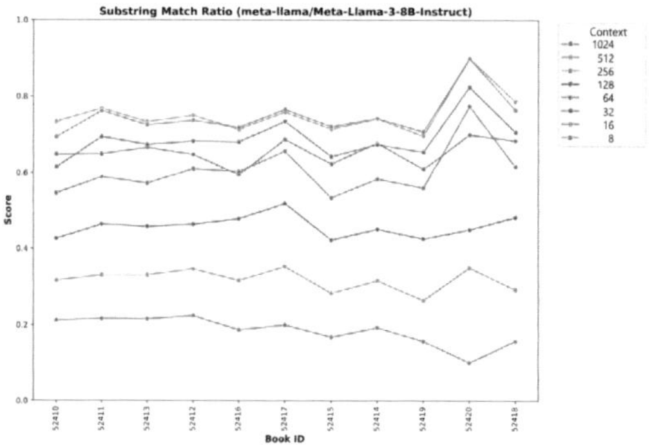

Figure 8: Variation in Substring Match Ratio by Context Length for `LLaMA-8B-Instruct`. This figure shows how the substring match ratio changes with different context lengths.

K Candidate Sets for Relaxed Speaker Name Matching

During the evaluation, we matched the predicted speaker names with the most corresponding name from the candidate sets. As shown in Figure 10, the substring match ratio using these sets was higher than in the initial evaluation. For book_id=52419, the evaluation became more consistent with the candidate sets.

Comparison of Paraphrase Set Acquisition with Wikipedia Redirects The Romance of the Three Kingdoms is well-known, resulting in many of its characters having dedicated Wikipedia pages. Therefore, using Wikipedia Redirects [18] to acquire paraphrase expressions is conceivable. However, our attempts revealed that paraphrase expressions could only be acquired for some characters.

Specifically, excluding the names we extracted as Main Name from our created paraphrase sets, only 1.83% of paraphrase candidates could be obtained using Wikipedia Redirects. Notably, expressions corresponding to "劉備" as "青年" or "應德" as "旅人" could not be obtained.

[18]https://en.wikipedia.org/wiki/Wikipedia:Redirect

Role	Content
user	次の物語（# Example Story）中のセリフに対して、誰が発言したのかを推測して、話者の名前のみを答えてください。
assistant	了解しました。以下の物語とセリフに基づいて答えを提供します。
user	# Example Story {Example Context}
assistant	物語を確認しました。では、セリフごとに誰が発言したのかを答えます。
user	次の発話は誰が発言しましたか？
assistant	セリフを教えてください。
user	おーい
assistant	漁夫
user	——そこの若い者ウ。なにを見ているんだい。いくら待っていても、そこは渡し舟の着く所じゃないぞ
assistant	漁夫
user	ありがとう
assistant	青年
user	おい、おい、旅の者
assistant	百姓
user	——そんな所で、今朝からなにを待っているんだね。このごろは、黄巧賊とかいう悪徒が立ち廻るからな。役人衆に怪しまれるぞよ
assistant	百姓
user	同様にして、次の物語（# Target Story）中のセリフに対して、誰が発言したのかを推測して、話者の名前のみを答えてください。
assistant	了解しました。以下の物語とセリフに基づいて答えを提供します。
user	# Target Story {Context}
assistant	物語を確認しました。では、セリフごとに誰が発言したのかを答えます。
user	次の発話は誰が発言しましたか？
assistant	セリフを教えてください。
user	{Line}

Table 10: Prompts for Speaker Identification (Original Version). This table represents the chat template prompts in Japanese. The {Example Context} and {Context} sections contain the story content, while the {Line} section specifies the dialogue for which the speaker is to be identified.

These results indicate the limitations of using Wikipedia Redirects for acquiring paraphrase expressions. Hence, combining other methods and data sources is essential for comprehensive paraphrase collection.

L Uncased Exact Match Evaluation

This section addresses evaluation variations arising from case sensitivity in English data. To mitigate such issues, we employ an Uncased Exact Match metric, normalizing generated text to be case-insensitive. As a result, mentions like "Old Woman" and "old woman" are treated as equivalent, ensuring a fairer comparison. Note that this adjustment is only applied to English datasets.

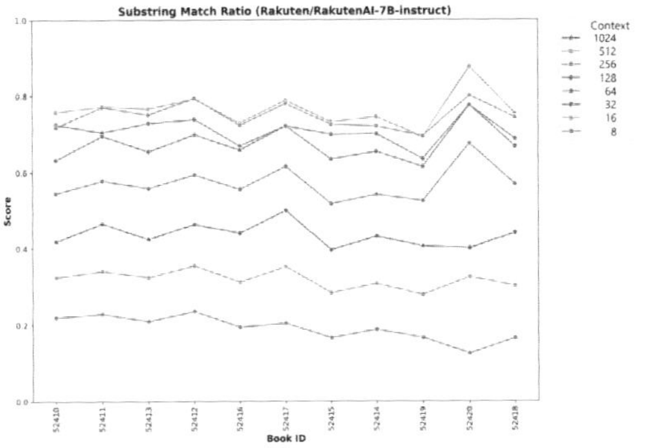

Figure 9: Variation in Substring Match Ratio by Context Length for RakutenAI-7B-Instruct. This figure shows how the substring match ratio changes with different context lengths.

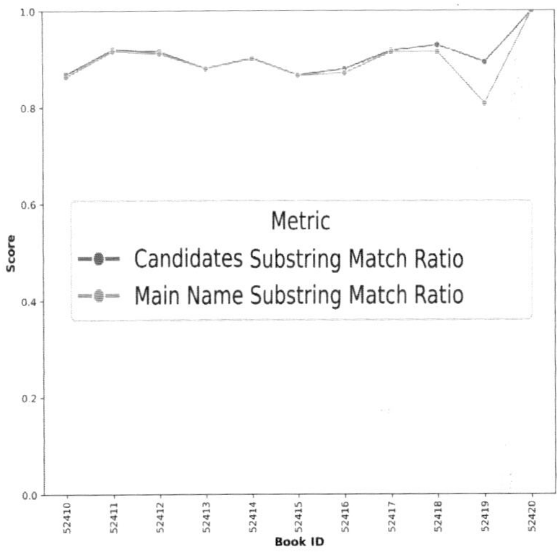

Figure 10: Comparison of the main name and its alternative candidates annotated through substring matching.

Figure 11 illustrates the impact of case sensitivity on evaluation by comparing the uncased substring match ratios for the English and Japanese versions of the story "Kintaro." Introducing uncased matching consistently improves accuracy. For instance, models such as calm3-22b-chat and LLaMA-3-70B-Instruct benefit notably from this approach. Additionally, the performance of Swallow-70B-Instruct aligns more closely with Swallow-70B, indicating that addressing case-related discrepancies reduces format-driven variance. Overall, uncased evaluation enhances the robustness and reliability of speaker identification metrics.

type	prompt
Japanese Example Story	後漢の建寧元年のころ。今から約千七百八十年ほど前のことである。一人の旅人があった。腰に、一剣を佩いているほか、身なりはいたって見すぼらしいが、眉は秀で、唇は紅く、とりわけ聡明そうな眸や、豊かな頬をしていて、つねにどこかに微笑をふくみ、総じて賤しげな容子がなかった。年の頃は二十四、五。草むらの中に、ぽつねんと坐って、膝をかかえこんでいた。悠久と水は行く——微風は爽やかに鬢をなでる。涼秋の八月だ。そしてそこは、黄河の畔の——黄土層の低い断り岸であった。「おーい」誰か河でよんだ。「——そこの若い者ウ。なにを見ているんだい。いくら待っていても、そこは渡し舟の着く所じゃないぞ」小さな漁船から漁夫がいうのだった。青年は笑くぼを送って、「ありがとう」と、少し頭を下げた。漁船は、下流へ流れ去った。けれど青年は、同じ所に、同じ姿をしていた。膝をかかえて坐ったまま遠心的な眼をうごかさなかった。「おい、おい、旅の者」こんどは、後ろを通った人間が呼びかけた。近村の百姓であろう。ひとりは鶏の足をつかんでさげ、ひとりは農具をかついでいた。「——そんな所で、今朝からなにを待っているんだね。このごろは、黄巾賊とかいう悪徒が立ち廻るからな。役人衆に怪しまれるぞよ」青年は、振りかえって、「はい、どうも」おとなしい会釈をかえした。
English Example Story	In the first year of the Jianning era of the Later Han Dynasty. This was about one thousand seven hundred and eighty years ago. There was a traveler. Apart from wearing a sword at his waist, his appearance was quite shabby. However, he had prominent eyebrows, red lips, especially intelligent-looking eyes, and full cheeks that always seemed to hold a smile, overall giving him an air that was not at all lowly. He appeared to be around twenty-four or twenty-five years old. He was sitting alone in a patch of grass, hugging his knees. Time flows like the eternal river—A gentle breeze brushed his sideburns. It was August, a cool autumn month. And this was the bank of the Yellow River—on a low clay cliff. "Hey there!" Someone called from the river. "—You there, young man. What are you looking at? No matter how long you wait, this is not where the ferry docks." A fisherman from a small boat said. The young man smiled and, "Thank you," he said with a slight nod. The fishing boat drifted downstream. But the young man stayed in the same spot, in the same posture, his eyes still looking into the distance. "Hey, hey, traveler." This time, someone passing by from behind called out. It seemed to be a farmer from a nearby village. One was holding a chicken by its feet, and the other was carrying farming tools. "—What have you been waiting for since this morning in a place like this? Lately, there have been bandits called the Yellow Turbans around. The officials will get suspicious of you." The young man turned and, "Yes, thank you," he replied with a gentle nod.

Table 11: Example Stories

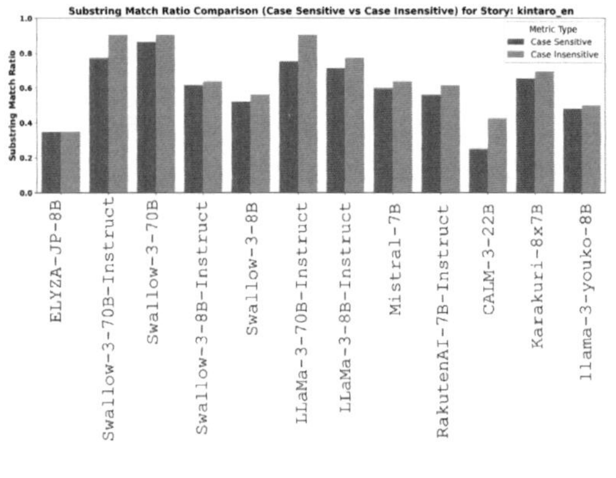

Figure 11: Comparison of Uncased Substring Match Ratio for story: kintaro_en.

Results Figure 12 compares substring match ratios across various models on the English-translated dataset. The English version achieves a substring match ratio of about 70%, approximately 20% lower than the performance on the Japanese data. We attribute this decrease to additional adjectives and extraneous terms introduced in English, which complicate identifying the core speaker references.

These results highlight the importance of translation quality and linguistic nuance when extending datasets to multilingual contexts. Although automated translation accelerates dataset construction, careful consideration of language-specific variations is crucial for maintaining annotation accuracy.

Expenses for Translation Conducting multiple checks and retries for format adherence and correctness increased the total number of tokens processed. The GPT-4o-mini model consumed about 30 million tokens, including retries, resulting in a total translation cost of $6.0. This demonstrates that even with thorough quality controls, automated translation remains a cost-effective strategy for building bilingual datasets.

M Use of AI Tools in Writing and Coding

We used AI tools to assist in the writing and coding processes for this project. Specifically, we employed ChatGPT[19] to help draft and refine the text, and we utilized GitHub Copilot[20] for code completion and suggestions during the coding tasks. These tools were incorporated into our workflow to support the efficient completion of the project.

[19] https://openai.com/chatgpt/
[20] https://docs.github.com/en/copilot

type	prompt
Speaker	Translate the following speaker's name into English, using terms that appear in the translated context. Provide the translation only: Example 1: Translated context: "The farmer walked through his fields, greeting the old man sitting by the road." Output: old man Example 2: Translated context: "In the small village, the young woman was known for her kindness." Output: young woman Example 3: Translated context: "The wise elder spoke to the gathered crowd with great wisdom." Output: wise elder
Dialogue	Extract the entire line that is most similar to this dialogue: 'original_dialogue', excluding the quotation marks. Ensure to extract the full sentence from the start to the end. Example 1: Original dialogue: "これからどうする？" Translated context: "They looked at each other, wondering about the next steps. One of them asked, 'What are we going to do now?' Another responded, 'We need to think carefully.'" Extracted line: What are we going to do now? Example 2: Original dialogue: "何を言えばいいかわからない。" Translated context: "He scratched his head, lost for words. He finally said, 'I have no idea what to say.' Another person nodded in agreement, 'It's a tough situation.'" Extracted line: I have no idea what to say. Failure Example 1: Original dialogue: "こっちへ行こう。" Translated context: "They were considering their options. One said, 'Let's go this way.' Another said, 'I think we should stay here.'" Extracted line: I think we should stay here. # The extracted line is incorrect as it does not match the original dialogue's intent to move.
Context	Translate the following context into English, ensuring consistency and that the provided dialogue is included. The translation should maintain a coherent narrative flow. Provide the translation only: Example 1: Original context: "彼は暗闇の中で独り、静かな夜の音を聞いていた。その時、彼は『おい、誰かいるのか？』と呼びかけた。" Translated dialogue: "Hey, is anyone there?" Translated context: "He sat alone in the darkness, listening to the quiet sounds of the night. At that moment, he called out, 'Hey, is anyone there?'" Example 2: Original context: "彼女は辺りを見回し、そして『ここに何があるの？』と尋ねた。周りには何もないようだった。" Translated dialogue: "What's here?" Translated context: "She looked around and then asked, 'What's here?' There seemed to be nothing around."

Table 12: Prompts for translation

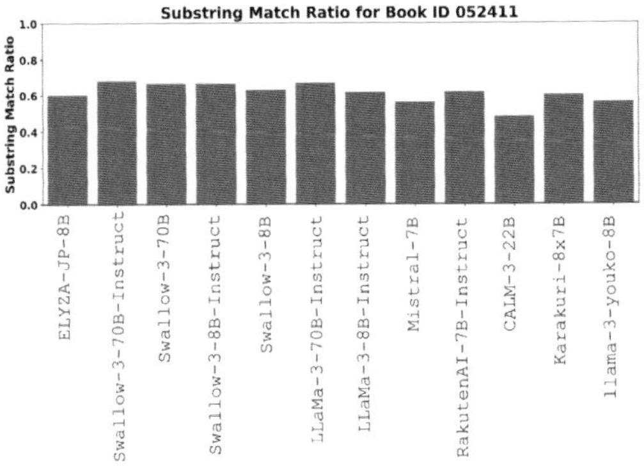

Figure 12: Substring match ratio comparison across models for GPT-4o-mini translated data.

Author Index